INFORMATION AND COMMUNICATION
TECHNOLOGY AND PUBLIC INNOVATION

Innovation and the Public Sector

The functioning of the public sector gives rise to considerable debate. Not only the efficiency and efficacy of the sector are at stake, but also its legitimacy. At the same time we see that in the public sector all kinds of innovations are taking place. These innovations are not only technological, which enable the redesign of all kinds of processes, like service delivery. The emphasis can also be put on more organizational and conceptual innovations. In this series we will try to understand the nature of a wide variety of innovations taking place in the public sector of the 21st century and try to evaluate their outcomes. How do they take place? What are relevant triggers? And, how are their outcomes being shaped by all kinds of actors and influences? And, do public innovations differ from innovations in the private sector? Moreover we try to assess the actual effects of these innovations, not only from an instrumental point of view, but also from a more institutional point of view. Do these innovations not only contribute to a better functioning of the public sector, but do they also challenge grown practices and vested interests? And what does this imply for the management of public sector innovations?

Series Editor:
Prof. Dr. Victor J.J.M. Bekkers
Erasmus University, Rotterdam, The Netherlands

Volume 12

Previously published in this series

This series is a continuation of "Informatization Developments and the Public Sector" (vols. 1–9, ISSN 0928-9038)

ISSN 1871-1073

Information and Communication Technology and Public Innovation

Assessing the ICT-Driven Modernization of Public Administration

Edited by

Victor Bekkers

Erasmus University Rotterdam, Faculty of Social Sciences, the Netherlands

Hein van Duivenboden

Capgemini & Tilburg University, Tias Business School, the Netherlands

and

Marcel Thaens

Ordina & Erasmus University Rotterdam, Faculty of Social Sciences, the Netherlands

IOS
Press

Amsterdam • Berlin • Oxford • Tokyo • Washington, DC

ISBN 1-58603-626-2
Library of Congress Control Number: 2006927913

Publisher
IOS Press
Nieuwe Hemweg 6B
1013 BG Amsterdam
Netherlands
fax: +31 20 687 0019
e-mail: order@iospress.nl

Distributor in the UK and Ireland
Gazelle Books Services Ltd.
White Cross Mills
Hightown
Lancaster LA1 4XS
United Kingdom
fax: +44 1524 63232
e-mail: sales@gazellebooks.co.uk

Distributor in the USA and Canada
IOS Press, Inc.
4502 Rachael Manor Drive
Fairfax, VA 22032
USA
fax: +1 703 323 3668
e-mail: iosbooks@iospress.com

Cover Design
Joost van Grinsven

PRINTED IN THE NETHERLANDS

Information and Communication Technology and Public Innovation
V.J.J.M. Bekkers et al. (Eds.)
IOS Press, 2006

Preface

The modernization of public administration is a recurring theme on the political and public agenda in many countries. Modernization presupposes innovation. However, is an innovative public administration a *contradiction in terminis*? According Aloïs Schumpeter, the founding father of innovation theory, the lack of competition in the public sector, the short term orientation of politicians and the bureaucratic nature of public organizations, focusing on creating stability, predictability, legal security and legal equality, frustrates the ability of public sector organizations to look for new ideas, new practices, new services and new organizations. However, if we look at the practice of public administration, and evaluate – from an evolutionary perspective – how public administration has transformed itself during the last 40 years, we actually see a variety of radical and incremental changes. Hence, innovation does take place. This book clearly demonstrates how public administration organizations try to adapt to changing circumstances in their environment in order to secure their legitimacy.

At the same time we see that public administration tries to respond and anticipate to new technological developments as well as to make use of them. In many countries e-government has become the symbol of the way in which ICT has penetrated in the nerves of ministries, local and regional government and all kinds of agencies. Moreover, a seamless web of information exchange, transaction and communication relations has been spun within and between all kinds of public, private and semi-public organizations which are involved in the formulation and implementation of public policy programs, the execution of public laws and regulations and the evolving delivery of public services. ICT can be seen as tool, which facilitates the implementation of all kinds of public innovations on the one hand; on the other hand the possibilities ICT offers can also be seen as a perspective of change. They can help us frame new possibilities or re-frame existing practices, thereby stimulating a process of 'creative destruction'.

However, how should we assess the added value of ICT to support public innovations? In this book a number of case studies have been presented in which different kind of ICT-driven innovations have been described and analyzed. All the chapters have been subjected to a review procedure in order to guarantee the quality of the contributions. In the selection of the chapters we have differentiated between several kinds of innovations in which ICT has been used in a substantial way. A distinction has been made between technological, service, organizational, conceptual and institutional innovations. Furthermore we have tried to ensure an international comparative overview of innovations. Case studies have been included from the United Kingdom, the Netherlands, Belgium, the United States of America, Denmark, Germany, Finland and Estonia.

We have tried to assess these innovations in two ways. From an instrumental perspective we have looked at the way in which ICT has supported the achievement of different innovations. What factors have contributed to the way in which the innovation goals have been accomplished? From an institutional perspective we have looked at the question, if the use of ICT has contributed to qualitative changes in public administration? Did ICT reinforce existing practices, or did it substantially generate new practices, new relationships and new concepts? Moreover, we have included some chapters that address these questions from a more reflective point of view.

We would like to thank Vivian Carter, Rebecca Moody and the translation service of Capgemini for their help with the editing of the chapters.

Rotterdam/Tilburg, April 2005

Victor Bekkers
Hein van Duivenboden
Marcel Thaens

Contents

Part 1

Setting the Stage

Information and Communication Technology and Public Innovation
V.J.J.M. Bekkers et al. (Eds.)
IOS Press, 2006

Public Innovation and Information and Communication Technology: Relevant Backgrounds and Concepts

Victor BEKKERS [a,1], Hein van DUIVENBODEN [b] and Marcel THAENS [c]

[a] *Erasmus University Rotterdam, Faculty of Social Sciences, the Netherlands*
[b] *Capgemini & Tilburg University, Tias Business School, the Netherlands*
[c] *Ordina & Erasmus University Rotterdam, Faculty of Social Sciences, the Netherlands*

Abstract. This chapter aim to explore the relationship between ICT and public innovation by looking by looking at a number of theoretical notions and empirical findings. A number of reasons is presented why the modernization of government is a returning issue and reflect on the nature of this modernization process. A necessary condition for modernization is innovation, but how innovative is the public sector. Some arguments for and against are given. We also distinguish several types of innovation. ICT innovations are very often used as incentives to modernize public administration. In order to understand the nature of these ICT driven innovations, it is important to question ICT itself as well as its added value.

Keywords. Modernization, Public Administration, New Public Management, ICT, Innovation, E-government

1. Introduction

"Government matters. We all want it to deliver policies, programmes and services that will make us healthier, more secure and better equipped to tackle the challenges we face. Government should improve the quality of our lives. Modernization is vital if government is to achieve that ambition". These are the opening lines of the vision statement which Mr. Tony Blair, the Prime Minister of the United Kingdom, presented to Parliament in March 1999 [1]. During the last decade modernization and public innovation programmes have been drafted in different European countries. Simultaneously, information and communication technology (ICT) has been perceived as an important driver for change. According to Blair: "Information technology is changing our lives: the way we work, the way we do business, the way we communicate with each other, how we spend our time. New technology offers opportunities and choices. It can give us access to services 24 hours a day, seven days a

---

[1] Corresponding Author: Erasmus University Rotterdam, Faculty of Social Sciences, Public Administration Group, P.O. Box 1738, 3000 DR Rotterdam, the Netherlands; E-mail: bekkers@fsw.eur.nl.

week. It will make our lives easier. Government intends to be at the head of these developments (…) Government must bring about a fundamental change in the way we use IT. We must modernize the business of government itself, achieving joined up working between different parts of government and providing new, efficient and convenient ways for citizens and businesses to communicate with government and to receive services" [1]. Hence, the massive penetration of ICT during the last ten years, especially the internet, in our daily work and lives, has opened up new horizons for modernized public administration. E-government has been one of the buzz words which has been used to frame this new perspective. E-government can be described as the use of ICT, and particularly the internet, a as tool to achieve better government [2]. Narrowly defined, e-government refers to the production and delivery of government (information, interaction and transaction) services through the use of ICT [3]. However, the modernization of public administration is much broader than the improvement of public service delivery as well as the use of ICT to achieve this. That is why it is important to see beyond the use of ICT to modernize public service delivery.

The general aim of this book is to investigate the innovation potential of ICT for different kinds of public innovations, the conditions under which these innovations take place and the innovative effects that actually have occurred due to the use of ICT. How should we assess the innovative potential of ICT?

Our investigation into the relationship between ICT and different types of public innovation begins with an exploration of the main theoretical concepts. First, we will start by giving some reasons why the modernization of public administration is a returning issue which attracts public, political and managerial attention. What are the main motives, at a more fundamental level, to modernize government? Some reasons will be put forward in section two. Second, we will explore the notion of innovation. What is innovation? What is the difference between innovation and modernization, although both concepts are often used as synonyms? What are the relevant characteristics? Is it possible to distinguish between several types of innovation? Section three will deal with these questions. Furthermore, it is important to look into the innovative potential of ICT (section four). How does ICT affect the different innovations that take place in public administration? How optimistic should we be about the innovative potential of ICT? Section five will provide a plan for the book, which has been based on categorizing different kinds of innovations. Also an indicative scheme for description and analysis will be presented which is used in the following chapters.

2. The Call for Modernization

What reasons can be given to modernize government? What is the nature of recent modernization projects throughout Western public administration? What results have been achieved? These questions will be answered in this section.

2.1. Public Administration under Pressure

The repeated call to renew public administration has a history of several decades. We will identify five lingering crises of the 'welfare state' that have contributed to this recurrent call for renewal. These crises have been and still are important drivers for change [4, 5].

The Financial Crisis of the Welfare State

The economic recession which started at the end of the 1970s and lasted until the mid-1980s brought about a crisis of the welfare state for almost every government in the Western world. This crisis can be understood as a financial crisis. The problem was not so much whether a comprehensive welfare system would be desirable or not, but whether it could be financed in a situation of increasing demands. Moreover, efficiency deficits in the implementation of welfare state regulations, in terms of bureaucratization and 'red tape', were also a major reason to raise questions. The result was a partial withdrawal of the state in providing these provisions [6: 9].

However, almost two decades later, the restructuring of the welfare state has not been finished yet. At the beginning of the 21st century the financial restructuring of the welfare state has returned onto the political agenda. Not only the economic recession – which started in 2001 when the dream of a 'new economy' was shattered – but also the growing aging of the population and the corresponding increasing demands on public provisions, like social security benefits, pensions plans and health care, has been an important motive to modernize government.

The Regulatory Crisis of the Welfare State

The implementation of all kinds of rules and regulations through which the provisions of the welfare state have been realized did also lead to a rather permanent regulatory crisis. Government intervention was primarily seen as using legislation and planning to provide these provisions. Hood talks about the rule-and-rote approach of government intervention, while Van Gunsteren refers to the dominance of the central rule approach in government, in which command and control were seen as important characteristics of the way government tries to influence societal developments, and in which policy-making was defined as the development of regulatory policies [7, 8]. However, these regulatory policies failed. One reason is that rule-oriented interventions can only work under specific conditions. Hood specifies these conditions [7: 21-22]. First, these rules must be knowable, discoverable by the participants before they make the decisions which these rules govern. Second, the purposes served by these rules should be broadly acceptable and easy to see. Moreover, the rules should in fact serve the purpose for which they are intended – i.e. they should incorporate valid cause-effect assumptions. Third, these rules must be completely consistent with one another, so as to avoid uncertainties bound up in 'umpiring' decisions as to which rules get priority in conflict-of-rule cases. Fourth, the conditions in which rules apply should be completely specified in advance, to limit uncertainty as to when or where the rules apply. Fifth, standards incorporated into rules should be capable of clear verification, so as to limit the scope for subjective interpretation. Finally, where rules divide behaviour or other items into categories, those categories should be robust and unambiguous. If you look at the practice of public administration, you see that most conditions cannot be met. As a result, more detailed regulatory policies were developed with more detailed instructions on how to behave or how to implement the norms which have been formulated [7]. The fact that government has been caught in a web of more detailed and even conflicting rules and regulations, as well as the fact that public organizations have been confronted with all kinds of administrative burdens, has led to the introduction of new regulatory and governance concepts.

Implementation Crisis of the Welfare State

Evaluation and implementation studies of public policies have shown that the implementation of regulatory policies is not a mechanical process. Implementation encompasses more than simply setting in motion the machinery of government through which the desired outcomes will be produced. Government agencies, but also citizens, societal organizations and companies that are confronted with all kinds of regulatory norms, do not behave as powerless and willing cogwheels in 'the machinery of government' which behave themselves according to the instructions that have been given. Policy implementation is not a technocratic and neutral issue; it is highly political. Moreover, implementation usually requires the involvement of multiple agencies, thereby reducing the probability of correct implementation, even if the agencies are willing to implement the policy [9]. Furthermore, implementation very often implies that tailor-made solutions have to be made, because of specific or changing implementation conditions. This implies discretion of the organization which has to implement a specific rule or programme.

However, discretion implies a transfer of tasks, responsibilities and competences from the centre to the periphery in order to guarantee such tailor-made implementation. This has been another modernization challenge.

The Complexity Crisis of the Welfare State

Effective government interventions presuppose that governments have a well-known insight into the causal relationships that are important to assess whether a specific kind of government intervention would produce the desired outcomes in terms of goals to be achieved [6]. From this point of view the causal relations (cause-effect relations) as well as final relations (means-end relations) should be known, when regulatory policies are drafted. Valid knowledge about possible causes, effects and side-effects is not available. We do not know what the outcomes of specific interventions would be, while at the same time there is normative confusion. Very often governments are not able to develop a hierarchy of norms and values which should be pursued. That is why most societal problems can be described as 'wicked problems' which fundamentally challenge the problem-solving capacity of governments.

An ongoing process of functional differentiation and societal fragmentation also challenges this capacity. This produces highly specialized and rather autonomous subsystems and organizations that at the same time are highly interdependent. The complexity of functional interdependencies and causal networks has grown immensely. This results in unpredictable direct and indirect effects, which originate in wide-ranging output-input relations between many actors. The network character of these relationships generates cognitive and manipulative problems, because we do not know the nature of this complexity. At the same time we do not know the desired and undesired outcomes of the possible interventions in these networks [6]. Moreover as a result of this process of differentiation and fragmentation, rather complex coordination and cooperation problems occur.

The Democracy Crisis of the Welfare State

Another crisis refers to the crisis of representative democracy in the welfare state. The traditional institutions of the liberal and constitutional democracy, which have legitimized the emergence but also the restructuring of the welfare state, are in a frail condition. Some scholars talk about a cleavage between citizens and politics. Elected representatives often do not represent 'the will of the people' and are prone to elitism [10]. This has led to a permanent search to renew democracy [10, 11]. Answers have been found in the (permanent) participation of citizens in the political and public debate in order to build a 'strong democracy', in which deliberation and political action by citizens are seen as important modernization goals [12]. Other answers have been found in addressing citizens primarily as consumers or clients of public services. The assumption is that a responsive public service delivery will restore the trust of the citizen in politics. That is why representative democracy should be complemented by a consumer democracy [13]. It can be regarded as a strategy for legitimizing and controlling the growth of the administrative state, by establishing greater popular control over the production and consumption of public services. It seeks to generate information about the citizens' preferences via marketing-like instruments, such as focus groups, complaint procedures and client research. Also, it seeks to improve the information position of citizens by giving them access to more and better information about the price and quality of public services and the conditions under which they are being produced.

The rediscovery of citizens as politically engaged citizens and as consumers, which goes beyond the traditional position of the citizen as a voter, can also be seen as the expression of the empowerment of citizens [14]. They have the ability and the resources to organize themselves as a pressure or issue group in order to advocate and protect their interests within the public and political arena.

Individualization and the collapse of the great ideologies of the 19th century have also contributed to this development. In general, these developments have eroded the legitimacy of claims and arguments that were put forward by government and politics on behalf of the citizen. The citizen himself, his individual interests, needs and beliefs have moved into the centre of the political and administrative system [11, 13].

2.2. New Public Management as a Reform Ideology

The rather permanent discussion about fundamental flaws in the functioning of public administration has led to a counter movement, with reform ambitions [4]. Established in the late 1980s, 'New Public Management' has evolved into a highly popular label for a wide variety of reforms in the public [15]. Pollitt [16: 27-28] identifies the following eight key elements of 'New Public Management' (NPM):

- A shift in value priorities away from universalism, equity, security and resilience towards efficiency and individualism, defining the role of a citizen as a 'homo economicus';
- A shift in the focus of management systems from inputs and processes towards results and outputs;
- A shift towards measurement and quantification, especially through the development of performance indicators and benchmarks systems;

- A preference for more specialized, 'lean', 'flat' and autonomous organizational structures;
- A substitution of formal, hierarchical relationships between or within organizations by contracts or contract-like relationships;
- A much wider deployment of markets or market-type mechanisms for the delivery of public services;
- An emphasis on service quality and a consumer orientation; and
- A broadening and blurring of the frontiers between the public sector, the market sector and the so-called third or non-profit sector.

The result of the popularity of NPM, as it has been embraced by politicians, policy makers and scholars of public administration during the last ten years, has been that "the so-called public sector is becoming more business-like, with the introduction of competition, output measures and corporate management styles" [17: 231]. This has also influenced the innovation agenda of public administration and the use of ICT in order to achieve these specific modernization goals. From an NPM perspective, public innovations should be focussed on creating a business-like public sector [17].

2.3. Modernization Goals and Results

In a recent review the OECD has documented the results of 20 years of modernizing the public sector. They conclude that major changes have been made [18: 10-12]. The following results have been listed:

Open government. Across OECD member countries, governments are becoming more open and transparent, accessible and consultative. This can be derived from the legal measures (e.g. Freedom of Information Acts, customer service standards) that have been taken and the institutions (e.g. Ombudsman) that have been established. E-government has also been an important driver which has enhanced open government.

Enhancing public sector performance. Governments have become more performance-focused, which has led to the development of formalized planning, reporting and control across government. Performance management and budgeting are important instruments that are being used.

Modernizing accountability and control. The main trend in control has been the move from ex ante to ex post control and the development of stronger processes of internal control. In practice there is a move from the inefficient but relative certainty of checking the regularity and legality of individual transactions to more efficient but relative uncertainty of verifying the proper operation of systems.

Reallocation and restructuring. The need for government to set outer limits for expenditure and to reallocate within those limits has changed national budgeting from a support function to the primary vehicle for strategic management. The budget process is frequently used as a vehicle for wider managerial reform. Also the ability to change organizational structures has been defined as essential for modern government, like putting agencies at arm's length from central government.

The use of market-type mechanisms. The introduction of market-type mechanisms of various kinds has contributed to efficiency gains. However, in some countries, there seems to be a distortion between private gains and public interest or public responsibility or accountability.

Modernizing public employment. The nature of public employment has significantly changed. The employment arrangements of public servants are becoming more like those of the private sector by altering the legal status and employment conditions.

Some Remarks

Several remarks can be made regarding the outcomes of this review. Although these results are quite impressive, reformers need to be aware of the possible effects of these rather managerial reforms on wider governance values [18: 10]. Public administration and public administration reform should not only be concerned with the improvement of the efficiency of the machinery of government. Not only economic values - in terms of efficiency, efficacy and coherence - play an important role in public administration, but also political values like liberty, equity and security, as well as legal values such as the rule of law [19]. The popularity of NPM and the results that have been achieved and have been listed by the OECD points to an interesting value-driven battle within public administration; a battle between 'management' on the one hand and 'politics' on the other, which also influences the current innovation and ICT agenda of public administration [20]. Moreover, one can observe that the described modernization results hardly address the democratic embedding of public administration and the functioning of the institutions of representative democracy. One could even state that the modernization agenda of public administration has a rather internal focus, while the ultimate test for the modernization of public administration is the way in which governments are able to respond to changing social, cultural and economic conditions and the 'wicked' policy problems which result from them.

Furthermore, we observe that the OECD review has a 'NPM bias'. Modernization has been defined as in accordance with the NMP ideology of renewal.

However, one can question the general claim of this ideology as Veenswijk does [21]. First, the one-sidedness on rationality, feasibility and plannability. A mechanistic perspective on the management and organization of government prevails, thereby neglecting the cultural and political dimension of public organizations. Second, the tension between the front stage rhetoric of NPM (showing convergence between government in different countries), laid down in all kinds of policy documents, official rules of conduct and performance reports on the one hand; and the daily and recurrent practices in government, which can be defined at the back stage of government (that is more varied than the front stage rhetoric would show us) on the other hand. Third, there is the universal claim of the modernization agenda of NPM. Successful modernization has been defined in accordance with criteria that have been based on the characteristics of NPM as we have described them. However, innovation studies show us the importance of taking into account the specific, i.e. local and historical context in which a government organization operates and in which innovations occur.

3. The Power of Innovation

In this section we address another relevant issue: innovation. What is innovation? Is it possible to distinguish different types of innovation? And, what is the innovative nature of public administration?

3.1. The Concept of Modernization and Innovation

Modernization and Legitimacy

The modernization of government can be defined as the ability of government to adapt to developments in different political, socio-economic, technological and cultural environments in which a government organization operates as well as the ability to respond to and anticipate the needs of different stakeholders in these environments, such as citizens, companies, societal organizations and other government organizations. The ultimate test of successful modernization is the ability of governments to act as legitimate political organizations. This refers to the binding allocation of public goods, resources and public values for a community as a whole [21: 278]. Politics and public policy are about communities trying to achieve collective goals that contribute to economic growth, such as the creation of safe neighbourhoods, a sustainable environment or a transport infrastructure [23]. This implies that the modernization of government ultimately adds to the input, throughput and output/outcome legitimacy of government.

Input-oriented modernization emphasizes the way in which 'government by the people' actually can be achieved in such a way that the 'will of the people' can be derived from the authentic preferences of the member of a political community. Participation and representation are important political values that should be taken into consideration [24: 6]. Examples of input-oriented innovations are interactive forms of policy formulation in which citizens play an active role in the planning of the new neighbourhoods or the rebuilding of old neighbourhoods.

We define throughput modernization in relation to the qualities of the rules and procedures by which governments try to solve problems. Checks and balances and the rule of the law are important political values that should be taken into account. Legal expert systems are for instance an example of a technological innovation, which adds to the legality of the bureaucratic decision-making processes, when a civil servant has assessed different requests to apply specific rules and regulation in order to issue a permit, to qualify for specific benefits, like social security benefits or a student loan.

The output/outcome-oriented perspective on modernization focuses on the notion of 'government for the people' [24: 11]. From this perspective, modernization tells us something about the capacity of government to produce certain output or outcomes that actually contribute to remedying collective problems. For instance, efficiency and efficacy are values that can be used to assess the specific modernization efforts. Many e-government innovations are focused to improve the quality of the service delivery process, thereby providing information services 24 hours a day.

Characteristics of Innovation

Innovation can be defined as a necessary condition for modernization. One of the founding fathers of modern innovation theory, Joseph Schumpeter, defines innovation as a process; as a process of creative destruction in which 'new combinations of existing resources' are being achieved [25]. However, in his view innovation cannot be separated from entrepreneurship. They are two sides of the same coin. He defines entrepreneurship as 'Die Durchsetzung neuer Kombinationen'; as the will and ability to achieve new combinations; new combinations that have to compete with established combinations. An innovation itself has been mostly defined as "an idea, practice or object that is perceived as new by an individual or unit of adoption" [26: 12].

Some authors also make a distinction between an innovation and an invention. An invention is the first occurrence of an idea for a new product or process, while an innovation is the first attempt to carry it out in practice. However, in practice this distinction is not always so simple. They are rather intertwined concepts [27].

Another relevant and related concept is change [21, 26]. Innovation requires change, but change is not necessarily innovative. The important factor is how radical the innovation is; what is the 'newness' of the change which has occurred? A distinction can be made between a) incremental innovations, which can be defined as minor changes in existing services and processes, b) radical innovations, which fundamentally change the existing ways of organizing or delivering services as well as producing fundamentally new products and services and c) systematic or transformative innovations, which are defined as major transformations which for instance emerge from the introduction of new technologies (like the steam engine or the internet) [28: 3]. According to McDaniel it is also important to make a distinction between evolutionary and revolutionary innovations [29: 62-64]. Evolutionary innovations occur within an organization rather incrementally, allowing an organization to adjust to small changes in its internal and external environment. Revolutionary innovations are not part of the normal process of adaption and change, but create major upheavals within an industry or policy sector. They represent major breakthroughs and create major changes.

3.2. Categorizing Innovations

In literature, several attempts have been made to classify innovations; to some extent these classifications vary; to some extent they are rather similar [25, 27, 28, 29]. Inspired by these different classifications and translating them to the realm of the public sector, we propose the following classification of public innovations:

- Product or service innovation, focused on the creation of new public services or products. A Dutch example is the so-called Integrated Environmental Licence, the so-called 'Omgevingsvergunning'. Different environmental permits, which deal with different legal obligations, based on different laws and regulations that have to be taken into consideration if a citizen or a company wants to build a new residence for its company (a shop, a plant or a farm) or want to change a home, have been integrated into one umbrella-like permit.
- Technological innovations that emerge through the creation and use of new technologies, such as the use of mobile devices and cell broadcasting to warn citizens in the case of an emergency;
- Process innovations, focused on the improvement of the quality and efficiency of the internal and external business processes, such as the redesign of the computer-supported application of rules and regulations and the redesign of service delivery processes. An example is the digital assessment of taxes;
- Organizational innovations, focused on the creation of new organizational forms, the introduction of new management methods and techniques, and new working methods. Examples are the creation of – mostly HRM, Finance or IT – shared service centres in which organizations share the same ICT systems and services and the use of quality systems;

- Conceptual innovations. These innovations occur in relation to the introduction of new concepts, frames of reference or even new paradigms. For instance, New Public Management and the notion of governance can be defined as conceptual innovations in public administration, because they provide a qualitative new perspective on the way government should organize itself or how government should steer societal developments;
- Institutional innovations, which refer to fundamental transformations in the institutional relations between organizations, institutions, and other actors in the public sector, and more specific in public administration. Examples are the introduction of elements of direct democracy, through referenda and the elections of public officials, such as mayors, in a representative democracy in which some officials have been appointed by the queen, which is for instance the case in the Netherlands.

However, it is important to note that these innovation types are not substantially exclusive. In practice we see that different types correlate which each other. For instance, the introduction of the internet as a technological innovation enables governments to redesign the information and transaction relations and processes with citizens and companies in order optimize working and information processing processes (in terms of process innovation).

3.3. An Innovative Public Sector?

Arguments Against

Some people state that innovation in the public sector is a contradiction in terms. In comparison with the private sector, the public sector may hardly be perceived as innovative. Several arguments are put forward to underline this statement. The most important one is that the public sector lacks competition, while competition is defined as a necessary condition for innovation. According to Schumpeter, innovation (as a process of creative destruction) is the cornerstone of any capitalist system. Companies can only survive if they are able to create new combinations: new products, new markets, new production methods, new organizations etc. [25]. The public sector is a sector in which there is no competition. Governments have the monopoly on the production of specific public and quasi-public goods and services, for which in some cases there has been a good reason, namely the failure of the market to provide public goods.

Moreover, the public sector is dominated by a bureaucratic culture in which standardization and formalization are important values; values which also refer to the 'Rechtsstaat' in which the rule of law, providing legal security and equality before the law, is an important asset. One the one hand standardization and formalization foster these values, because standardization and formalization add to stability and predictability; on the other hand they discourage individual initiative and risk-taking [25: 207]. Standardization and formalization can, therefore, hardly been defined as fruitful conditions for innovation. They can be seen as important characteristics of so-called mechanistic organizations. In a classical study, Burns and Stalker have compared the characteristics of mechanistic organization structures with organic ones. They conclude that there is a strong positive relationship between the organic nature of organizations and the capacity to adapt and to innovate. Characteristic for organic structures are a dynamic and complex organizational environment, horizontal coordination and communication mechanism and less standardization and formalization, thereby creating more variety and competition between ideas [30]. And, variety is also being defined as a necessary condition for innovation. Through variety it is possible to search for 'new combinations'. Scott even states that the state and state organizations in general do not like variety, which they perceive as a threat to their control, deliberately destroying the variety of locally developed solutions for wicked problems as well as the local and contextual intelligence and wisdom that have been used to develop these solutions [31].

Furthermore, the political nature of public administration, rooted in representative democracy, is also being viewed as a handicap for innovation. Three reasons are given. First, the democratic and political nature of public administration is in many cases a culture of compromise in which different political values and different rationalities should be reconciled. Those compromises can hardly be defined as innovative, because they have a rather incremental character, thereby referring to Lindblom's notion of policy-making as the 'science of muddling through' [32]. The second reason is the negative perception and assessment of risk and risk-taking. Bureaucratic and political cultures are perceived as risk avoiding culture. They are rather dynamic in their conservatism [8]. Moreover, in a bureaucratic and political culture in which political and public accountability has become a very sensitive and risky issue (also in combination with the 'hyper' attention of mass media to follow the actions of politicians and public managers), there will be fewer natural incentives left to take specific risks by looking for 'new combinations'. The third reason is the short-term orientation of politics [8]. Drucker has stressed the importance of 'systematic innovation and entrepreneurship', which implies that organizations should develop a long-term, goal-oriented and systematic perspective on how to mobilize internal and external resources - such as knowledge, people and funds - in order to look for 'new combinations', thereby creating fruitful conditions for innovation. Investments in research and developments and setting up research & development departments are examples of systematic innovation [33]. However, in public administration this long-term orientation does not exist [8]. Politics is characterized by a short-term orientation, focused on winning the hearts of (possible) voters and interest groups through 'quick wins'. That is why Schumpeter was rather sceptical about the innovative nature of democracy [25: 93].

Arguments For

However, if we look at the practice of public administration we see a large number of innovations. Innovation as a process of creative destruction is also a process which takes place in the public sector, although the public sector is not perceived as innovative. If we want to study the innovative character of public administration it is important to use another perspective on innovation. According to Zouridis and Termeer it is important to switch from a rather dominant revolutionary perspective on innovation to a more evolutionary perspective [34]. If we look at the different perspectives on the role and position of government with regard to the steering of societal developments (in terms of modes of governance), the way government has organized itself during the last five decades, the way in which public administration has introduced all kinds of quality, budgeting and performance management systems, they way in which citizens participate in policy-making processes, the way in which public administration tries to improve its service delivery process, they way in which ICT has been used, we see numerous (incremental and radical) changes and innovations. Hence, we must conclude that the public sector is also an innovative sector. What arguments can be given to support this statement [34]?

Developments in the environment of public administration, as well as the political and public problems which emerge from them, can hardly be described as rather stable and simple. Ecological problems, problems regarding social quality in cities, the fight against crime and terrorism, the economic development of regions, the growing aging of the populations in relation to the provision of social benefits, social and economic integration of ethnic minorities are all examples of 'wicked problems'. However, the way in which these social problems are translated into political and public problems, combined with the way in which solutions are formulated and measures are taken, creates permanent pressure on government organizations. The emerging turbulence is in many cases an important incentive to look for new combinations in order to be innovative, because it could, in the end, lead to changes in electoral voting, to changing political coalitions. Elections, mass media attention and the growing empowerment of citizens to raise their voices and to go into action, if their interests are really at stake, put government under pressure to innovate.

Moreover, the pressure to innovate and to look for new combinations is also being stimulated by the multi-rationality of public administration. Policy problems can be understood in terms of a permanent struggle between different rationalities [35]. A distinction can be made between political rationality (focusing on the question 'who gets what how and when'), legal rationality (stressing the importance of the 'rule of the law'), economic rationality (stressing the importance of an efficient allocation of costs and benefits) and professional/scientific/technological rationality (putting forward the values which relate to professional and scientific acquired knowledge, based on e.g. professional standards and professional theories of action). The tensions which emerge from the confrontation of values can create a kind of dialectical process, in which compromises between these values are reached on a higher level, thereby creating new combinations of problem definitions and problem-solving strategies.

Innovation also refers to new ways of 'framing and naming', thereby creating new discourses, introducing new sensitizing concepts, opening the way to look for innovative solutions in order to overcome conflicts between these rationalities. Verbal innovation can be regarded as an important innovation strategy within public administration, because language and rhetoric are very important and powerful instruments in public administration to create new coalitions that advocate new frames of references [34, 36, 37]. An example of this kind of conceptual innovation is the notion of sustainability, which tries to combine economic and ecological values.

Another factor that adds to the innovative nature of public administration is the convergence between the public and private sector, which stimulates a more intensive copying of private sector management, organization and technology concepts by the public sector organizations. Moreover, public sector organizations are also more eager to learn from each other, which can be derived from the popularity of benchmarking and best practice studies. Therefore, innovation and learning by copying or mimicking best practices from the private sector and from other public sector organizations can also be seen as a potentially effective innovation practice [38].

4. The Innovation Potential of ICT

Technological developments can stimulate public innovation, especially if one acknowledges that modern ICT has rapidly and substantially penetrated the primary processes of public administration. It has become substantially intertwined with the formulation and implementation of public policy processes, with budgeting and accounting processes, with the delivery of public services, with law enforcement, which are in essence information and knowledge-intensive processes. In this section we want to explore the added value of ICT to achieve innovation in the public sector.

4.1. Perspectives on ICT-driven Innovation

Three complementary perspectives can be distinguished, which tell us something about the possible contribution of ICT to modernize public administration.

The Technological Perspective

First, we can define ICT as a set of tools or instruments that can be used to achieve specific goals. The innovation effort lies in the combination of the goals to be achieved and the specific attributes of the technology to be used. The following developments tell us something about relevant attributes.

First, the capacity of ICT to process increasing quantities of data in speedier and more intelligent ways. Second, due to the process of digitalization, information (not only in terms of data sets, word documents, but also in terms of images and sounds) can not only be more easily transported from one location to another, but can also be more easily manipulated in a tailor-made way. Third, ICT - especially chip technology - has become smaller and smaller and has become more embedded in other materials, which opens up new possibilities. Examples are all kinds of mobile devices which give rise to a shift from electronic, internet-based forms of public service delivery (e-government) towards mobile and wireless forms government (m-government). Moreover, the miniaturization of ICT has led to the fact that ICT has become embedded into the fabric of our daily lives and daily working. It has become an integral part of the devices which we use every day: cars, radio, refrigerators, elevators, etc. etc.

The last development is the integration of computer technology with other communication and information-processing infrastructures, application and devices. Examples are mobile phones and personal digital assistants (PDAs) that can be used to e-mail and surf the World Wide Web. Moreover, they have become equipped with global positioning systems (GPS) and with cameras. Another example is interactive television that can also be used to surf the World Wide Web.

The Organizational Perspective

We can also look at the (inherently) organizational capacities of ICT that make it possible to redesign the information, communication and working processes and relationships within and outside public administration in new ways. Concepts such as business process redesign, e-government and virtual organization express this potential.

The following organizational qualities of ICT are of relevance. The first quality is the ability to connect, thereby creating new information exchange and communication linkages. Presence availability, which implies that people should share time and location to communicate with each other, is no longer a necessary condition for effective organizing. Organizational, functional and temporal boundaries have lost their significance. The result is that the access to (dispersed) information and knowledge of people is no longer a serious problem. The second quality is transparency. It has become rather easy to share and combine existing and dispersed information and knowledge (e.g. through the coupling of databases, data profiling and data mining), which makes it possible to create 'new' information and knowledge. Policy makers may get a more detailed and integrated picture of relevant policy results, policy processes and target groups. However, in many cases transparency opens the door to another relevant quality, which is monitoring and control. The fifth quality is communication. For instance, e-mail makes it possible for people to interact with each other in (hopefully) sensible ways, thereby interlocking and coordinating behaviour.

The Conceptual Perspective

The technological attributes and organizational qualities of ICT can also be used as a set of inspiring and conceptual lenses to look at existing practices or to develop new practices. From this perspective, ICT can be used to frame and to reframe. For instance, in the Dutch city of Tilburg, the police use instant mobile messaging to alert the inhabitants of a neighbourhood to be aware of burglars or to look for a child reported missing. In that way the police make use of the concept of mobilizing 'many eyes' and 'many ears', just a few minutes after something has occurred, which in the case of a missing child for example is quite important.

4.2. Results

If we look at the meaning which politicians, public managers but also citizens attach to the contribution of ICT to actually change public administration, optimism prevails. How realistic is this optimism? What is the actual contribution of ICT to public innovation? What outcomes does research show us?

   Research into the effects of ICT in public administration shows that there are hardly any general effects and changes. Changes are rather specific and context-driven. Effects are limited to the specific setting in which ICT is introduced. Hence, we must be reserved against general claims about the innovation and change potential of ICT [Overviews: 39, 40, 41].

   The reason why these effects are limited and context-driven is that the introduction of ICT in public administration is a social intervention in a policy and organizational network, which influences the position, interests, values and (information) domains of the actors involved. Thus, the introduction and use of ICT is not a neutral but a political intervention in a specific context. Choices with respect to ICT influence the access, use and distribution of information and communication and information relations and patterns between the actors in the policy network, and thus the effects that will occur [42]. For instance, Dutton and Guthrie have analysed the development of the Santa Monica Public Electronic Network as an 'ecology of games', in which an interrelated system of actors within a certain territory develop a number of games with changing players that influence the use of ICT [43]. McLoughlin draws attention to the dynamic interaction between organizational and individual power in order to understand the effects of technology interventions in organizations. Referring to the effects of e-mail, he concludes that there is little point in talking about the impacts of e-mail by focusing on the inherent technical features of e-mail, but rather on the emergent properties of e-mail which result from the micro-political interaction between the technical features of e-mail and the organizational context in which e-mail is introduced and used. The effects of e-mail that have occurred have not been as general as previously claimed. They are limited and contradictory [44]. Evaluating the success and failures of business process redesign by ICT, Davenport also questions the general claim of business process redesign, in which ICT plays an important role [45]. He concludes that the effects that occur can only be understood sensibly by looking at the co-evolving interactions and relations between a diversity of actors, their practices, values and technology within a specific and local (hence unique) environment. It is important to stress that social and technological aspects of an environment co-evolve, ultimately determining the effects of ICT-driven innovations.

Although effects have been documented, there is still another question to be answered: which actor benefits from the changes that actually did occur? Research shows that the use of ICT in the public sector very often strengthens the existing frames of reference, power relations and positions within a policy sector [39]. In many cases ICT tends to extend and reinforce the prevailing biases of governmental structures and processes. However, this so-called reinforcement hypothesis stems from the period before the massive introduction of network technology such as the internet. Does this hypothesis survive the age of the internet? Up until now research findings have been scarce, and if they are present they are ambiguous and based on a single or a few case studies. However, some preliminary observations can be made, which up until now support this reinforcement hypothesis to some extent. For instance, Taylor and Hurt have looked at e-government initiatives of parliaments by looking at their websites [46]. They conclude that a parliament-centric view prevails. The information they provide is information about the parliament, its history, its functioning, its agenda, its members. Access is also given to relevant documents which are discussed in the parliament. However, internet and web technology is hardly used for debate and for participation of citizens, in terms of participation services. The explanation, which Taylor and Hurt give, refers to the dominance of the institutionalized paradigm of representative democracy, in which strong citizenship and active participation of citizens is seen as a threat to the institutions of the representative democracy. However, only 'young democracies' with an emerging new parliamentary tradition, such as the Estonian, Scottish and Slovenian parliaments, used the internet for discussion and citizen participation, emphasizing the importance of looking at the institutional context in which also the new technologies such as the internet are being introduced and used. Hence, the conclusion is drawn by several scholars that the potential of innovation (in terms of contributing to strong, participatory democracy and enhancing the responsiveness of democracy) up till now has not been used fully to address the crisis in the established representative democracies [46, 47, 48]. These examples also illustrate that the effects of ICT are rather ambiguous. They are influenced by the complex and dynamic institutional setting in which it is developed, introduced and used. Moreover, ICT tends to reinforce existing practices, frames of reference and power positions.

5. Plan of the Book

The contents of this book make clear that it is an edited volume, in which a number of case studies will also be presented. The research material that will be presented has originally been produced in separate research projects and has been documented in various forms (e.g. research reports and conference papers). However, it all has in common that it is focused on documenting different kinds of public innovations and tries to gain an insight into factors that account for the success of these innovations. Moreover, it gives us an indication of the actual changes that have occurred.

Framework for Description

We have asked the authors to rewrite and reanalyze their original work by using the following indicative framework for description and analysis.
- What are the aims and orientation of the innovation project and how can this project be understood in relation to specific characteristics of the institutional embeddedness of the project (e.g. degree of politicization, professionalization, fragmentation, type of actors, their interest and strategies, etc.)? Why should this modernization project be understood as an innovative one?
- What is the role of ICT in the modernization project? How is ICT used in the project and what is the expected contribution of ICT in order to achieve the specific goals of the project?
- If we were to make an instrumental assessment of the innovation, how would it look?
  - o   Were the goals of the modernization project accomplished and which factors were critical for success or failure?
  - o   Did ICT contribute to the goals of the innovation and which factors were crucial for the contribution of ICT?
- If we were to make an institutional assessment of the innovation, how would it look?
  - o   Which institutional factors (such as the political or organizational culture, the legal regime or the relationships between the actors involved) have influenced the way in which ICT has been used as well as the results that have been achieved?
  - o   Did the use of ICT challenge existing, grown practices and positions?
  - o   Did the use of ICT contribute to a reinforcement of existing practices, positions and relations in public administration?
  - o   Did the use of ICT contribute to new practices, positions and relations in public administration?
- What do these instrumental and institutional assessments teach us about the relationship between ICT and public innovation?

Outline of the Book

This chapter and the following chapter (part 1) set the stage for the contents of this book. In chapter two Bekkers and Korteland describe the role of ICT in several European modernization and public innovation programmes in which the governments of the United Kingdom, Denmark, the Netherlands and Germany try to redefine their positions, leading to several shifts and modes of governance.

Part 2 consists of several chapters in which ICT is predominantly used to redesign public service delivery processes. The emphasis in these contributions lies on process innovation. Snijkers (chapter 3) makes a comparative assessment of two major business process redesign projects in the Belgian social security sector in which ICT was one of the major drivers to create change and innovation. The general idea was that ICT was able to tackle problems of fragmentation, compartmentalization and a lack of efficiency and effectiveness as well as to improve customer orientation. Some interesting results will be presented. In the following chapter (4) we will broaden our scope. The experiences of eight innovative public service delivery processes in eight European countries (Denmark, Estonia, Finland, the Netherlands, France, Germany, Slovenia and Spain) will be listed. Did the investments made in these projects actually lead to innovative results. What kind of instrumental and institutional factors account for the costs and benefits which have been reported? Process innovation was also a major topic in the redesign of the Dutch social security sector. In chapter 5 Thaens, Bekkers and Van Duivenboden compare two innovation projects, but they address especially one important characteristic of ICT-driven forms of process innovation, namely how to achieve a flexible information architecture which ensures a smooth sharing of cross-organizational information. What instrumental and institutional factors have contributed to the shaping of a flexible architecture?

The characteristics of the technology itself can also be a major incentive to review existing practices and an interesting source of inspiration to develop new practices. That is why we focus in part 3 on technological innovation. Bekkers and Moody devote attention to the role of geographical information systems in the development of public policy programmes. Especially the ability of geographical information system to enhance the transparency of policy problems (through the combination of data and databases) and the possibility of visualizing effects generates interesting policy development practices in different countries (chapter 6). In chapter 7 we look at three innovative projects in the United Kingdom with interactive digital television as a technological innovation which aims to modernize the public administration. The background to the emergence of interactive television is the development of new ICTs and the subsequent convergence of different technologies, including: telephony, computing, photography and television.

In part 4 we shift our attention to another kind of innovation: organizational innovation and the role of ICT in establishing new organizational arrangements. Wagenaar et al. make an assessment of a number of considerations and factors which should be taken into account if organizations cluster similar activities and functions, such as ICT and human resource management services in a so-called shared service centre (chapter 8). Soeparman and Wagenaar look at the role of ICT as a catalyst for the establishment of horizontal organizational arrangements in the Dutch police system and the role of intermediary co-coordinative organizations in it (chapter 9).

In part 5 the emphasis lies on conceptual and institutional innovation. Did ICT contribute to the development of new ideas about how to modernize public administration, for instance to bridge the democratic and participatory gap between government and citizens or to develop new ideas about public service delivery (which go beyond the redesign of existing public service delivery processes). Did ICT contribute to an institutional renewal? Four chapters are dedicated to this central question. Edwards looks at a number of innovative partnerships between local government, citizens and the civic society in Cleveland, in which local communities try to empower themselves to become a full partner in environmental decision-making, making use of ICT (chapter 10). Burt and Taylor take us in the following chapter to the United Kingdom and show how in the UK new concepts of public service delivery are being developed based on new coalitions between the public, private and voluntary sectors (chapter 11). In chapter 12 we see an interesting combination of technological innovation and conceptual innovation. New developments in ICT, such as the use of biometrics, the sharing of data and all kinds of surveillance technologies, have profound implications for the way in which the identity of the citizen can be determined, while at the same time modern technology offers citizens interesting possibilities to manipulate an identity or create additional identities. This implies that our traditional concept of identity has become footloose, giving rise to all kinds of challenges. Lips, Taylor and Organ explore these challenges. E-government as such can be seen as a new concept of how ICT can be used to redefine the relationships which governments have with citizens, companies, other governments, societal organizations and their own employees. But how should we assess the contribution of this new concept?

In part 6 we try to assess, in a more general way, the described ICT-driven innovations. What is the state of affairs of ICT-driven public innovation? And what conclusions can be drawn? What is the image of public innovation if we look at the way in which ICT is used to modernize public administration. For instance, did e-government lead to institutional innovations, to the establishment of new practices, to fundamentally changing existing power positions and relationships? This question will be addressed in the chapter written by Meijer and Zouridis (chapter 13). Van Duivenboden, Bekkers and Thaens will compare the main results of the previous chapters and will present an outlook (chapter 14).

References

[1]   Ministry of the Cabinet Office, *Modernizing Government*, Stationery Office, London, 1999.
[2]   OECD, *The E-Government Imperative*, OECD, Paris, 2003.
[3]   M. Moon, The Evolution of E-Government among Municipalities: Rhetoric or Reality?, *Public Administration Review* **4** (2002), 424-433.
[4]   M. Fenger and V. Bekkers, The Governance Concept in Public Administration, in: *Governance and the Democratic Deficit*, V. Bekkers, A. Edwards, M. Fenger and G. Dijkstra (eds.), Ashgate, Aldershot, 2006 (forthcoming).
[5]   V. Bekkers and V. Homburg, E-Government as an Information Ecology: Backgrounds and Concepts, in: *The Information Ecology of E-Government*, V. Bekkers and V. Homburg, IOS Press, Amsterdam/Berlin/Oxford/Tokyo/Washington DC, 2005, 1-20.
[6]   R. Mayntz, Governing Failures and the Problem of Governability, in: *Modern Governance*, J. Kooiman (ed.), Sage, London, 1993, 35-50.
[7]   Ch. Hood, *Administrative Analysis,* Harvester, Brighton, 1986.
[8]   H. van Gunsteren, *The Quest for Control*, Wiley, London, 1976.
[9]   J.L. Pressman and A. Wildavsky, *Implementation. How Great Expectations in Washington are Dashed in Oakland*, University of California Press, Berkeley, 1973.
[10] B. Hague and B. Loader, *Digital Democracy: Discourse and Decision Making in the Information Age*, Routledge, London, 1999.
[11] V. Bekkers and S. Zouridis, Electronic Service Delivery in Public Administration, *International Review of Administrative Sciences* **65**(2) (1999), 183-195.
[12] B. Barber, *Strong Democracy: Participatory Politics for a New Age*, University of California Press, Berkeley, 1984.

[13] Ch. Bellamy, Modelling Electronic Democracy, in: *Democratic Governance and New Technology*, J. Hoff, I. Horrocks and P. Tops (ed.), Routledge, London/New York, 2000, 33-53.

[14] H.P.M. van Duivenboden, Citizen Participation in Public Administration. The Impact of Citizen Oriented Public Services on Government and Citizen, in: *Practicing e-Government: a Global Perspective*, Khosrow-Pour, Medhi (ed.), Idea Group, Hershey, 2005, 35-47.

[15] Ch. Hood, Contemporary Public Management: a New Global Paradigm?, *Public Policy and Administration* **10**(2) (1995), 104-17.

[16] C. Pollitt, *The Essential Public Manager*, Open University Press, Maidenhead, 2003.

[17] A. Lawton, Public Service Ethics in a Changing World, *Futures*, **37**, 231-243.

[18] OECD, *Modernising Government: The Way Forward*, OECD, Paris, 2005.

[19] A. Ringeling, *Het imago van de overheid*, VUGA, Den Haag, 1992.

[20] J. Clarke and J. Newman, *The Managerial State*, Sage, London, 1997.

[21] M. Veenswijk, Cultural Change in the Public Sector: Innovating Frontstage and Backstage. Organizing Innovation, in: *Organizing Innovation*, M. Veenswijk (ed.), IOS Press, Amsterdam/Berlin/Oxford/Tokyo/Washington DC, 2006.

[22] D. Easton, *A System Analysis of Political Life*, Wiley, New York, 1965.

[23] D. Stone, *The Policy Paradox. The Art of Political Decision-Making*, Norton and Company, New York/London, 2002.

[24] F.W. Scharpf, *Governing in Europe: Effective and Democratic?*, OUP, Oxford, 1998.

[25] J. Schumpeter, *Capitalism, Socialism and Democracy*, Harper, New York, 1942.

[26] E. Rogers, *Diffusion of Innovations*, Free Press, New York, (5th edition), 2003.

[27] J. Fagerberg, D. Mowerey and R. Nelson (eds.), *The Oxford Handbook of Innovation*, OUP, Oxford, 2005.

[28] G. Mulgan and D. Albury, *Innovation in the Public Sector*, Strategy Unit Cabinet Office, London, 2003.

[29] B.A. McDaniel, *Entrepreneurship and Innovation. An Economic Approach*, Sharpe, New York, 2002.

[30] T. Burns and G. Stalker, *The Management of Innovation*, Tavistock, London, 1961.

[31] J.C. Scott, *Seeing Like a State*, Yale University Press, New Haven/London, 1998.

[32] C. Lindblom, The Science of 'Muddling Through', *Public Administration Review* **19** (1959): 79-88.

[33] P. Drucker, *Innovation and Entrepreneurship*, Harper & Row, New York, 1985.

[34] S. Zouridis and K. Termeer, Never the Twain Shall Meet. Een oxymoron: innovatie in het openbaar bestuur, *Bestuurskunde* **14**(7/8) (2006), 13-23.

[35] I.Th.M. Snellen, *Boeiend en geboeid*, Samsom H.D. Tjeenk Willink, Deventer, 1987.

[36] M.J.W. van Twist, *Verbale vernieuwing: aantekeningen over de kunst van de bestuurskunde*, VUGA, Den Haag, 1995.

[37] M. Edelman, *Political Language. Words that Succeed and Policies that Fail*, Academic Press, New York, 1977.

[38] P.J. DiMaggio and W.W. Powell, The Iron Cage Revisited: Institutional Isomorphism and Collective Rationality in Organizational Fields, in: *The New Institutionalism in Organization Analysis*, W.W. Powell and P.J. DiMaggio (eds.), UCP, Chicago, 1991, 63-83.

[39] K. Kraemer and R. King, Computing and Public Organizations, *Public Administration Review* (1986), 488-496.

[40] I.Th.M. Snellen and W.B.J.H. van de Donk (eds.), *Public Administration in an Information Age*, IOS Press, Amsterdam/Berlin/Oxford/Tokyo/Washington, 1998.

[41] K.V. Andersen and J.N. Danziger, Impacts of IT on Politics and the Public Sector: Methodological, Epistemological, and Substantive Evidence from the "Golden Age" of Transformation, *International Journal of Public Administration*, **25**(5) (2001), 129-159.

[42] R. Kling, Computerization as an Ongoing Social and Political Process, in: *Computers and Democracy*, G. Bjerkness, P. Ehn and M. Kyng (eds.), Ashgate, Aldershot, 1987, 117-136.

[43] W. Dutton and K. Guthrie, An Ecology of Games. The Political Construction Of Santa Monica's Public Electronic Network, *Informatization and the Public Sector* **1**(1) (1991), 279-301.

[44] I. McLoughlin, *Creative Technological Change*, Routledge, London, 1999.

[45] Th. Davenport, *Information Ecology*, OUP, Oxford, 1977.

[46] J.A. Taylor and E. Hurt, Parliaments on the Web: Learning Through Innovation, in: *Parliament in the Age of the Internet*, S. Coleman, J. Taylor and W. van de Donk (eds.), OUP, Oxford, 1999, 141-155.

[47] S. Coleman, J. Taylor and W. van de Donk, Parliament in the Age of the Internet, in: *Parliament in the Age of the Internet*, S. Coleman, J. Taylor and W. van de Donk (eds.), OUP, Oxford, 1999, 3-8.

[48] B.N. Hague and B.D. Loader, Digital Democracy: an Introduction, in: *Digital Democracy: Concepts and Issues*, B.N. Hague and B.D. Loader (eds.), Routledge, London, 1999, 3-22.

Information and Communication Technology and Public Innovation
V.J.J.M. Bekkers et al. (Eds.)
IOS Press, 2006

Governance, ICT and the Innovation Agenda of Public Administration: A Comparison of Some European Policy Initiatives

Victor BEKKERS[1] and Evelien KORTELAND
Erasmus University Rotterdam, Faculty of Social Sciences, the Netherlands

Abstract. This chapter explores what kinds of shifts of governance are being proposed in several European modernization programs and what the alleged role of ICT is here. It is argued that the innovative potential of ICT, defined as a neutral tool, is primarily used in relation process innovation, stressing the importance of efficiency and service delivery, thereby facilitating a consumer democracy which is based on a redesign of the machinery of government. However, one can question if the broader innovation potential of the governance concept and the role of ICT, has been fully acknowledged.

Keywords. Governance, Modernization, e-government, European Policy Initiatives

1. Introduction

During the last ten years, several modernization and public innovation programs have been drafted in different European countries as a response to new ideas about the organization and management of public sector organizations - like New Public Management (NPM) and the discussion about 'governance' - as well as a reaction to major cut-back operations due to public finance considerations.

In these programs ideas have been developed about the need for change within the public sector. From a governance point of view, these programs could be assumed to develop a perspective on state-society relations in a world that is growing ever more complex, interdependent and therefore, hard to govern. Questions have been raised about the efficacy and efficiency of government. Answers have been found in a plea for public innovation. One of these innovations is the paradigm shift from 'government' to 'governance', which can be seen as a conceptual innovation.

From a policy analysis perspective, it is important to look at the dominant frames of reference which lay behind the drafting of these programs and the reform agenda

---

[1] Corresponding Author: Erasmus University Rotterdam, Faculty of Social Sciences, Public Administration Group, P.O. Box 1738, 3000 DR Rotterdam, the Netherlands, E-mail: Bekkers@fsw.eur.nl.

which accompanies them; a reform agenda which presents arguments why it is necessary to question the role and position of government in relation to specific shifts and modes of governance. Two grounds can be given. First, it is important to reveal the specific biases which lay behind the drafting of modernization programs, the myths that are fostered and the claims and demands that have been formulated [1, 2, 3, 4]. How valid are those? The second ground is that language, rhetoric and symbolism play an important role in public administration, because they contribute to the creation of a shared frame of reference in order to enact a desired political reality, because of its persuasive power [5, 6, 7].

In this chapter we will focus on the assumptions - the language and rhetoric which are used to express them - that lay behind a number of shifts and modes of governance, which are presented as desired roads for the modernization of government in several European countries. Moreover, we focus on the use of ICT as a vehicle for modernization. The first research question will be: What are the basic assumptions behind the shifts in, and modes of governance that have been formulated in a number of strategic policy documents on government modernization in four countries, namely Denmark, United Kingdom, Germany and the Netherlands? The second question refers to the role of ICT in the accomplishment of these modernization goals. How is this role being perceived?

In section two the notion of governance will be explored. Shifts and modes of governance will be described. In section three we will elaborate on the role of ICT, while in section four a description will be presented of our research strategy in order to select and compare relevant public innovation policy programs. Moreover, attention will be paid to the kind of assumptions which have to be taken into consideration while studying these programs. Next in section five we will describe the modernization and public innovation programs of Denmark, the Netherlands, the United Kingdom and Germany. In section six a comparative analysis will be made and some conclusions will be drafted. Finally, in section seven some reflections will be put forward.

2. Shifts and Modes of Governance

2.1. From Government Towards Governance

In the last decade, the concept of 'governance' has become a popular theme in the theory and practice of public administration [9]. Following Van Kersbergen and Van Waarden [10: 151-152], it could be argued that all these applications of the governance concept within public administration have three elements in common. First, the governance concept refers to pluricentric rather than unicentric systems. Traditionally, governments have been put in the centre of all kinds of societal developments and problems. They were supposed to be able to effectively intervene in societal developments and solve societal problems from a centralised and hierarchical position, detached from society, and consistent with to the goals laid down in a policy programme. Ineffective government interventions were primarily seen as flaws in the 'machinery of government', as the result of imperfect knowledge on the nature and effects of the problem, and as the product of a mis-match between the policy instruments that were used and the policy goals that were formulated. From the 1990's this idea was subject to a lot of criticism. Moreover, government and society are not an entity but a conglomerate of actors which all together try to influence societal developments. This change in thinking can be understood in terms of a shift from government towards governance.

Second, networks, whether inter- or intra-organizational, play an important role and they make two things visible. They express the fragmentation of society and government and their dependencies. Moreover, these networks organize relations between relatively autonomous, but interdependent actors. In these networks, hierarchy or monocratic leadership is less important or even absent. Formal government may be involved, but not necessarily so, and if so, it is merely one – albeit an important – actor among many others [10: 151-152]. As a consequence, the state "can no longer assume a monopoly of expertise or of the resources to govern, but must rely on a plurality of interdependent institutions and actors drawn from within and beyond government" [11: 11-12].

Third, the focus is on processes of governing instead of the structures of government, in terms of continuing and game-like interactions between all kinds of (semi-)public and private actors within several societal domains and at different levels. These processes refer to practices of negotiation, compromise-seeking, concerted action, and cooperation rather than the traditional processes of coercion, command and control [10: 151-152, 12: 53]. The practices are very often rooted in trust and regulated by rules of the game negotiated and agreed upon by the actors involved, based on the notion of self-regulation [12: 53].

How can governance practices be made visible? How can we identify the empirical manifestations of governance more clearly? The emergence of governance practices in public administration can be made demonstrable in two ways.

2.2. Shifts in Governance

The first way is that all these practices have in common that problem-solving capacity is transferred from the traditional state institutions towards other levels or institutions. According to Van Kersbergen en Van Waarden [10] the following shifts in governance capacity can be identified:

- An upward vertical shift from nation-states to international public institutions with supranational characteristics such as the EU, the WTO, and the IMF. This upward vertical shift can also be observed within specific state functions, like the judiciary and the police.
- A downward vertical shift from national and international to sub-national and regional levels. In part, this is related to the previous shift, because international bodies rely on local agencies to implement and enforce their regulations. But also within states there is a growing tendency to decentralize tasks, authorities and responsibilities to the regional level and from the central to the decentralised level of government, in favour of other territorial bodies of government, like municipalities and regions.
- A horizontal shift between the executive, legislative and judicial power. In many countries, the judiciary is assuming a more active role in rule interpretation, and de facto also in rule formation.
- A horizontal shift from public to semi-public, autonomous organizations and agencies. "Policy-making, implementation, enforcement and control have become differentiated as separate functions. For reasons of efficiency and effectiveness in complex situations and political prudence or credibility, some of these sub-tasks

have been delegated to more autonomous semi-public or even private institutions"[10: 154].

- A horizontal shift from public to private organizations. For instance, in Dutch public administration the reintegration of sick and disabled persons which formerly were tasks of public organizations has now been shifted to private companies.
- A horizontal shift from the central public level to the civil society. In several countries, governments try to replace regulation by 'self-responsibility' of its citizens. The intellectual roots of this governance practice lie in notions like communitarianism, 'civil society' and 'the third way'. All these notions deny the central importance of bureaucracies in the delivery of public services and instead look for means of 'coproduction', personal involvement and citizen engagement as the way to make government perform better. Bureaucracies may still be necessary, but the people themselves can play a larger role in helping themselves.
- A shift to the withdrawal of the state from certain activities, replaced by an appeal to the self-regulating capacity of citizens. In most instances, this appeal to self-regulation is inspired by the wish to decrease the number and complexity of state regulations that create a high administrative burden for citizens and organizations.

2.3. Modes of Governance

The shift in problem-solving capacity can lead to the emergence of specific modes of governance [13, 14, 15].

Governance from a Distance: Deregulation, Performance and Accountability

In this mode of governance the relationship between the organizations which steer and the organizations which are the object of steering is still hierarchical, but the organizations steered are given a (substantial) amount of discretion to develop and implement their own policies, based on the recognition of self-regulation [13]. The internal processes of an organization (the throughput) are no longer the objects of detailed government intervention, but the results (output and outcomes), which an organization should produce. This implies a retreat of government, which only governs from distance. Kooiman [14] talks about 'hierarchical governance': giving more discretion in order to enhance the necessary flexibility of organizations to respond to, for instance changing implementation conditions, but within a hierarchical framework. As a result of this retreat of government, deregulation is an important instrument, which can be used to reduce the administrative burden, in order to provide the necessary administrative freedom or discretion [15]. The fundamental assumption of the move towards deregulating government has been that if some constraints on bureaucratic action are eliminated, government could perform its functions more efficiently. The problem is not the people in government; the problem is the system, meaning the rules and regulations that inhibit swift and effective action [15]. Deregulation can be seen as a prerequisite for de-bureaucratization which opens the door for public entrepreneurship.

It is in this mode of governance that the ideas about New Public Management (NPM) and governance meet. Both paradigms emphasize the shift from process accountability towards accountability in terms of results, which have been achieved [16].

If we look at the accountability issue we see a shift in this mode of governance in the way accountability has been organized. Traditionally accountability is organized in a vertical, hierarchical way, in which for instance government agencies are being held accountable for the results they have achieved by a minister or by Parliament. Nowadays, we also witness more public ways of accountability, in which information about results of agencies are also made accessible and transparent for other societal groups than administrative and political superiors, like citizens as consumers of public services or professional peers [17]. These public accountability arrangements are complementary to the more political, rather 'classical' accountability arrangements, which recognize the fragmentation of the network society with its proliferation of stakeholders.

Self-Governance, Level Playing Fields and Competition

In this governance mode, government interventions are focussed on the shaping of a level playing field which facilitates self-regulation, like the development of a collective quality system within a policy sector or the sharing of information between different service providers in order to create a transparent market for privatised public services. One could say that a level playing field or an arena is created in which interdependent stakeholders meet and negotiate with each other in order to realize cooperation or collective action [13].

Kooiman defines this mode of governance as self-governance [14]. Steering interventions can be focussed on allocation of (equal) positions in the arena, the process of inclusion and exclusion of actors, and the definition of the boundaries of the arena. Moreover, steering can also be focussed on the definition of playing rules to which the actors in the arena should comply with, in the bargaining processes between them in order to achieve collective action. Government interventions are not related to define the definition of the specific outcomes of the collective behaviour within the arena or level playing field. The content itself is the product of self-regulation between the parties involved. It is restricted to the shaping of relations (stipulating interdependency) and the definition of playing rules, which could facilitate cooperation and stimulate self-regulation. In the practice of public administration we see that this mode of governance is rather dominant in the liberalisation of traditional public monopolies, e.g. due to legislation of the European Community. From this point of view, the introduction of market models in the public sector (also called market governance) has been seen as a strategy of reforming government. Its primary intellectual root is in the belief that a market model or an analogous competitive model will contribute to a more efficient allocation of resources, like public health services, in society [15].

Participation, Linking and Cooperation

In this mode of governance, steering is focussed on facilitating a shared understanding between the organizations or stakeholders in a policy network in order to create a common, and trustworthy policy practice through interaction, communication, negotiation and exchange [13, 14, 15]. Kooiman defines this mode of governance as co-governance [14]. The positions, tasks, interests and frames of reference of relevant (public and private) stakeholders are linked together in order to create competitive perspectives on the nature of the problem and of possible solutions. In this mode of governance the focus lies on the active participation of a variety of interests involved, which can be discerned around (rather complex and wicked) policy problems like the reconstruction of an urban area, in which private and public partners should cooperate, or the prevention of juvenile crime in which all kinds of public organisations and societal organizations should work together. The bringing together of these stakeholders does not only add to the acceptance of the policy program (in terms of support), once it has been drafted, but it also enhances the collective problem solving quality due to the possible new combinations of knowledge, information and experience. The fundamental concept behind this version of participation, which is also called 'discursive democracy' [18] or 'strong democracy' [19] is that the 'experts' in a bureaucracy do not have all the information, knowledge or even the right type of established policy answers to deal with a specific challenge. Therefore isolating important decisions from public and plural policy involvement could lead to policy errors.

Governance as New Public Management

In the public administration discipline, there has been some debate on the nature of the relation between the ideas of the New Public Management (NPM) on the one hand and the governance paradigm on the other. Perhaps it is possible to define NPM as a specific governance practice, with an emphasis on market governance and governance from distance. Developed in the late 1980's, the 'New Public Management' has evolved into a highly popular label for a wide variety of reforms in the public sector that share two common features: "lessening or removing differences between the public and the private sector and shifting the emphasis from process accountability towards a greater element of accountability in terms of results" [16:94]. More in specific, Pollitt [20: 27-28] identifies the following eight key elements of the 'New Public Management' (NPM):

- A shift in value priorities away from universalism, equity, security and resilience towards efficiency and individualism, defining the role of a citizen as a 'homo economicus';
- A shift in the focus of management systems from inputs and processes towards results and outputs;
- A shift towards measurement and quantification, especially through the development of performance indicators and benchmarks systems;
- A preference for more specialized, 'lean', 'flat' and autonomous organisational structures;
- A substitution of formal, hierarchical relationships between or within organisations by contracts or contract-like relationships;
- A much wider deployment of markets or market-type mechanisms for the delivery of public services;
- An emphasis on service quality and a consumer orientation;
- A broadening and blurring of the frontiers between the public sector, the market sector and the so-called third or non-profit sector.

3. On the Role of ICT

In this section we aim to understand the role of ICT in the modernization programs in public administration. In many policy documents, and not the only one that we have studied, we see that the use of technology is very often seen as an important trigger for modernization and public innovation. How can we assess the relationship between modernization and ICT?

Assessing the Role of ICT

Several approaches can be distinguished. First, one can see ICT as a set of neutral and powerless tools which can be used as an instrument to accomplish specific modernization goals, like the improvement of public service delivery. In this approach the emphasis lies on the capacity of ICT to handle large quantities of data in a speedier and cheaper way, while at the same time the processing of this data takes place in a more sophisticated, more integrated way. Efficiency-improvement is the main justification of the use of ICT. In the second approach ICT is defined from an organizational perspective. Specific organizational qualities are given with the technology itself, like the capacity to improve control, to create transparency or the ability to link or to connect people, organizations, groups, information and knowledge. These organizational qualities not only provide more efficient ways to process data, but they can also facilitate the design of new organizational arrangements, e.g. the creation of portals or online fora, or the redesign of existing business and policy process (e.g. like BPR). In the third approach to ICT, which can be defined as a political approach of the use of ICT, ICT is seen as a powerful and scarce resource, which actors within and without public administration can use to protect or enlarge their specific interests, positions and biases [6: 21]. The fourth approach, which can be seen as a more institutional approach, focuses on the specific values and meanings which are embedded in technology itself (like the power to control or the promise of progress), which are being attached to the use of ICT by actors; values and meanings which challenge other existing values and meanings within public administration as well as established practices, routines and procedures (in terms of 'rules') which are facilitated by ICT or surround the functioning of ICT [22, 23]. Hence the first question should be: How do stakeholders, who are involved in the drafting and implementation of modernization programs, define the role of ICT at forehand?

Assessing the Effects of ICT

The next question raised is what effects will be actually realized through the use of ICT within public administration? What factors, in the end, shape the effects that take place when ICT is used in public administration? Are these questions being raised in the documents studied? The answer to this question refers to another debate which is often called the technology debate. The first position is the deterministic position that reflects the idea that ICT is an autonomous, exogenous power. The effects that will occur are given with the characteristics of the technology, and they shall occur. Technology is a defining technology [24]. Very often the notion of the information society, as the manifestation of the defining power of ICT, is used as a future from which nobody can escape. The voluntarists presuppose that ICT is a neutral set of tools that enable individuals to realize their goals. Technology is viewed as an enabling technology, as a set of instruments that are willing instruments in the hands of their masters and the goals they want to accomplish. The effects that ICT will realize are primarily goal-driven and are dependent on the effective and efficient use of ICT. ICT is seen as a set of instruments that can be controlled by the people who use them. The challenge is to apply the right tools in the right manner. Both positions can be combined by the following assumption which is dominant in all the documents. The emergence of the information society produces new technologies which cannot be denied, and because they are available they should be applied in the most proper way so that they can be seen to produce effects that support the reinvention of government.

However, research into the effects of ICT in public, but also private organizations shows that the effects that are generated by the use of ICT in public administration are not general, but specific and context-driven [22, 25, 26, 27, 28, 29] . In the policy documents studied, the existing political, socio-organizational and institutional setting in which ICT and e-government is introduced, is neglected. So we can question the claim of a more open, client-oriented and more responsive government, realized by the proper use of ICT. There are hardly any general effects. Effects are limited to the specific setting in which ICT is introduced.

The reason why these effects are limited and context-driven is that the introduction of ICT in public administration is a social intervention in a policy and organizational network, which influences the position, interests, values and (information) domains of the actors involved. Thus, the introduction and use of ICT is not a neutral, but a political intervention. Choices with respect to ICT influence the access, use and distribution of information and communication and information relations and patterns between the actors in the policy network, and thus the effects that will occur [22, 30, 31] Evaluating the success and failures of business process redesign by ICT, Davenport and Prusak also question the general claim of business process redesign [31]. They conclude that the effects that occur can only be understood sensibly by using an 'information ecology' approach. An information ecology can be described as the evolving interactions and relations between a diversity of actors, their practices, values and technology within a specific and local (thus unique) environment. It is important to stress that social and technological aspects of an environment co-evolve [31, 33, 34].

Assessing Who Benefits?

Not only is it important to understand why the effects that have occurred did take place, but it is also important to raise the question: Who benefits from these limited effects? Research shows that ICT in the public sector very often strengthens the existing frames of reference, power relations and positions within a policy sector [27]. ICT tends to extend and reinforce the prevailing biases of governmental structures and processes. However, this so-called reinforcement hypothesis stems from the period before the massive introduction of network technology like the Internet. Does this hypothesis survive the age of the Internet? Up till now research findings are scarce, and when present they are ambiguous and based on a single or a few case studies. But the results of scarce empirical studies show us that breakthroughs can sometimes be noticed, but in general the reinforcement hypothesis has not been fundamentally challenged. Internet technology also tends to reinforce existing positions and practices [e.g. 34, 35, 36].

4. Research Strategy

We have argued why it is important lo look at the assumptions behind the public innovation programs which have been formulated in a number of European countries during the last five years. These assumptions refer to the following ideas.

Assumptions Relating to Possible Drivers for Modernization

The nature of the societal problems which governments should address, is one set of assumptions which should be analyzed, because they can be seen as possible drivers for modernization. The perception of these problems challenge the problem solving capacity of government. And thus the role and position of government vis à vis other public and private actors. Examples are the aging of the population, the empowerment of the citizen, the rise of the information society or the globalization of the economy, the importance of the European Union.

Assumptions Related to Goals of Modernization and Shifts of Governance

Given these problems, which modernization goals have been formulated as an answer to these problems? Do these problems lead to specific shifts in governance and what kind of governance arrangements should be established in order to accomplish these goals? For instance, should governments aim to be more open and responsive to the needs of citizens and does this imply a shift in governance in favour of more citizen participation? What kind of political values are being addressed and sponsored by the modernization goals that have been formulated and the shifts of governance which have been promoted?

Assumptions Related to Specific Measures and Actions

The next group of assumptions refer to the specific actions that should be implemented in order to establish these new governance arrangements in order to meet the desired modernization goals. For instance, the empowerment of citizens as consumers implies that citizens should be given more personal freedom to choose. How is this freedom of choice realized? What instruments should be deployed? One step could be to improve the transparency of government in which citizens through the Internet could compare the prices of government services?

Assumptions Related to the Role of ICT

Special attention will be paid to assumptions which lay behind the role of ICT as an important instrument that can contribute to the modernization of government. How is added value of ICT being perceived? For instance, is the added value of ICT primarily perceived as contributing to efficiency, transparency, accountability or participation? Is ICT defined as an instrument which can be controlled and which presents new possibilities? Who should benefit from the use of ICT and are they able to do so?

We have tried to reconstruct these assumptions through a qualitative analysis of the content of policy programs. In order to analyze the assumptions behind these modernization programs, we have compared and analyzed strategic policy programs of four OECD countries that have formulated national modernization programs. We selected the following countries: Denmark, the Netherlands, the United Kingdom and Germany, which fit in a specific 'idealtype' state and governance tradition [37]. These state traditions can be summarized in the following table.

Element\tradition	Anglo Saxon	Germanic	French	Scandinavian
State-society Relations	Pluralistic	Organic	Antagonistic	Organistic
Form of political organization	Limited federalism	Integral/organic federalist	Centralized and indivisible (Jacobean)	Decentralized unitary
Basis of policy style	Incrementalist, 'muddling through'	Legal corporatist	Legal technocratic	Consensual
Form of decentralization	State power (US); local government (UK)	Cooperative Federalism	Regionalized unitary state	Strong local autonomy

Table 1. Elements of State Traditions

If we look at the selected case studies we see that Denmark, the United Kingdom and Germany fit in the state traditions which were named after them. The Netherlands can be seen as a combination of German and Anglo-Saxon elements. The lack of English written modernization programs has made it difficult for us to study French modernization programs or modernization programs of countries which could fit the French tradition of public administration.

5. Modernizing Government: the European Public Innovation Agenda

In this section we will describe and analyse a number of modernizing initiatives which have taken place during the last years in a number of European countries in accordance with the scheme presented in the previous section. Although we recognize the fact that these programs should be understood from an historical and institutional perspective, and that they elaborate on past experiences, we only focus on the 'broader' programs, which present a helicopter view on the modernization. In some cases these programs have been worked out in more specific programs, which will not be address.

5.1. Denmark

In May 2002 the Danish government launched its public sector modernization program titled 'Citizens at the Wheel'. The program provides a framework for renewal and describes the goals of the public sector for the future as well as examples of measures that are being implemented. The document should be seen as an isolated document, but it fits in a continuous line of earlier modernization projects.

Drivers for Modernization

What are the main reasons for this renewal? If we analyze the document, a clear motive can not be identified. It is stated that 'the public sector needs modernization' (p. 1). The document refers to 'major challenges in the coming years', but only pays attention to the rising number of the elderly, while the number of persons of working age remains unchanged. This will exert considerable pressure on state expenditure, while more people will need to provide for care (p. 19). Externally this will lead to a rising demand upon existing and for new public services. Internally, within public administration a large number of people will retire, which can affect the functioning and organization of the public sector. In order to manage this problem the public sector should become more efficient and more attractive for younger people (p. 19).

Modernization Goals and Shifts in Governance

If we look at the goals of this modernization program, we see that a new governance paradigm has been presented in order to achieve a welfare society based on freedom and solidarity. In 'Citizen at the wheel', the emphasis lies on the establishment of a major shift in governance, in favor of the citizen. It must ensure that the public sector a) is based on the free choice of citizens, b) is open, simple and responsive en c) provides value for money and is thus more efficient (p. 5). This implies that citizens should stand at the wheel (p. 31).

The solutions which are brought forward refer to the ability of the public sector to adapt in order to suit the needs of the citizens – not the other way around – which should lead to a critical examination of existing structures and responsibilities (p. 5). In order to do so, government has to generate simpler and more transparent rules and to eliminate systems which obstruct the expression of individual initiative (p. 5). However, the increased choice of alternatives does not mean that an individual citizen can get whatever he or she likes. Freedom of choice, which implies to have alternatives to choose between – especially in key social service areas between private, state- as voluntary organization (p. 6, 8), must exist within an order of priorities and a politically determined service level (p. 7). Politically elected politicians will decide on the services and the level of quality, which will be maintained by public authorities (p. 7, 22), while operations and the organization of the work within individual institutions will be the responsibility of the institution's management (p. 22). Accordingly, costs and results must be made evident, because political prioritization of public funds requires that expenditures should be made visible and transparent (p. 22). Moreover, government should create a framework to allow different suppliers to offer innovative solutions and to create diversity in the services provided (p. 8).

Does this also affect other governance relations? In order to meet the needs of the Danish citizen, collaboration between different parts of the public sector is necessary, especially between municipalities but also between the public sector and voluntary organizations. The interplay between the latter could contribute to the development of solutions that are more responsive to the needs of citizens (p. 23).

Measures and Actions

How should this new governance paradigm be implemented? If we look at the modernization agenda of the Danish government we see that the following measures will be taken. The first cluster of measures deals with the actual freedom of choice. A prerequisite for the freedom of choice is that there are alternatives to choose between. Government should therefore provide for are alternative suppliers. Furthermore, there should be an adequate level of information concerning the various choices and services made available. Also, the quality of services to be rendered should be satisfactory (p. 8). In addition to these measures, the legal position of citizens should also be improved (p. 10).

The second cluster of measures relates to a more open, simpler and user-friendlier administration. Rule and administrative simplification and the reduction of administrative burdens are important proceedings to be taken, not only for citizens but also for the business community (p. 12, 13, 17). In order to realize this, information and communication technology plays an important role. As e-government becomes more widespread, it is the Danish government's aim to allow citizens and businesses to monitor the progress of their own cases via the Internet, and to be able to receive information on case procedures, decision and case processing times. The responsiveness of government is not only based on the creation of a more open and transparent administration, but also on the active involvement and consultation of citizens and users (p. 17). This will be more far-reaching than the influence which citizens currently enjoy through user boards, etc. It is defined as a fundamental matter of every public institution, which also presupposes that it will assume a certain degree of responsibility and to make an active contribution towards helping to shape the public sector (p. 17).

In order to stimulate the necessary changes, the Danish government wishes to reward institutions to their efforts. In some areas the amount of financing will depend on the number of citizens who choose for the supplier of particular services. In this way, the supplier of these services will enter into healthy competition to increase quality (p. 23). Moreover, more competition will emphasize the need for each institution to work systematically to improve quality and efficiency and to organize their work in a holistic way (p. 23). The importance of competition also implies that private companies should have the opportunity to challenge the efficiency of the public sector. That is why local and central government should be able to explain why a given task should be undertaken by the public sector, if a company makes the case that it can perform better and at a lower price (p. 24).

The Role of ICT

If we look at the role of ICT we see that in the Danish view ICT is primarily seen as an instrument to improve public service delivery, by efficiency as well as the openness of government. The Danish government aims to bring Denmark to the forefront of developments as a modern IT and knowledge-based society, and is aiming new technology to alter the way that work is performed in the public sector. The aim is to provide citizens and businesses with better services and to release public employees for tasks that contribute directly to the welfare of citizens (p. 20). Furthermore, it has been stated that the investments made in e-government can eliminate manual, routine case processing and reduce administration times. The goal is the establishment of more efficient public working practices, as well as faster and more correct case administration, for the benefit of citizens and businesses" (p. 20). Moreover, ICT will underpin the creation of a more open, user-oriented and democratic administration. As e-government becomes more widespread, it is the government's aim to allow citizens and businesses to monitor the progress of their own cases via the Internet, and to be able to receive information on case procedures, decisions and case processing times. The government also desires that information technology is used to strengthen the level of dialogue between citizens and politicians (p. 17).

5.2. The Netherlands

In 2003 the Dutch government presented a perspective on how to modernize government, which was defined as 'Andere Overheid' (translated: Another government) The main document is an Action program, which was accompanied by a vision document on behalf of the Cabinet, which conceptually tries to legitimize the actions of the Action program and which came after the formulation of the Action program.

Drivers for Modernization

In the Action Program it is said that changing societal conditions have been the motive that the Dutch government likes to reflect on its role and position (p. 3). Government has been forced into a position in which it is expected that it should solve of all kinds of small and major societal problems through rather detailed regulations. However, many problems cannot be solved which should lead to a re-formulation of the role of government, in terms of retreat, and a re-formulation of the role and position of the citizen, which should be seen as an empowerment of the citizen who is (or should be) willing to participate in society and who is (or should be) self-responsible. This should lead to the drafting of a new social contract between government and society, which enables government to attack only the core problems of Dutch society, which refer to the core competences of government, while at the same time the handling of other problems are joint responsibility of government, the private sector and the civil society (p. 4). But what are these changing social problems and conditions? In the Cabinet vision some are mentioned. The main argument is that the emancipation of the citizen has not taken place successfully. On the one hand citizens have empowered themselves, but on the other hand this empowerment did not lead to a situation in which citizens translated their emancipation in terms of taking more responsibility for the way societal problems can be attacked (p. 6). This should lead to a new balance between the duties and rights of the citizen versus government (p. 7) in which the grown close (financial) relationships between government and citizens should become rather loose ties – especially in the non-profit sector. An other reason, not so prominent as the previous one, to modernize government is the relationship between the Netherlands and the European Union, the avalanche of all kinds of restrictive and detailed regulations - which in some cases have European roots - that causes all kinds of enforcement problems, administrative burdens and legal procedures (p. 7).

Modernization Goals and Shifts in Governance

In the Action program (p. 4) and in the Cabinet vision (p. 11-12) the outline of the Dutch modernization and governance strategy has been sketched as follows. A modern government should, first, be reserved in things it wants to regulate. It should take a distant position and should focus on the headlines and general frameworks. Second, government should create room for self-regulation for citizens, companies, agencies and the organizations of the civil society so that these actors can have a greater responsibility. This implies a new distribution of responsibilities between government and other societal sectors. In the civil society of the emancipated citizen the responsibility of government ought to be rather limited. As a consequence, there will be some responsibilities left which should be picked up by government. Government should guarantee basic public interests and the rule of the law. Hence, the major shift in governance which can be distinguished is a shift towards the civil society. The final goal is that government should provide a high quality of those services which have been defined as public services and cannot be provided by private or non profit organizations.

Measures and Actions

Four lines of action have been identified in the Action program, which have been worked out in all kinds of sub-lines and projects. What one can observe is that there is some distance between the concrete level of action and the governance strategy which has been worked out. The notion of self-regulation by the civil society has not substantially been worked out in the Action program. The emphasis lies on increasing the efficiency of public administration. The first line of action is the improvement of the quality of public services in terms of improving efficiency, more demand-driven and in a more customer-friendlier way. ICT should play an important role in order to realize these goals (p. 7-14). The second line is a reduction of the number of regulations (deregulation) and the development of new and other regulatory regimes, which focus on the definition of broad frameworks, which offer more room for self-regulation (p. 16-22). This should lead to a reduction of the administrative burden for companies and citizens. The third line is that government will organize itself in a different way. Attention should be paid to the number of ministries and the core competencies of these central departments, the elaborated policy advice system and a new civil service, the number of executing agencies, the quality and organization of law enforcement, and the internal administrative system and financial management system (p. 22-33). The last line of action is the improvement of the relationship between central government on the one hand and the local and regional government bodies on the other hand. Not only should these bodies obtain more freedom, but the cooperation between them and with the central government should improve also through chain management approaches, while at the same time the performances of the bodies should be made transparent and comparable (p. 35-38).

Role of ICT

In the Dutch Cabinet vision (p. 9-10) ICT has been primarily defined as an instrument which possibilities have not been fully used, especially and primarily in relation to improving public service delivery, although some attention has been paid to improving the monitoring of public performance (p. 14) and the possibility ICT can offer to increase the public and political participation of citizens (p. 14) However, hardly no attention has been paid to, neither in the action program, why this is the case. The focus in the Action program (p. 7-9) has been on the realization of a number of goals of which the improvement of the quality and efficiency of public service delivery (e.g. improving the whole person concept, developing pro-active and demand orientated public service strategies, one stop virtual counters which are open 24 hours per day, as well as reducing administrative burdens) is the most important one. Also, a lot of attention has been paid to the role of ICT as an instrument for business process redesign in implementation chains and networks in which the exchange and sharing of information between different layers of government and agencies as well as semi-public and private organizations is important to improve public service delivery as well as the enforcement of law and regulations (p. 37).

5.3. The United Kingdom

On March 30, 1999, the British government launched a major public sector reform initiative by tabling its 'White Paper on Modernising Government' (Prime Minister and Minister for the Cabinet Office, 1999). The White Paper states the government's vision for the public sector for the years ahead, and incorporates a wide-ranging set of reforms.

Drivers for Modernization

Modernizing government to get a better government and getting government right in order to make life better for the people of Britain have been defined as a vital part of the renewal of Britain (p. 4, 9). In order to do so government should face the challenges it meets. The basic line in the document is a loud call for transformation. But what are these challenges? These challenges are hardly defined. Only two arguments have been put forward. First, that one is aware that better government is about much more than whether public spending should go up or down. The main focus of past reforms has been on improving value for money too much. Modernizing government should be about finding new and better ways, which meet the needs of the people as consumers and citizens, who have become more demanding (p. 5, 15). Second, ICT and the rise of the information age is revolutionizing our lives, which offers "a new scope for organizing government activities in new, innovative and better ways and for making life easier by providing public services in integrated, imaginative and more convenient forms" (p. 9). Moreover, the document notices that the distinction between services delivered by the public and private sector is breaking down, which opens the road to new ideas, partnerships and opportunities (p. 9).

Modernization Goals and Shifts in Governance

Looking at the 'tabula rasa' of observations, intentions and goals in the document, we observe that all the arguments which are brought forward concentrate on the following five goals. In the first place things should change in relation to the kind of policy-making that is taking place. It is important that policies produce outcomes that matter, that meet the rising demands of the people and business, and are not reactions on short-term pressures. The separation between policy and delivery, in relation to a fragmented organization of public administration and a risk averse culture, has prevented this. The second challenge is to deliver responsive public services that will meet the needs of citizens and not the convenience of service providers (p. 23). This implies that government should listen and be sensitive to the concerns of people and businesses and involve them in decisions on how services should be provided. Moreover, services should be provided in a more integrated way that reflects people's real lives, which prevents that people do not have to hunt down services by a process of trial and error (p. 25). Another goal is to improve the quality of public services. In the document it is stated that efficient public services will be provided, which are of high quality and that mediocrity will not be tolerated. In order to achieve these previous goals, the development of information age government has been seen as the main driver for modernization. ICT should contribute to the joined up working between different parts of government and provide new, efficient, and convenient ways for citizens and businesses to communicate with the government and to receive services (p. 45). The last goal is focused on a re-valuation of the civil service. Government should be committed to public services and public servants and should not denigrate them. This has been neglected for too long. It is important to establish a culture of improvement, innovation and collaboration, which asks for new skills, new talent and new standards (p. 56). What are the main shifts in governance which can be derived from these challenges? The answer can be mainly found if we look at a number of measures which have to be taken in order to achieve these goals.

Measures and Actions

The British document on 'Modernising government' is rather ambiguous, because measures are difficult to find. The document, which is highly rhetorical, consists of all kinds of intentions which tumble over each other. In order to improve the quality of public policy making, attention should be paid to design policy around shared goals and carefully defined results and not around the organizational structures or existing functions. The goals should focus on the outcomes to be delivered, which should also lead to a better appraisal of costs and benefits (p. 16). Moreover, it is important to develop new partnerships between the Whitehall, the devolved administrations, local government and the voluntary and private sector. Consulting experts, those who implement policy and those affected by it, early in the policy process can contribute to develop policies that are deliverable from the start (p. 16). This implies that government should regard policy-making as a continuous learning process, not as a series of one-off initiatives. More attention should be paid to the organization of the feedback process (p. 17). In order to design more responsive services, government should listen more to the needs of citizens and businesses and try to involve them in the decisions on how these services should be delivered. Therefore government should consult and work with them, especially in relation with specific target groups like elderly people, women, small businesses and ethnic minorities and with specific areas (p. 27-29). Moreover it is important to deliver joined up delivery of services that have measurable outcomes that provide a better value for money.

The quality of the services to be delivered can be improved by focusing on the results that matter to people, by developing general standards, and by monitoring and auditing results (p. 35). It is also important to use competition in order to deliver improvements. This means that government should look at what services government can provide itself, what should be contracted out to the private sector and what should be done in partnership (p. 35). Information age government which has been defined as a major goal is at the same time the main instrument to achieve many of the described goals. ICT is defined as a set of tools to offer new ways of service delivery, new ways of communication, new ways of sharing information which enable new forms of collaboration and improving the access to and organization of information (p. 46).

The improvement of the public service is primarily seen as the development of another culture, in which innovation and collaboration are important values. In order to achieve this a new human resource policy should be developed that especially brings in skills and experience from outside (p. 56).

In this section several shifts in governance and modes of governance can be discerned. Because of its focus on public service delivery the main shift can be understood in terms of a shift towards the citizen which has higher expectations of the services to be provided and the way he or she should be consulted in designing these. Moreover, improving public service delivery also implies a better working together between different parts of government. Attention should also be paid to the outcomes of the policy programs which should provide a better value for money.

Role of ICT

In the UK document ICT has been defined as a goal as well as an instrument. E-government (defined as information age government) is an aspect of modernizing government which has only one purpose: to make life better for citizens and business. The emphasis lies on the improvement of electronic service delivery in such a way that it reflects real lives and delivers what people really want, and on a more effective use of the government's information resources. In order to accomplish these goals, all parts of government have to work better together: joined-up government is needed (p. 45). Up till then, government did not use the possibilities which ICT offers sufficiently. This should fundamentally change (p. 45-47). The UK would like to use new technology to meet the needs of citizens and business, and not trail behind technological developments (p. 45). This is why attention should be paid to a more effective and efficient use of ICT (p.45-47).

5.4. Germany

In December 1999 the German Federal Government launched the program 'Modern State – Modern Administration'. It is a joint political program of the federal government to modernize the state and administration on the basis of the concept of the enabling state, which has been described as a future-oriented perspective, taking into account the different understandings of the roles of the state and administration. Together with an actively participating society it will be able to successfully steer a middle course between a leaner state and a state which reduces state intervention and excessive regulation (p. 7). What are the assumptions behind this idea of the enabling state and the shifts in governance which become manifest in this concept?

Drivers for Modernization

The main reasons for introducing the program are not very clear and concrete. It is only stated that 'the state and the administrative system must redefine their tasks and competences taking into account the changed conditions within society' (p. 6).

Moreover, the concept of the "lean state" which was pursued in the past, has been defined as limited to reducing public tasks too much, i.e. it only focussed on a set of perceived negative goals, which were seen as a rather isolated approach of internal modernization (p. 7) not responding to changed societal conditions.

Modernization Goals and Shifts in Governance

The concept of the 'enabling state' has been grounded on four pillars. The first one is a new distribution of responsibilities between state and society. On the one hand the state should continue to protect the freedom and security of its citizens as its core task for which it remains solely responsible (e.g. internal security, legal protection, and tax collection). On the other hand there are many tasks which so far have been deemed to be public tasks, which are equally important but need not be fulfilled by the state itself. Here, however, the state must ensure that they will be fulfilled (p. 8). In that case the reform of the state and its administrative system should be based on a model that creates a new balance between the duties of the state, individual initiative and social commitment. "This will shift the focus in such a way that the state becomes less of a decision taker and producer and more of a mediator and catalyst of social developments which cannot and must not control on its own. The enabling state means strengthening society's potential for self-regulation and guaranteeing the necessary freedom of action. Above all, it requires the concerted action of public, semi-public and private players to achieve common goals. This interaction needs to be developed and enhanced. In this context, it is the special responsibility of the federal government to create the legal framework for a state geared to the needs of its citizens, acting like a partner for them and endowed with an efficient administrative system" (p. 8).

The second pillar is a responsive public service, which implies that the interests and motives behind government decisions need to be transparent, and that players in society have better information at hand (p. 8). "Therefore, the federal government wishes to enhance the transparency of public administration and boost participation by the people. To this end, the state and the administrative system will have to prepare themselves for the transition from a society based on industrial production to a knowledge-based society, and use the possibilities offered by information technologies as a basis for keeping citizens informed and for communicating with them" (p. 8).

The third pillar is that a better cooperation between the different tiers or bodies of public administration, because they have to work together more closely as well as respect each other. In order to achieve this, the document presupposes more freedom of decision, based on the principle of subsidiarity. Moreover, it tries to foster diversity within the federation by reducing the number of federal government provisions (p. 9) and to offer the 'Länder' a chance to reform their administrative systems if federal government provides them with more room to manoeuvre (p. 9).

The fourth pillar is an efficient administration, based on a better use of the limited financial resources through the development of more performance-oriented and cost-efficient procedures so that superfluous 'red tape' can be eliminated. This can be achieved through competition and benchmarking (p. 9), while at the same time government should modernize its human resource policies through the introduction of more performance related elements into the numeration and career schemes of the public service and to elaborate on human resource development (p. 10).

Measures and Actions

Given these modernization goals and the measures to be taken, they concentrated themselves on four areas of reform, which can be defined as a set of sub-goals of the modernization goals which already have been sketched. The improvement of the effectiveness and acceptance of legislation is the first area of change. More attention should be paid to the consequences of legal provisions and to the identification and dismantling of obstacles for new services.

Furthermore, the cooperation between the bodies of government, in which the federal government defines itself as a partner, should be based on the removal of barriers which hamper independent actions by the 'Länder' and local authorities. The aim is to extent their scope of action and to strengthen local self-government, which should lead to a shift in competences. It is also important to improve the cooperation with the private sector. In line with the argument above, "the federal government will create scope for the development of self-initiative and self-regulation and will promote voluntary work. It will also remove restrictions and create new forms of cooperation between the state, the private sector, the welfare organizations and other non-profit-making institutions" (p. 13).

Thirdly, measures should be implemented that contribute to a competitive, cost-efficient and transparent administrative system with higher performance targets while cutting expenses. In order to achieve this, government has to adapt more and more to competitive conditions, making use of instruments of business administration, such as accurate accounting and controlling. However, an administration can become more efficient only if it improves the way in which the citizens are involved in administrative decision making and provided that it makes administrative actions more transparent (p. 14). It also implies that government will be engaged in a concrete dialogue with the citizens and to reveal red tape. To this end, the federal government will make use of modern information and communication technologies on a broad basis, thus accomplishing the transition towards the 'electronic government' (p. 14-15).

The last area of reform is the creation of a highly motivated employee force in which "personal responsibility, better career opportunities and flexible, self-determined working structures (collaborative working) ensure that the existing potential for modernization is actually being used" (p. 16).

Role of ICT

In the federal German program not much attention has been paid to the role of ICT. The most interesting remarks have been made in relation to the goal of creating a more responsive public service. It has been stated: "Therefore, the federal government wishes to enhance the transparency of public administration and boost participation by the people. To this end, the state and the administrative system will have to prepare themselves for the transition from a society based on industrial production to a knowledge-based society, and use the possibilities offered by information technologies as a basis for keeping citizens informed and for communicating with them" (p. 8).

6. A Comparison of the Initiatives

In this section we will compare the programs that we have studied and try to search for striking resemblances and differences on which will be reflected.

Assumptions regarding\ country program	Denmark	Germany	The Netherlands	United Kingdom
Drivers for modernization	Major challenges in the coming years, which is only elaborated in relation to the growing number of elderly people which also gives rise to a large demand on existing and new services and in relation to meet the needs of citizens	A need to redefine tasks and competences in relation to changed conditions in society. Moreover the former concept of the 'lean state' is a too limited approach for modernization	Redefinition of the role of government in relation to changing societal conditions and lacking efficacy to solve societal problems. Citizens are not willing to take their own responsibility in solving these problems. They are too dependent on the state	To face challenges implies transformation. Focus on two challenges: a) meeting the increasing needs of citizens, b) reacting on the possibilities of ICT
Goals	Public sector based on a) the free choice of citizens, b) is open, simple and responsive and c) provides value for money.	Modernization by a) new distribution of responsibilities between state and society, b) responsive public service which is transparent and boosts participation, c) more collaboration between government bodies, d) an efficient administration	Modernization by a) retreat in regulation, b) a shift of responsibilities towards self-regulation by the civil society, c) a focus on essential public interests and the rule of law, d) improving high quality public services	Modernising government implies a) focussing policy making on outcomes that meet the demands of citizens and businesses, b) responsive public service delivery of a higher quality c) information age government, d) improving quality of civil service
Measures and actions	Creation of alternatives to choose between and improving information about alternatives Administrative simplification and reduction of administrative burdens Strengthening role of ICT	Shifts in competences to improve self-government Improving quality of legislation Improving cost-efficiency through performance management, citizen participation in defining 'red tape' and ICT	Improving quality of public services, deregulation and self-regulation, other way of organization of the central government, and new relationships with local and regional government	Focus on outcomes to be delivered in services and policies, improving feedback mechanisms; improving consultation and participation of users; central role of ICT; an new human resource policy for the public service

	Improving competition between service providers	Modernizing human resource policy		
Dominant shift	Towards citizens	Towards society, other decentralized layers of government, towards citizens	Towards the civil society in order to improve self regulation by citizens	Towards citizens
Dominant modes	Market - governance, governance at a distance, network governance	Multi-level government, network government	Governance at a distance; market-governance; and societal self-governance	Multi-level government, network government
Dominant political values	Responsiveness Freedom of choice Efficiency Value for money	Self-organization of decentralized government Responsiveness Efficiency Value for money Accountability	Self-organization of the civil society Efficiency	Responsiveness Efficiency Value for money
Role of ICT	Primarily focussing on improving the quality of public service delivery, internal and external efficiency and openness of government	Primarily focussing on responsive public service delivery	Primarily focussing on public service delivery, internal and external efficiency as well as business process redesign in implementation chains and networks	Primarily focussing on improving public service delivery

Table 2. A comparison of initiatives

What conclusions can we draw from this comparison?

Modernization Drivers

If we look at the main drivers for modernization, we observe that in the policy documents references have been made to changing societal conditions, but that a profound analysis of these developments and their consequences for the role and position of government has not been made. Conditions that have been mentioned are the rising number of elderly people (Denmark), the increasing needs of empowered citizens (UK), the uncompleted emancipation of the citizen (Netherlands) and the emergence of the information society (UK). This implies that the drivers for modernization have a rather internal bias.

Two explanations can be given. The first one is that internal efficiency goals are the hidden motives of the modernization programs; the second one is that modernization programs can be seen as a ritual in public administration, through which governments periodically make clear – for internal and external reasons – that they are able to meet new emerging normative reforms or socio-political ideologies, like New Public Management (e.g. UK and Germany), communautarism and the civil society (e.g. the Netherlands) or neo-liberalism (e.g. Denmark). It is also interesting to see that only Denmark and the Netherlands have paid some attention to the rising power of the European Union as a relevant layer of government, which is primarily seen as a source of detailed regulation.

Modernization Goals

A comparison of the programs show us that the main emphasis lies on the improvement of the quality of public service delivery. Demand-orientation, public participation and improving openness and responsiveness are all relevant aspects which return in the documents studied. In all the programs this was one of the main goals mentioned. We also observe that there is a need to redefine the responsibilities of the state, which is primarily the case in Germany and the Netherlands. In Germany, this has been phrased in terms of self-government – especially in relation to other layers of government – while in the Netherlands the uncompleted emancipation of the citizen should be compensated through giving citizens more responsibility that has been based on the notion of self-regulation. Moreover, we see in most programs that improving efficiency and getting more value for money are also goals which should be realized. Sometimes these goals have been formulated explicitly (Netherlands, Germany), sometimes they have been hidden away, but if one looks at the measures and actions that will be taken, then one sees that these goals are quite prominent, e.g. in relation with administrative simplification, improving competition, improving performance management methods and feedback mechanisms. What one can observe is that New Public Management as a management theory has been an important source of inspiration for the design of these concrete measures.

Shifts in and Modes of Governance

These modernization goals also affect the shifts of governance which come about. We notice a shift towards self-government and self-regulation which has been elaborated in several ways. The first expression of self-government has been decentralization in favour of other bodies and layers of government. This has been especially mentioned in the German and Dutch cases and in a lesser degree in the Danish case. At the same time a plea has been made to improve the cooperation between these layers of government in all of the four countries studied, very often in relation to the provision of integrated, holistic services like in Denmark, the UK and the Netherlands.

The second expression of self-government has been the idea that the private sector and the civil society in terms of the non-profit sector, should also have more liberty and autonomy to provide (semi-)public services, which should substitute or compete with the services provided by government. This is especially the case in Denmark, the

Netherlands and Germany. Deregulation and privatisation are instruments which can be used to realize the goals.

The third expression refers to shifts to give citizens a greater responsibility. Three options can be discerned. The first one is to address citizens as consumers of public services and to improve the information position of the citizen in order to act as a rational consumer. This orientation is dominant in the Danish case. The second option is to design more responsive public service delivery which actually meets the needs of citizens and companies, which is present in all the four cases, but especially in the UK. In order to realize this, it is necessary that citizens as a consumer can participate in the design of the public service delivery process. The final option is to stimulate the self-responsibility of the citizens, not only as a consumer but also as an engaged 'citoyen', who takes up his own responsibility as co-producer of solutions for societal problems. This is the dominant Dutch perspective on self-regulation, based on ideas about the civil society.

Shifts in Political Values

These shifts in governance can be understood in terms of shifts towards specific layers of government or target groups, but they can also be understood in terms of a shift in political values. In the documents studied, the following political values are rather present. The first one is liberty, referring to giving more freedom and autonomy to other layers of government and to citizens in order to act as rational consumers of public services or in order to take more responsibility for the functioning of society. But liberty also presupposes accountability for the outcomes of the autonomy and liberty which has been given, especially in relation to the outcomes which have been realized by local and regional government bodies. Many of the measures which have been formulated are focussed on improving accountability, like the introduction of performance management methods and bench marking. Liberty is also a necessary condition for efficiency, which is another political value which should be mentioned. A trade-off between liberty and efficiency can be found, if one looks at the possibilities that are being offered for private and non-profit organizations to take over former public tasks and provide all kinds of public services as well the idea to increase the competition within the public sector itself, between public service agencies. Another trade-off between efficiency and liberty can be found in the idea of deregulation and rule simplification, which cannot only contribute to more freedom and to act more responsible but can also reduce the administrative burdens for citizens and companies so that they can operate more efficient. If we look at this change in political value orientation, we see that they match neo-liberal ideas about the way government should modernize.

The Role of ICT

Looking at the way the role of ICT in the modernisation of government has been put forward in the various documents, we see that ICT is primarily seen as a tool which can be used to realize specific goals, and corresponding public values. Sometimes it stated that this tool has not been used properly and that there are barriers which should be overcome to implement in a more effective way (The Netherlands, UK). The emphasis lies primarily on improving public service delivery (e-government in a narrow sense), which can be understood in relation to a shift in governance to empower the position of the citizen, and on improving internal and external efficiency (the latter in relation to redesign of the transaction and communication processes with citizens and companies). In some cases ICT is put in relation to the omnipresence of the information society which should also affect the way in which government should use the possibilities of ICT (UK, Denmark). Moreover, in most cases, with an exception of the Danish case, we can see that the use of ICT has not been related to specific shifts in governance or specific modes of governance. It has primarily been related to the goal of improving public service delivery.

7. Reflections on the Nature of Modernization

How should we understand the conclusions which are drawn in the previous sections? In this section we will present some reflections which can help us to understand the assumptions which lay behind the modernization agenda in the countries studied; reflections which have been primarily based on an institutional perspective on the modernization of public administration, focussing on the practices that emerge.

7.1. Ongoing Modernization and Institutional Isomorphism

If we look at the modernization goals and the shifts in governance which are related to them, we observe, although the institutional embeddedness of the Danish, German, UK and Dutch government is quite different (see section 4) that there is a striking resemblance. This is also the case for the way in which ICT has been defined. It is perceived as a set of tools which can be used to realize the quality of public services (as a goal) and internal and external efficiency (as a goal as well as a public value). What kind of explanations can be given for this striking similarity of the different modernization agenda's?

This drive for modernization can be understood in terms of all kinds of policy challenges that have to be addressed, like the rising demands of citizens, the growth of the number of elderly people and the evolving claim on existing and new services or the lack of efficiency within public administration, but it can also be understood as the outcome of a sociological process of functional rationalization. As a general theoretical concept the term modernization has its roots in Weber's modernization theory, in which modernization refers to the further rationalization of organizations and social systems in general. From Weber's point of view the rationalization process of the Western society takes shape through a process of bureaucratization, in which power is being exercised on clearly defined and well known - thus formal and standardized - rules. At the same time we see that in many modernization programs, a plea has been made for de-bureaucratization, for rule-simplification. Perhaps the drive to enhance the modernization of public administration can be understood in a more proper way by relating modernization to Mannheim's concept of functional rationality as opposite to the concept of substantial rationality. Functional rationality refers to the extent to which a series of actions is organized in such a way as to lead to predetermined goals with maximum efficiency [38: 33]. Or, in the words of Mannheim, functional rationality refers to the organization of a series of actions in such a way that it leads to a previously defined goal, in which every element in this series of action receives a functional position and role [39: 53]. The call for a more managerial approach, like NPM, in public administration can be understood as the expression of this functional rationality. Therefore, public management reforms consist of deliberate changes to the structures and processes of public sector organizations with the objective of getting them, in some sense, to run better [40: 8]. Efficiency and efficacy are important values in order to judge whether these reforms contribute to a public administration that runs better; values which also stress the importance of the output side of public administration. Opposite to the notion of functional rationality, Mannheim has introduced the notion of substantial rationality. Substantial rationality refers to an act of thought which reveals intelligent insight into the interrelations of events in a given situation [39: 53]. In the case of public administration, the notion of substantial rationality refers to the process of goal formulation in which there are all kinds of trade-offs between different political values, for instance, between liberty versus equality, security versus liberty. Within public administration a growing tension can be observed between the values which are related to the functional rationality, like efficiency, and more substantial values which refer to political values like liberty, equity, security, participation, etc. [41]. To some extent this tension can also be understood in terms of a confrontation between 'management' and 'politics' [42] or between the market model and the polis model of policy making [43]. This additionally influences the legitimacy of public administration in general and the legitimacy of governance practices in specific, in which the confrontation between substantial and functional rationality takes place.

Another reason, closely related to the previous reflections, is that government organizations, in order to survive as legitimate organizations, are forced to comply with specific administrative and management ideologies which can be seen as the expression of functional rationalization as a specific, yet dominant, pattern of meaning. New public sector management techniques and reforms like NPM, e-government as well as the notion of 'governance' can be seen as myths and ceremonies, which, provided adopted and performed, add to the legitimacy of an organization towards its environment. Conformity implies success; non-conformity implies failure. Meyer and Rowan have shown us the importance of 'myths' and 'ceremonies' that legitimise the transformation of organizations to meet changing environmental conditions in order to secure success, survival and resources [44]. DiMaggio and Powell refer to the same process, which they label 'institutional isomorphism' [45]. The learning strategy which lies behind this is that of imitation, of mimicking. Organizations tend to reduce uncertainty by imitating the ways of other organizations that they use as models. By doing this the organization will not cause to stand out or to be noticed as different. Organizations also copy specific management reforms because they could enhance their status as being progressive and innovative.

7.2. Instrumentality and Reinforcement

In the policy documents, there is a strong belief and trust in the promises of modern ICT. Optimism prevails on the progress the information society and Internet technology will bring. The dominant view on technology that lies behind the several policy documents is a combination of determinism and voluntarism. The deterministic position reflects the idea that ICT is an autonomous, exogenous power. The effects that will occur are given within the characteristics of the technology, and they shall occur. Technology is defining technology and is given together with the rise of the information society. The voluntarists presuppose that ICT is a neutral set of tools that enables individuals to realize their goals. The challenge is to apply the right tools in the right manner. However, it is the question whether government should adopt a more realistic view on the way ICT should be defined in order to understand undesired effects, like failing modernization, which reflect the other positions in the technology debate (see section 4).

Moreover, we see that ICT is primarily defined as a tool for achieving public service delivery and efficiency. In relation to these goals the modernization potential of ICT has been narrowed down tremendously. It is primarily seen as an instrument to achieve process innovation, for instance as an instrument to redesign public service delivery processes, which are more transparent, more integrated and more efficient. In the modernization programs studied it is to be seen that ICT has hardly been put forward in relation to specific societal problems, like the quality of the health care and educational sector or the rising number of elderly people, and other relevant, non-economic, public values. Moreover, the innovation potential of ICT has not been related to institutional innovation, for instance in breaking down grown practices and positions. Although the Danish modernization program aims to empower citizens as rational consumers, it is within the framework of the existing practices of Danish public administration. This brings us to another point. The focus of innovation has been primarily on the role of the citizen as a consumer, while other roles have been neglected. In most cases they are mentioned but worked out poorly. Hence, we can formulate the hypothesis that the contribution of ICT to the modernization of government in terms of shifts in modes of government up till now will probably reinforce the existing structures, positions and processes within public administration.

7.3. Consumer Democracy and the Machinery of Government

Following the observations made in the previous section, we see that the shift of governance towards the citizen has two consequences. First, we see the emergence of a consumer democracy, blended with ideas about New Public Management, complementary to the existing democratic order. Modernization primarily takes place through a shift of governance towards the citizen as a consumer, who a) should be empowered so that he is able, more than before, to act as a 'homo economicus' who actually has a choice (Denmark), b) can obtain more client-friendlier and more cost efficient services (Denmark, UK, Netherlands, Germany), c) can participate as co-producer in the way services should be provided (Denmark, UK) in order to strengthen the responsiveness and need-orientation of the public service delivery process (Denmark, Germany, UK).

In a consumer democracy the power and scope of the administrative system is being limited not by restoring a civil society of the homo publicus (which is present in the Dutch cabinet vision but not in the Action program) but by seeking the realm of the homo economicus [46: 40]. The consumer democracy model shares with economic liberalism and rational choice theory the assumptions that individuals are to be regarded as active, competent and instrumental and rational in the making of choices and the expression of preferences, at least as far as their consumption of public services is concerned. This also implies a strong claim for information on public service entitlements as well as to the means of enforcing those entitlements [46: 41]. ICT is either used to improve the information base of citizens to make more rational choices or is used to improve the information base of government in order to deliver more tailor-made, integrated ways of service delivery which recognize the dynamics of the needs of citizens.

The second implication is that government can only meet the challenges of a more integrated, more responsive way of delivering public services, if it functions as an efficient machine, which can be achieved by a) deregulation, b) reducing 'red tape' and c) monitoring the outcomes which are produced by the machinery of government in terms of value for money, focussing on quality and efficiency, d) improving the collaboration between the 'cogwheels in the machinery of government' (collaboration between layers of government and agencies), e) through the introduction of more 'management techniques' which come from the private sector and f) strengthening the central control of the functioning of machinery of government by on the one hand giving more autonomy but on the other hand focussing on specific parameters. From this point of view ICT is primarily seen as an instrument to improve the functioning of the cogwheels in the machinery of government, because service delivery processes can be redesigned in a more efficient and effective way, while at the same time it offers new possibilities to design an administrative system which functions as a cybernetic system in which more and better information, for instance about the outcomes of the service delivery process and the needs of citizens, enables government to govern more effective. From this point of view government is seen as an 'information processor' in which the use of ICT is primarily defined as information management [47, 48].

The emergence of a consumer democracy which asks government to organize itself resembling a machinery, can be seen as an important step to modernize government. However, it is the question whether this, rather one-dimensional modernization agenda does recognize the multiple faces of government and the multiple roles of citizens, especially if we relate it to the discussion on the decreasing legitimacy of government and relate it to other modes of governance which have been distinguished in section two, focussing on participation, linking and the co-production of shared policy practices in policy networks. This also poses consequences for the role of ICT.

8. Conclusion: the Emerging Public Innovation Agenda

In the modernization programs of Denmark, the Netherlands, United Kingdom and Germany a retreat of government is to be seen. We have noticed a shift towards self-government, market-governance and self-regulation. This can be described as a conceptual innovation: introducing a new steering paradigm in which government is not primarily seen as the principal actor that shapes societal developments. More cooperation between layers of government and between public, private and societal organizations is being promoted. Moreover, more attention is being paid to the role of the citizen as a client c.q. consumer of public services. The empowerment of the citizen as a consumer forces public administration to become more responsive towards these citizens and to become more transparent and efficient. It is also stated that governments should be made more accountable for the products and services it produces and the outcomes realized. The political values these shifts in governance express are efficiency, accountability and liberty. ICT is primarily seen as an instrument which can be used to achieve these goals and values, especially in relation to the redesign of public service delivery processes. On the one hand ICT is used to redesign the machinery of government in a more efficient and transparent way. On the other hand ICT is used to improve the information position of the citizen (as an empowerment strategy) in a more substantial way, which opens the door for the establishment of a consumer democracy, which can be seen as an institutional innovation. However, the potential of ICT in order to achieve institutional innovation has not been fully acknowledged. Two reasons can be given. First, an internal perspective on modernization prevails. Innovation, and the potential of ICT in order to facilitate this, has hardly been related to a number of complex and wicked societal problems. The internal problems of government dominate, which primarily ask for a redesign of existing processes and organizations. Second, the potential of ICT has primarily been aimed at the role of citizen and companies as consumers or clients of public products and services, who as tax payers expect customer friendly, high quality and efficient products and processes; at the same time government is primarily being portrayed as service company. Other roles of the citizen as well as of government organizations have not substantially been addressed. However these other roles can offer additional possibilities for innovation; innovation which is aiming at introducing governance practices in which e.g. participation, linking and cooperation are important political values.

References

[1] M. Edelman, *The Symbolic Use of Politics*, University of Illinois Press, Urbana, 1967.
[2] M. Edelman, *Political Language. Words that Succeed and Policies that Fail*, Academic Press, New York, 1977.
[3] F. Fisher and J. Forester (eds.), *The Argumentative Turn in Policy Analysis and Planning*, UCL Press, London, 1993.
[4] W. Parsons, Public *Policy: An Introduction to the Theory and Practice of Policy Analysis*, Edward Elgar, Cheltenham, 1995.
[5] K. Weick, *The Social Psychology of Organizing*, Addison-Wesley Publications, Reading, Mass., 1969.
[6] J. Pfeffer and G.R. Salancik, *The External Control of Organizations*, Harper & Row, New York, 1978.
[7] J.G. March and J..P. Olsen, *Rediscovering Institutions*, The Free Press, New York, 1989.
[8] G. Majone, *Evidence, Arguments & Persuasion in the Policy Process*, Yale University Press, New Haven/London, 1989.
[9] H.G. Frederickson,. Whatever Happened to Public Administration? Governance, Governance Everywhere, in: *The Oxford Handbook of Public Management*, E. Ferlie et al., Oxford University Press, Oxford, 2005.
[10] K. van Kersbergen and F. van Waarden, Governance as a Bridge between Disciplines: Cross-Disciplinary Inspiration regarding Shifts in Governance and Problems of Governability, Accountability and Legitimacy, *European Journal of Political Research* **43** (2004), 143-171.
[11] J. Newman, *Modernising Governance. New Labour, Policy and Society*, Sage, London, 2001.
[12] R. Rhodes, *Understanding Governance*, Open University Press, Buckingham, 1997.
[13] I.Th.M. Snellen, *Boeiend en geboeid*, Tjeenk Willink, Deventer, 1987.
[14] J. Kooiman, Governance and Governability: Using Complexity, Dynamics and Diversity, in: *Modern Governance*, J. Kooiman (ed.), Sage, London, 1993, 9-20.
[15] G.B. Peters, *The Future of Governing*, University Press of Kansas, Lawrence, 1996.
[16] Ch. Hood, Contemporary Public Management: a New Global Paradigm, *Public Policy and Administration* **10**(2) (1995), 104-117.
[17] A. Meijer and M. Bovens, Public Accountability in the Information Age, in: *The Information Ecology of E-Government*, V. Bekkers and V. Homburg (eds.), IOS Press, Amsterdam/Berlin/Oxford, 2005, 171-182.
[18] J.S. Dryzek, *Deliberative Democracy and Beyond*, Oxford University Press, Oxford, 1990.
[19] B. Barber, *Strong Democracy, Participatory Politics for a New Age*, University of California Press, Berkely, 1984.
[20] C. Pollitt, *The Essential Public Manager*, Open University Press, Maidenhead, 2003.
[21] T.H. Davenport, *Information Ecology: Mastering the information and knowledge environment*, Oxford University Press, Oxford, 1997.
[22] R. Kling, Computerization as an Ongoing Social and Political Process, in: *Computers and Democracy*, G. Bjerkness, P. Ehn and M. Kyng (eds.), Ashgate, Aldershot, 1987, 117-136.
[23] P. Frissen, *Bureaucratische cultuur en informatisering*, Sdu, Den Haag, 1988.

[24] S. Zuboff, *In the Age of the Smart Machine*, Basic Books, New York, 1998.
[25] W.E. Bijker, Th. P. Hughes and T.J. Pinch (eds.), *The Social Construction of Technological Systems*, MIT Press, Cambridge Mass., 1981.
[26] J.N. Danziger, W.H. Dutton, R. Kling and K.L. Kraemer, *Computers and Politics*, Columbia University Press, New York, 1986.
[27] K. Kraemer and R. King, Computing and Public Organizations, *Public Administration Review*, 1986, 488-496.
[28] C. Bellamy and J. Taylor, *Governing in the Information Age*, Open University Press, Buckingham, 1998.
[29] I.Th.M Snellen and W.B.J.H. van de Donk (eds.), *Public Administration in an Information Age*, IOS Press, Amsterdam/Berlin/Oxford/Tokyo/Washington, 1998.
[30] W. Dutton and K. Guthrie, An Ecology of Games. The Political Construction of Santa Monica's Public Electronic Network, *Informatization and the Public Sector* **1**(1) (1991), 279-301.
[31] V.M.F. Homburg, *The Political Economy of Information Management: A Theoretical and Empirical Analysis of Decision Making Regarding Interorganizational Information Systems*, Labyrint publication, Capelle a/d IJssel, 1999.
[32] T.H. Davenport, R.G. Eccles and L. Prusak, Information Politics, *Sloan Management Review* **34**(1) (1992), 53-65.
[33] B.A. Nardi and V.L. O'Day, *Information Ecologies*, MIT Press, Cambridge Mass., 1999.
[34] V. Bekkers and V. Homburg, E-Government as an Information Ecology: Backgrounds and Concepts, in: *The Information Ecology of E-Government*, V. Bekkers and V. Homburg (eds.), IOS Press, Amsterdam/Berlin/Oxford, 2005, 1-20.
[35] J.A. Taylor and E. Hurt, Parliaments on the Web: Learning through Innovation, in: *Parliament in the Age of the Internet*, S. Coleman, J. Taylor & W. van de Donk (eds.), OUP, Oxford, 1999, 141-155.
[36] S. Coleman, J. Taylor & W. van de Donk, Parliament in the Age of the Internet, in: *Parliament in the Age of the Internet*, S. Coleman, J. Taylor & W. van de Donk (eds.), OUP, Oxford, 1999, 3-8.
[37] J. Loughlin and B.G. Peters, State Traditions, Administrative Reform and Regionalization, in: *The Political Economy of Regionalism*, M. Keating and J. Loughlin (eds.), Frank Cass, London, 1997, 41-61.
[38] W.R. Scott, *Organizations*, Prentice Hall, Upper Saddle River, 1998.
[39] K. Mannheim, *Man and Society in the Age of Reconstruction*, Routledge, London, 1980.
[40] C. Pollitt and G. Bouckaert (eds.), *Public Management Reform*, OUP, Oxford, 2000.
[41] A. Ringeling, *Het imago van de overheid*, VUGA, Den Haag, 1992.
[42] J. Clark and J. Newman, *The Managerial State*, Sage, London, 1997.
[43] D. Stone, *The Policy Paradox. The Art of Political Decision-Making*, Norton and Company, New York/London, 2002.
[44] J.W. Meyer and B. Rowan, Institutionalized Organizations: Formal Structure as Myth and Ceremony, *American Journal of Sociology* **83** (1997), 340-363.
[45] P. DiMaggio and W. Powell, The Iron Cage Revisited: Institutional Isomorphism and Collective Rationality in Organizational Fields, *American Sociological Review* **48** (1983), 147-160.
[46] C. Bellamy, Modelling Electronic Democracy: towards Democratic Discourses for an Information Age, in: *Democratic Governance and New Technology*, J. Hoff, I. Horrocks and P. Tops (eds.), Routledge, London/New York, 2000, 33-54.
[47] R. Zincke, Administration: The Image of the Administrator as an Information Processor, in: *Images and Identities of Public Administration*, H. Kass, and B. Catron (eds.), Sage, Newbury Park, 1990, 183-201.
[48] S. Zouridis and M. Thaens, Reflections on the Anatomy of E-Government, in: *The Information Ecology of E-Government*, V. Bekkers and V. Homburg (eds.), IOS Press, Amsterdam/Berlin/Oxford, 2005, 21-36.

Part 2

Process Innovation

Information and Communication Technology and Public Innovation
V.J.J.M. Bekkers et al. (Eds.)
IOS Press, 2006

Process Innovation in the Public Sector: Two Belgian Crossroads Bank Initiatives

Kris SNIJKERS[1]

Public Management Institute, Katholieke Universiteit Leuven, Belgium

Abstract: Process innovation promises radical improvements in service delivery processes. It is argued that, starting from a clean slate, processes should be redesigned, using information and communication technologies as an enabler for efficient and effective service delivery processes. In this chapter the author examines the potential and critical success factors of process innovation in the public sector. Two Belgian cases are studied: the Crossroads Bank for Social Security and the Crossroads Bank for Companies. In both cases ICT was used to redesign processes. Yet, both cases show that a pure rational process innovation is not possible. The institutional embeddedness of the processes has to be taken into account. In these processes, several actors are involved that all have different goals and interests at stake. The success of a process innovation project depends on the attention that is given to goals and interests, communication and trust.

Keywords: process innovation, public administration, e-government, crossroads bank, Belgium

1. Introduction

The innovation of public sector processes through the use of ICT is seen as a solution to the shortcomings of the classic Weberian bureaucracy. Problems of fragmentation and compartmentalization, a lack of efficiency, effectiveness and customer orientation have to be tackled by introducing ICT into the public sector. Belgium has not been able to escape from this e-government hype. In this chapter we will analyse and discuss two Belgian innovation projects. The first is the Crossroads Bank for Social Security (CBSS). This is a process innovation project in the Belgian social security sector. The project started officially in 1990 and was aimed at making a breakthrough improvement in the information management of the social sector. The second is the Crossroads Bank for Companies (CBC) and was started in 2003. The Crossroads Bank for Companies was aimed at innovating processes in economic policy, ICT played an important role in both reform projects and was used to improve existing processes.

In the first section, we will analyse the way in which ICT can be used to innovate public sector processes. We will look at the theory and principles of process innovation. The second section will describe the aims and institutional embeddedness

---

[1] Corresponding Author: Public Management Institute, Katholieke Universiteit Leuven, Edward van Evenstraat 2 A, B-3000 Leuven, Belgium, E-mail: kris.snijkers@soc.kuleuven.be.

of both the CBSS and the CBC. In the third section we will look upon the role of ICT in both projects. How was ICT used to reform and improve the existing processes? In the fourth and fifth sections, we will assess the results of the projects. This assessment will be an instrumental assessment (did the projects achieve their intended (or unintended) goals?) as well as an institutional assessment (did the projects change existing institutions?). We will conclude with some critical factors regarding their success and failure.

In both cases, the institutional embeddedness plays an important role. The case of the CBSS as well as the case of the CBC show that pure rational process innovation is not possible. There is no mathematical or best way to innovate processes. In both projects different actors, from the public as well as from the private sector, were involved who all had their own goals and strategic interests. The success, and also failures, in these projects depended on the way in which this institutional embeddedness was taken into account.

2. ICT and Process Innovation in the Public Sector

The innovation of processes is a crucial issue for the improvement of public service delivery. The Weberian bureaucracy, with its specialized administrations, strict task allocation, formalization and hierarchy has led to a fragmented, compartmentalized and supply-oriented policy and public service delivery. Information or services regarding a citizen's problem are scattered throughout 'the administration'. Citizens have to search through different departments or levels of government to find a solution to their specific problem. Each time they have to provide the same information over and over again. This information can range from general information (e.g. name, address, date and place of birth) to more specific information (e.g. income). This situation causes an inefficient and ineffective administration. The administrative burden for citizens and companies is high, and often, citizens and companies just can't find (or even do not know about) the services they need or are entitled to. Even when they are aware of a service, or are obliged to make use of one, the administrative forms they have to fill out are too complex.

ICT is seen as an enabler for the innovation of processes in the public sector. f ICT makes innovation possible in the front-office as well as in the back-office. ICT can be used in the front-office to integrate services and information. Electronic service delivery, one-stop-shops and integrated counters have been developed to overcome fragmentation problems. Nevertheless because of international benchmarking practices, governments often tend to make their existing services available on-line without reforming the underlying processes [1]. In this way, classic fragmentation and compartmentalization makes way for an electronic fragmentation and compartmentalization. It does not lead to many changes on the effectiveness, efficiency and customer orientation level. In order for reforms to take place in the front-office they have to be supported by innovating back-office processes.

The business process re-engineering movement made an important contribution in the field of the innovation of back-office processes. The general idea in business process re-engineering is that one should start by determining the intended output of a process after which the total process should be redesigned. Davenport and Short define a process as "a set of logically related tasks performed to achieve a defined business outcome" [2]. According to Hammer and Champy a process is, "a collection of activities that takes one or more kinds of input and creates an output that is of value to the customer" [3]. Both of these definitions see a process as a chain of tasks and activities aimed to create a valuable output. Thus, a process is a value-chain in which different actors perform different tasks and activities.

Process innovation differs from automation. In the case of automation a specific task or activity can be automated by the use of ICT. However, the problem is that although the efficiency of a specific task may increase through automation the effectiveness of the entire process does not. Thus, when ICT is used for specific tasks it only makes incremental improvements possible. To radically improve public service delivery the entire process should be reviewed. During the past several years, many e-government projects did not extend any further than incremental improvements of service delivery because they only automated a certain part of the total process. Take, for example, electronic tax filing. If electronic tax filing is conceived as an on-line tax-form to be filled out by taxpayers, the quality of the service will not greatly increase. The largest improvement will be for the tax-administration which will no longer have to manually enter the data into its own system. Suppose now that the entire process were to be redesigned and the output of the process was a pre-filled tax-form. In order to do so all of the administrations which already obtain information about the income of citizens (e.g. social security) would have to cooperate with each other and share information. This would decrease citizen's administrative burden.

The innovation of a process means that all tasks and activities of the process are reviewed. Do they all have an added value in the process or, are some of them useless or duplicate? Can some tasks be reshuffled or even abolished? There are several principles in process innovation. An important principle is the electronic exchange of information between different administrations. Administrations often re-enter data manually in their own information systems. Administrations are used to collect the information they need from the citizen. Administrations often have an automated information system but when they exchange information with another administrations, this happens on paper and not electronically.

The principle of electronic information exchange is linked to the principle, 'capture information only once at the source' [4]. When administrations do not exchange information, they always have to ask the citizen for this information. Thus, there is an administrative burden for the citizen who has to provide the information, as well as for the administrations, which have to collect and manually re-enter the same information repeatedly. The principle 'capture information only once at the source' means that a specific piece of information is only collected by one administration that stores it in a database. This means that the information can be electronically shared with other administrations which has a lot of advantages. First, the administrative costs for the citizen as well as for the administration decrease. Second, the quality of information increases because it is no longer possible to provide different information to different administrations (by accident or on purpose). Third, it is much easier to keep the information up-to-date. For example, when someone moves, and their address is stored in several databases all of these databases have to be updated. This is not the case when these data are stored in only one database. Fourth, data verification has to happen only once, i.e., at the moment of their capture. When administrations individually collect their own data, they have to build-in their own control procedures.

Other principles in business process re-engineering are changing the sequence of a process from sequential activities to parallel activities, better information management, better monitoring systems, integration of activities and the elimination of intermediary functions [5].

The ideas concerning process innovation seem very logical and rational at first. However, can these principles be applied to the public sector? When we take a closer look at the principles of process innovation they may even seem naïve. Process innovation departs from a purely rational perspective. One of the assumptions is that all of the actors involved in a certain process agree on the output of the process. Is this always the case? It is very probable that some actors have a different view on the process, and do not share the same goals and have other interests at stake. Are all actors willing to give up a certain task or to eliminate an intermediary function in order to improve the overarching goal? In practice, we can expect that a rational process innovation often clashes with existing institutions and practices.

3. Two Belgian Innovation Projects: the Crossroads Bank for Social Security and the Crossroads Bank for Companies

In this paragraph we will discuss two Belgian innovation projects: the Crossroads Bank for Social Security and the Crossroads Bank for Companies. The Crossroads Bank for Social Security is an initiative in the social sector, while the Crossroads Bank for Companies is an initiative to improve processes in economic policy.

Institutional Embeddedness

Crossroads Bank for Social Security

The social security sector used to be a classic example of a fragmented and supply-oriented public service delivery. The Belgian social security system is very specialized: there are several dozens of administrations, and all of these administrations have specific tasks and responsibilities. A lot of these administrations are part of the Belgian federal government (e.g. the National Service for Sickness and Disability, the National Service for Pensions, the National Service for Social Security). These administrations are steered by a board comprising two parties: the trade unions and the employer organizations. The federal government has a representative on this board. As a result, every reform in the Belgian security sector has to be based on collaboration, negotiations and agreements between the government, the trade unions and the employer organizations.

Besides these federal administrations, there are also other actors involved in the implementation of the social security policy. In Belgium, the trade unions are responsible for the payment of the unemployment benefits [6]. The regulation and control of unemployment benefits is the responsibility of the National Administration for Employment, but the actual payment of the unemployment benefits are dealt with by the trade unions. This means that citizens wanting to obtain an unemployment benefit have to be or become a member of a trade union. A citizen can choose between three trade unions: the liberal trade union (ACLVB), the socialist trade union (ABVV) or the Christian-democrat trade union (ACV). Besides these trade unions, the federal government has organized a small administration where citizens can obtain their unemployment benefits without intermediation of a trade union (HVW), but this federal administration's service is far more restricted than that of the trade unions. The trade unions provide services for the unemployed and assist them when, for example, the National Administration for Employment rejects their claim. Therefore, most of the unemployed choose to become a member of a trade union to get their unemployment benefit. It is clear, that the payment of the unemployment benefits is an important strategic resource for the trade unions as this is an important way of attracting members.

Other important actors in the Belgian social security system are the 'mutualities'. These mutualities are private sector health insurance organizations that are responsible for the payment of the health care benefits to citizens. The regulation and funding of this health insurance is the responsibility of the federal government, but the actual payments are made by the mutualities. As is the case of the unemployment benefits, the federal government has organized a small federal administration (HZIV) that pays citizens' health care benefits without the mediation of a private sector health insurance organization. However, the services of this administration are limited in comparison to the services provided by the health insurance organizations.

The trade unions and mutualities are mainly organized along socio-political lines (Socialist, Liberal, Christian-democrat or Independent). They are the inheritance of strong pillarization in the history of Belgian society. The role of these actors in the present social security system is one of intermediary between the federal social security administrations and the citizen for specific services (payment of unemployment benefits and health care benefits). Besides their role of implementing social policy, trade unions are important actors in the development and decision-making process in the Belgian social sector, as all social security administrations are steered by a board comprising of trade unions (50%) and employer organizations (50%).

Crossroads Bank for Companies

The administrative burden for companies in Belgium was very high. Nevertheless, in a globalized economy, a country's administrative environment is an important variable when companies make their investment decisions. In 2003, the World Bank investigated the administrative burden of starting-up a new company in several countries. The World Bank looked at two variables: the number of procedures you have to go through (fragmentation) and the time needed to complete these procedures (integration and efficiency of processes). According to the World Bank's study in Belgium, to start-up a new business you had to go through several procedures with different administrations [7]:

- Deposit 'societal capital' with a bank;
- Deposit financial plan with the notary;
- Register with the Court of Commerce;
- Apply for a business license with a Chamber of Crafts and Trade;
- Register with the Commercial Register;
- Apply for a VAT-number with the fiscal administration;
- Apply for a social security number with the social security administration.

Regarding the level of fragmentation, Belgium was positioned 17 in the international ranking of the World Bank. In the list of procedures a strong fragmentation is evident. Public (e.g. fiscal and social security administration) as well as private (e.g. banks) administrations are involved in the start-up of a new company. During the further life cycle of a company, this fragmentation continues to cause problems: companies have to repeatedly provide the same information (e.g. identification information) to different administrations. An extraordinary part of the procedures to start up a new company is the difference between the VAT-number and the social security number: two sectors of the Belgian federal administration use a different number to identify a company.

However, the biggest problem was the amount of time needed to comply with these procedures. It took an average of 57 working days to start up a new business (Belgium was ranked 77th in the international ranking). At the time of the study, in Australia, Canada, the USA and Denmark these processes had already been innovated and you only needed an average of 2 to 4 working days to start up a new company. These examples show that is possible to use ICT to overcome fragmentation (reduce in the amount of procedures), and to integrate procedures to obtain a more efficient service delivery for companies. In Canada, for example, people have access to a Business Start-Up Assistant. The federal, provincial and territorial governments have a portal site that integrates information about how to start up a new business. Furthermore, it is possible to register a business on-line through an application provided by the Canada Revenue Agency and several provinces.

The Crossroads Bank for Companies was introduced to solve these problems. The Crossroads Bank for Companies was a priority initiative of the federal government. When a new federal government took office after the elections in 1999, the prime minister, Guy Verhofstadt declared in parliament that: "The government will immediately develop a system in which each company and self-employed has a unique identification number. The government will also develop an integrated counter to prevent that companies have to repeat unnecessary administrative formalities. With less regulation, a decreased administrative burden and more support of the individual initiatives, a strong increase of the amount of companies and employment is possible" [8].

The Crossroads Bank for Companies received a lot of press coverage in the Belgian media. In March 2002 the federal minister of Economy, Charles Picqué (socialist), and the federal minister of SMEs, Rik Daems (liberal), introduced the project to the press. They argued that the Crossroads Bank for Companies should be operational by the 1st of January 2003. This deadline was important at the political level given the Belgian federal elections in June 2003. The Crossroads Bank for Companies, as an instrument in the battle against the administrative burden for companies, was an important political goal for the liberal parties in the federal government.

Innovative Potential of ICT

Crossroads Bank for Social Security

In the 1970s a first attempt was made to tackle the problem of fragmentation in the social sector. The National Labour Council recommended the creation of a 'central social information database' with all the relevant information concerning social security benefits [9]. This idea was repeated in the Law concerning the general principles of the social security for employees in 1981. Although the creation of a central database could solve many problems, it was met with great resistance. It was argued that by collecting all information concerning social security benefits in one centralized database was threatening to the privacy of the Belgian citizen. As long as specialized administrations held specific pieces of information, privacy was not an issue. However, if information were to be registered in one database, all sorts of techniques like profiling could be possible. In addition to the privacy problem, various administrations within the social sector feared that they had to give up their autonomy or would lose power.

In 1990 another idea was developed and implemented. Instead of a central database, a clearing-house was set up: the Crossroads Bank for Social Security (CBSS). The goals of the CBSS are threefold: better service delivery for citizens, better protection of privacy and, better information management to support social policy. A clearing-house has the advantage that the information is not centralized, but stays within the different administrations. Information can be exchanged through the CBSS between different administrations. In this system every citizen has a unique identification key which is based on the identification number in the Belgian National Register. In principle, by using this identification number all information relating to a citizen can be coupled or exchanged. To be able to exchange information the CBSS maintains three reference directories: a directory of persons (which administration has a file concerning a specific person?), a data availability table (which data are available concerning a specific person?) and an access authorisation table (which administration has access to which type of information?) [10]. There is a division of tasks between the different administrations. Information can only be collected once by the appropriate administration. If an administration needs a certain type of information that has already been collected by another administration, it is obliged to use this information, instead of asking the citizen again for the information. Privacy is protected because administrations are restricted in their access to information (accessibility table and control by an independent committee of the privacy commission).

Crossroads Bank for Companies

The goals of the CBC are twofold: one is to improve the service delivery to companies, the other is provide more efficient information management about companies within the (federal) government [11]. A central database was set up to achieve these goals which integrated a lot of smaller databases of different administrations. In this database a unique identification number identifies every company called the 'Company Number'. The database holds a number of data concerning a company,: for example the name, address and the company's licenses. Most of the information in the database is for identification purposes. Specific information such as social security information, fiscal information or the balance sheet of the company is not registered in the database, but is kept by other administrations (in this case National Administration for Social Security, the fiscal administration and the National Bank). However, all information concerning a company can be linked or exchanged because all of the different administrations holding information about companies now have to use the Company Number to identify a specific company. Before the CBC was introduced, a lot of administrations used their own number (e.g. the fiscal administration used the VAT-number and, the RSZ used its own number). This, of course, made it difficult to exchange information.

Besides creating the central database in the back-office, there were also changes in the front-office: Company Counters were set-up. Company Counters were the first step on the way to an integrated counter for companies. In the future, these Company Counters would function as an integrated front-office where companies could obtain all sorts of services (e.g. information, subsidies, and permits). Currently, the Company Counters fulfil two tasks: they register new companies in the central database and they control the business license of companies. These two tasks used to be performed by two different administrations, the Commercial Register and the Chambers of Crafts and Trade, which were abolished. It is important to mention that the federal government does not organize the Company Counters in the front-office itself. Company Counters are set-up by private sector organizations: employer organizations, social secretariats, chambers of commerce and merchant's organizations. Company Counters are subject to regulation and control by the federal government.

The decision to put the front-office in the hands of the private sector was subject to political debate [12]. The socialist parties in the federal government believed that the tasks to be performed by the Company Counters were public , and therefore should be performed by the government itself. However, the liberal parties were in favour of involving the private sector in the front-office of the project. They argued that this would create competition between the different Company Counters. In the end, this competition would lead to a better service delivery to companies.

4. Instrumental Assessment

Have the goals of the projects been accomplished? Such an evaluation is quite complex. One possibility is to look at the official goals of the project and try to assess whether the outputs and outcome of the project meet these goals. However, a project, or actors involved in the project, can also have unofficial goals. Furthermore, it is important to take unintended or side effects into account. The official goals of e-government projects often refer to the improvement of efficiency, effectiveness and customer orientation [13, 14]. This focus on 'economic' goals is strongly rooted in the New Public Management movement. Besides this economic perspective on e-government, there are also other perspectives: an administrative perspective and a democratic perspective. In an administrative perspective on e-government, ICT is used to enhance the uniformity of the implementation of regulation and to reduce uncertainty. A democratic perspective on e-government emphasises the potential of ICT to improve transparency and equity between different actors in public administration. Therefore in order to be able to evaluate an e-government project, we first have to analyse the official goals of each project through the lens of these different perspectives. Afterwards we can assess the unofficial goals and side effects of the projects.

Crossroads Bank for Social Security

As stated previously, the official goals of the CBSS were threefold: a better service delivery to citizens, a better privacy protection and an improved information management to support policymaking. It can be argued that the main goals of the CBSS cover economic as well as administrative and democratic goals. The improvement of service delivery is an example of an economic goal. Through the CBSS, the efficiency and customer orientation of the social sector in Belgium have increased.

First, administrations do not have to re-enter the same data into their own systems over and over again as they now exchange data electronically. In 2004, there were 378,3 million electronic transactions between the administrations in the social sector [15]. In the past, all these transactions between different administrations happened on paper.

Second, the administrative burden for citizens and companies has diminished. Citizens and companies do not have to provide the same information to different administrations in the social sector. It is forbidden by law for administrations that are connected to the CBSS to ask citizens or companies for information that is already available through the CBSS. Information such as, for example, data on working hours and employees' income. Employers have to send electronically this information quarterly to the National Administration for Social Security. This information is then accessible through the CBSS to other administrations that need it (e.g. the National Administration for Retirement to enable them to calculate a citizen's retirement benefit). Furthermore, 50 out of 80 forms were abolished and the length of the remaining forms has been reduced [15].

Third, through the exchange and combination of data, it is possible to provide proactive services. This means that an administration does not react as a result of a citizen's question, but provides a service proactively. For example, by automatically reducing contributions to health care for widows or persons with a physical handicap. Thus, a citizen does not have to know about a service, allowance or a reduction, this is done for them.

From a democratic perspective, the CBSS offers new possibilities for generating a wide array of information to support the social policy. Hence, the transparency of the social policy increases and a better evaluation and feedback loops become feasible.

An example of an administrative goal is better privacy protection. The improvement of efficiency and customer-orientation could not be realized at any price. This was one of the reasons for working with a clearinghouse instead of a central social information database. The access authorization table limits access to information to those administrations and civil servants that are authorized to do so. Furthermore, there is an independent committee that supervises the exchange of information and has to give its permission to start up new information exchanges between administrations.

The detection and prevention of fraud was not an official goal of the CBSS. It was argued that, if the fraud detection was one of the official goals, the trade unions would be unwilling to support the project. They were not willing to support an instrument that would be used to 'hunt' their clients. Given the institutional setting of the social security system in general, and specifically the CBSS, their attitude is quite understandable. First, the trade unions play an important role in the management of the social security administrations; the support of the trade unions was crucial to the development of the project. Second, clients in the social sector are often members of the trade unions. Thus, it is logical that the trade unions were not willing to harm their own interests by openly supporting a project that had a 'negative' goal such as fraud detection. Consequently, the official goals of the CBSS were formulated in a positive way and focused on more efficiency, more customer orientation and better policy support. Nevertheless, in practice, the CBSS plays an important role in the detection and prevention of fraud. By using the CBSS, a civil servant can find out whether a citizen obtains an allowance from another administration. Street-level bureaucrats (e.g. social workers) are no longer dependent on the goodwill of citizens to inform them correctly about their situation as more and more information is exchanged between different administrations in the social sector.

Crossroads Bank for Companies

The CBC had mainly economic goals of efficiency and effectiveness: reducing the administrative burden for companies and better information management [11]. A year after launching the project, the average number of days needed to start up a new company had been reduced to 34 [16]. The ultimate goal of the Belgian government is an average of three days, which is comparable with Canada, the United States and Denmark. The number of procedures has also diminished. Prior to setting up the CBC a company had to go to the Commercial Register and to a Chamber of Crafts and Trade. After the CBC was implemented a company could deal with these procedures through one Company Counter where also registration with the fiscal administration and the social security can be done.

The single collection of identification information in one database has a positive impact on administrative goals. Identification information is more accurate. In the past, it was often the case that certain information changed (e.g. if a company moved or was sold), but the information was not updated in all of the different databases where it was kept. The single collection of information diminishes this problem. However, the fact that one company could have different information (e.g. address) in different databases made the integration of the old databases in the new one rather difficult [12]. The integration of identification information in one database and the ability to exchange other information between the fiscal and social administration and the National Bank makes it easier to detect fraud.

The project endured several problems during its implementation in 2003. The proposed date of January 1st, 2003 did not seem realistic [12, 11]. The government wanted to launch the project before the federal elections in June 2003, but due to technical and organizational issues this seemed impossible. A new deadline was set for July 1st, 2003. The project was indeed launched on this date, but only a few days later, the system crashed because all of the Company Counters tried to enter data into the central database. Due to time constraints, the connection between the Company Counters and the CBC was not tested appropriately and these tests started only two weeks before the deadline. At the start-up, the system was unable to deal with all of the information from the different Company Counters. This resulted in the system crashing and the Company Counters were unable to enter data straight into the central database. This obliged them to e-mail their data to a team at the CBC which had to manually enter data into the database. This resulted in the Company Counters having to deploy more staff to get the work done and a longer waiting period for companies. The Company Counters accused the federal government of a lack of communication and bad preparation of the project. Some of the Company Counters even threatened, as a compensation for their extra costs, not to transfer 50% of the registration fees to the federal government. Besides solving the technical problems of the CBC, the federal government appointed a crisis manager. The crisis manager's most important task was to restore communications between the federal government and the Company Counters.

5. Institutional Assessment

Did both modernization processes challenge the existing institutions? The interaction between technology and institutions is complex [17]. On the one hand, technologies offer new possibilities to restructure existing administrative practices in more efficient and effective ways. On the other, existing institutions can use technologies to reinforce their own position. Thus, the way in which an ICT-project develops is dependent on the capabilities of the existing institutions to use technology to their own advantage.

Crossroads Bank for Social Security

In the case of the CBSS, there was no large re-organization of the organizational structures in the social sector. The social sector in Belgium was very fragmented, and still is. The CBSS did not involve the organizational structure: the CBSS functions as a clearing house between the existing organizations. Yet, there were some changes in the task allocation between the different administrations [18]. There is an administration responsible for each kind of information (e.g. information on income). This administration has to retain the information and verify it before exchanging it with other administrations. Besides this task allocation there were also changes in the concepts and the definitions that were used in the social sector. Before the CBSS was set-up different administrations used different concepts, or defined a concept in a different way. For example, this was the case for the concept 'income'. The income of an employee was defined and calculated differently by several administrations. In order to share information regarding a citizen's income, it was necessary to develop common concepts and definitions, so that each administration could use the same information. The development of these common concepts was crucial for the project because this effected the way in which an administration processed information.

In the social sector in Belgium, the trade unions and the health insurances function as intermediary structures between the federal social security administrations and the citizen. The Dutch commission *'ICT en overheid'* argues that these intermediate structures will fade away through the use of ICT [19]. Intermediate structures function as a broker to match supply and demand in cases where the suppliers and customers are not capable of doing this themselves. Yet, ICT diminishes the added value of intermediaries because by using ICT it is easier to distribute or find services or information. So, in the case of the CBSS the role of the trade unions and health insurers as intermediary structures can be questioned. In practice however, their role was never under discussion. One argument is that competition between the trade unions (for unemployment benefits) and health insurers (for health care benefits) would lead to a better service delivery for the citizen. Another argument is that the intermediate structures are familiar with the needs and wants of citizens and can adapt their services to such needs and wants [20]. Griffin and Halpin support this argument [21]. They argue that ICT leads towards a renewed importance of intermediaries. They see public service delivery as a value chain in which several actors add value. According to Griffin and Halpin, an intermediary can fulfil four tasks in a value chain: (1) facilitating the demand side by providing information on services, (2) matching supply and demand of services and information, (3) stimulation of trust between suppliers and customers who do not interact on a regular basis and (4) the aggregation of services and information of different producers focused on a specific group of citizens. Theoretically, this framework can be applied to trade unions and to health insurers. There are arguments to support their role as an intermediate. However, besides these theoretical reflections on the role of intermediaries there are other reasons why the CBSS did not cause a disintermediation. Contact with citizens is an important source of power for these intermediaries. The trade unions, which have a powerful position in the management of the federal social administrations, certainly would not have supported the CBSS if this meant that they would lose their intermediating role.

Crossroads Bank for Companies

In contrast to the CBSS, the implementation of the CBC was accompanied with an institutional reform. The introduction of the CBC had consequences for the existing administrations [11]. First of all, the Commercial Register was abolished. This register was located at the Federal Public Service Justice, but now the register is a part of the CBC, which is located in the Federal Public Service Economy. The Federal Public Service Justice was not terribly disappointed about losing the Commercial Register. The Commercial Register was never a core task of the Federal Public Service Justice nor was it an important strategic register for this specific Federal Public Service. It was not only a question of the marginal strategic relevance of the register, the Federal Public Service Justice could keep the staff and the budget of the Commercial Register either. The second institutional reform was the abolishment of the Chambers of Crafts and Trade. The chambers were an inheritance of the past, but no longer had any strategic importance. The staff and budgets of the chambers were transferred to the Federal Public Service Economy.

The CBC shows the importance of the front-office. As mentioned earlier, the front-office has been outsourced to private sector organizations. Why did these organizations collaborate with the government? The government did not oblige them to do so, nor can these private sector organizations make large profits out of the Company Counters (the fees of the Company Counters are fixed by the federal government and, moreover, the Company Counters have to deposit 50% of the fee with the federal government). However, the private sector organizations that have established a Company Counter see the importance of such a counter in the fact that they offer access to companies [11]. Companies which make use of a Company Counter are often also interested in other services that these private organizations behind the Company Counter offer (e.g. insurances or HR-services). In this way, the Company Counters are an important gateway to the market of companies which have just come onto the market.

During the parliamentary debates on the law concerning the CBC and the Company Counters, there was a lot of protest from the Belgian Association of Accountants and Tax Advisors. The association supported the goals of the CBC and the Company Counters, namely the reduction of the administrative burden for companies. However, they did not agree with the Company Counters' task description as it was formulated in the proposed enactment [22]. As said previously, these Company Counters are located in the private sector. The government wanted to create competition between the different Company Counters to obtain a better service delivery. In the enactment put forward by the government, it was stated that the Company Counters could provide a range of services to companies in addition to their official tasks. In the government's view, Company Counters should be able to provide advice to companies on financial and tax matters. In Belgium, the profession of accountant is protected. This means that anyone who wants to exercise this profession has to meet certain criteria (e.g. education). The Association of Accountants and Tax Advisors argued that the government wanted to undermine their position by giving the Company Counters the opportunity to give advice to companies in matters that should only be dealt with by official accountants. In the end, the enactment was amended in favour of the Association of Accountants and Tax Advisors.

The Belgian federal structure makes it difficult to establish truly integrated counters. At present, the Company Counters are not truly integrated counters because they only provide services which come from the federal government. At the time of the establishment of the Company Counters, the Flemish regional government established its own counters (Houses of the Flemish Economy, recently reformed into the Flemish Agency for Entrepreneurs). Due to the reform of the Belgian federal state, the regions and communities attach great importance to their autonomy. So, in this case, they have developed their own policy concerning integrated public service delivery for companies. At these Flemish counters, companies can obtain services and information from the Flemish government. Therefore, the institutional structure of the Belgian federal state hinders the development of a truly integrated service delivery for companies. Nevertheless, in the back-office, the Flemish government uses the 'federal' Company Number to identify companies. This enables the exchange of information between the federal and regional levels of government. It seems that collaboration in the front-office, which is very visible to citizens, is sometimes more difficult than collaboration in the back-office. Different levels of government seem to want their own counter, carrying their own logo. Yet, the fact that these two levels of government use the same identification number will enable the innovation of a lot of transboundary processes in the future. In the long run, this strategy is probably more effective than sharing a shallow front-office without a real 'deep' innovation of processes.

6. Conclusions

The innovation of processes in the public sector is much more complex than the classic theory on process innovation suggests. Public sector process innovation is an exercise in a minefield of existing institutions, interests and practices. Two Belgian cases, the Crossroads Bank for Social Security and the Crossroads Bank for Companies show the possibilities as well as the pitfalls of a process innovation project in the public sector. In both projects, public service delivery suffered from fragmentation, compartmentalization, inefficiency and ineffectiveness. ICT was used to overcome these problems through the innovation of processes.

The CBSS was initiated in 1990, quite some time before the e-government hype. Therefore, there was not a lot of political pressure or media attention for the project. The CBSS is strongly embedded in the Belgian social security system that was designed in the aftermath of World War II. This is a complex system in which some actors (e.g. trade unions and health insurers) hold crucial positions and quite an amount of power. Thus, the way in which the CBSS developed has not only been determined by rational principles or technical elements, but also by the interests of the existing institutions.

The CBC began in 2003, during a period in which e-government was a priority of the Belgian government. The tremendous political pressure behind the project is seen as one of the reasons why the project encountered many technical problems during its implementation. The number of reshuffles and abolishment of several organizations is quite remarkable in this project in comparison with the CBSS. The difference in this project was that the abolished organizations were of no strategic relevance to the stakeholders in the project.

What are these projects' critical factors of success and failure ? The first critical success factor is the attention given to the goals and strategic interests of all of the partners involved in the project. Project innovation is often motivated by economic goals such as the improvement of effectiveness, efficiency and customer orientation. This was also the case in the two Belgian examples. However, in practice they not only have an economic effect, but they also increase the possibilities for control by the government (e.g. detection of fraud). This was never an explicit goal of these projects. Especially in the case of the CBSS, the government was not eager to motivate the CBSS with this 'negative' goal because it would decrease the support of the project by some actors. The trade unions and the health insurance organizations play an important role in the Belgian social security system, and their support was necessary for the project. This is also the reason why the project did not lead to a disintermediation: the trade unions and health insurance organizations still are responsible for the payment of unemployment and health care benefits.

The second critical success factor is the role of communication. This became particularly clear in the case of the CBC when the new system crashed only a few days after its launch. The private sector Company Counters accused the federal government of bad communication. They argued that they were poorly informed of their specific tasks and the problems that arose after the crash. The federal government responded to this crisis not only by repairing the technical infrastructure, but also by appointing a crisis manager who had to improve communications with the Company Counters.

The third critical success factor is the role of trust. The partners involved in a process innovation project have to trust each other. They have to be sure about each other's capacities and reliability. Process innovation projects always bear a certain risk. Absolute certainty is impossible in these projects. However, the partners have to be confident that risk is managed as well as possible. In the case of the CBC, this seemed not to be the case. Good tests of the entire system would have probably prevented the crash which caused problems for the Company Counters.

References

[1]   D. Janssen, S. Rotthier and K. Snijkers, If You Measure It They Will Score: An Assessment of International E-Government Benchmarking, *Information Polity* **3**(4) (2004), 121-130.
[2]   Th.H. Davenport and J.E. Short, The New Industrial Engineering: Information Technology and Business Process Redesign, *Sloan Management Review* **4** (1990), 11-27.
[3]   M. Hammer and J. Champy, *Reengineering the Corporation*, Nicholas Brealey Publishing, London, 1993.
[4]   M. Hammer, Reengineering Work: Don't Automate, Obliterate, *Harvard Business Review* **4** (1990), 104-112.
[5]   Th.H. Davenport, *Process Innovation. Reengineering Work through Information Technology*, Harvard Business School Press, Boston, Massachusetts, 1993.
[6]   *Jaarverslag 2004* (Annual Report 2004), RVA, Brussel, 2005.
[7]   World Bank, *Doing Business in 2004. Understanding Regulation*, The World Bank, Washington D.C., 2003.
[8]   *Regeringsverklaring* (Policy declaration), Federale Regering, Brussel, 1999.
[9]   J. Viaene, F. Robben, D. Lahaye, and J. Van Steenberge, Algemene schets van een rationele informatieverwerking in de sociale zekerheid, *Belgisch Tijdschrift voor de Sociale Zekerheid* **4**(5) (1986), 399-473.
[10] J. Deprest and F. Robben, *E-Government: The Approach of the Belgian Federal Government*, Fedict, Brussel, 2003.
[11] Advisor to the minister of SME's, Interview, Gent, 27-10-2003.
[12] Director of a Company Counter, Interview, Brugge, 20-4-2004.

[13] H. van Duivenboden and M. Lips, Responsive E-Government Services: Towards 'New' Public Management, in: *The Information Ecology of E-Government*, V. Bekkers and V. Homburg, (eds.), IOS Press, Amsterdam, 2005, 141-154.

[14] S. Zouridis and M. Thaens, Reflections on the Anatomy of E-Government, in: *The Information Ecology of E-Government*, V. Bekkers and V. Homburg, (eds.), IOS Press, Amsterdam, 2005, 21-36.

[15] F. Robben, E-government in de Belgische sociale sector, presentation prepared for the Dutch Minister of Social Affairs, Kruispuntbank van de Sociale Zekerheid, Brussel, 2005.

[16] World Bank, *Doing Business in 2005. Removing Obstacles to Growth*, World Bank, Washington D.C., 2004.

[17] W.B.J.H. van de Donk and I.Th.M. Snellen, Towards a Theory of Public Administration in an Information Age?, in: *Public Administration in an Information Age. A Handbook*, I.Th.M. Snellen and W.B.J.H. van de Donk (eds.), IOS Press, Amsterdam, 1998, 3-20.

[18] Vice General Manager of a Federal Social Security Administration, Interview, Brussel, 23-10-2003.

[19] Eenmalige Adviescommissie ICT en Overheid, *Burger en overheid in de informatiesamenleving: de noodzaak van institutionele innovatie*, Ministerie van Binnenlandse Zaken en Koninkrijksrelaties, Den Haag, 2001.

[20] General Manager CBSS, Interview, Brussel, 22-9-2003.

[21] D. Griffin and E. Halpin, Local Government: A Digital Intermediary for the Information Age?, *Information Polity* 4 (2002), 217-230.

[22] Ph. van Eeckhoute, *Ondernemingsloket: welke rol voor de accountant en de belastingconsulent?*, Standpunt van het I.A.B. inzake het Wetsontwerp tot oprichting van de Kruispuntbank van ondernemingen, tot modernisering van het handelsregister en tot oprichting van erkende ondernemingsloketten, Instituut voor Accountants en Belastingconsulenten, Brussel, 2002.

Information and Communication Technology and Public Innovation
V.J.J.M. Bekkers et al. (Eds.)
IOS Press, 2006

Public Service Innovation in Europe

Hanneke DRIESSEN[1]

Capgemini, Consulting Services, The Netherlands

Abstract. Based on proven practices in Europe, this chapter gives an insight into the lessons that can be learned from public service innovation with ICT. The chapter describes four cases in which both procedural and organizational improvements have been achieved by means of ICT, proving that ICT supports efficiency and customer satisfaction objectives. Institutional changes have been found to focus on (i) the distribution and ownership of information and (ii) public and public-to-private cooperation. Although the latter may be difficult to effect in practice, customer demands and technical opportunities are important factors determining the success of such cooperation.

Keywords. E-government, public service delivery, best practices, cooperation, returns of e-government, institutional changes

1. Introduction

It is generally assumed that public services and democratic processes can be improved by the use of ICT and accompanying organizational changes ("e-government"). A study carried out in 2004 by Capgemini and TNO under the authority of the Dutch Ministry of Internal Affairs shows that investing in the use of ICT for public services in Europe is rewarding. The study involved eight cases of public service innovation by means of ICT in Europe and provides an insight into the type of benefits that can be achieved with ICT. The cases focus on process and organizational innovations. In each case, procedural and organizational back-office changes were made together with the implementation of ICT in order to improve services to citizens, as well as for public and private organizations. The actual benefits range from tangible returns, such as reduced process time and reduced costs, to less tangible returns, such as improved service levels and more transparent government.

Section 2 of this chapter takes a closer look at four successful public service innovations in Europe, each varying according to the type of innovation. For each case, its goals, changes made and approaches to changes are described. Instrumental as well as institutional factors that have had an impact on success are analysed and discussed in sections 3 and 4 respectively. This chapter concludes with a summary of important lessons learned in section 5.

---

[1] Corresponding Author: Capgemini, Consulting Services, P.O. Box 2575, 3500 GN Utrecht, The Netherlands, E-mail: hanneke.driessen@capgemini.com.

2. Proven Practices of Public Service Innovation in Europe

From the eight initial case studies, four will be described here, since these cases best represent the diverse areas of public service. In each case, different ICT innovations were implemented to improve public services.

2.1. Online Administration of Student Grants in Denmark

In Denmark, the State Education Fund (SU-Agency) of the Ministry of Education is responsible for the administration of student grants. In addition, two other ministerial agencies, the Central Customs and Tax Administration and the Agency for Governmental Management, as well as educational institutions, are involved in the administration of student grants. The three ministerial agencies launched a joint project, the "Service Community", to improve the administration of student grants. As a result of the project, the SU-Agency set up a web-based system, 'My SU', giving students a single point of access and contact with the Agency. The system also features a joint log-in service for students with a digital signature, creating a one-stop-shop service for the three ministerial agencies. Students can log onto a single website to use services of the three ministries or to enter or change data, receiving immediate automatic feedback from the system on entries and changes made.

Goals

My SU was set up to ease the administrative workload and costs of educational institutions and to provide better services to students in respect of grant administration. Another, important, objective was more efficient government, to be achieved by reducing staff levels by 10% over four years.

Approach

The main use of ICT has been the simplification and digitization of procedures. On the one hand this was achieved by eliminating certain steps and reducing the number of institutions involved. For example, as a result of My SU, there was a reduced need for a private company that was previously employed by the government to carry out data input activities. Administrative tasks have been transferred from government to educational institutions and then to students themselves. Also, a demand-driven service taking students as a starting point was set up.

Success and Failure Factors

The objective of the Danish government to cut staff levels by 10% was a major driver for success in the My SU case. Translation of the political sense of urgency to cut costs into a quantitative objective proved decisive. Furthermore, the fact that the three ministerial agencies shared the objective of improving services offered to students was a driver for change.

Because My SU took the student as a starting point, cooperation between public and private organizations was necessary in order to provide students with an integrated service, instead of several products that are not fine-tuned or coordinated. This resulted in a transparent and user-friendly system. In the previous situation cooperation regarding this demand-driven approach had been more challenging because of conflicts of interests and a traditional (supply-driven) approach. A barrier delaying success was the lack of a common starting point between the three ministerial agencies. The agencies, who needed to cooperate closely, did not invest sufficient time to fully understand the role of each party and the objectives involved. Therefore, My SU was started without a common strategic plan. Also, governmental hierarchy and formal procedures within the ministries presented difficulties for the decision-making process. The biggest technical limitations were encountered in respect of installing the digital signature feature, as a result of security problems and inefficient ordering processes.

Results

In the My SU case, efficiency objectives have largely been accomplished. The costs of services of the private sector data input bureau were drastically reduced and staff levels at the SU Agency have decreased by 18% since 2001, when the first changes were made. Within the Agency for Governmental Management, administration staff levels were reduced by 12% – which is even more impressive considering the fact that the number of students has increased by 15%.

As My SU was a success, the three ministerial agencies continued their common strategy to give citizens a single point of access to government services. The Service Community has been continuously improved to reach higher quality of service for students. It is intended that other services will also be digitized. The three ministries are also considering expanding their partnership both internally and externally.

At the SU Agency and the Agency for Governmental Management, cost efficiency was achieved as job descriptions changed drastically as a result of the ICT implementations. Instead of having to collect, retype and store grant applications data, working time can now be spent on technology development and maintenance. The informational function of the agencies has also been reduced. Students are more flexible, control their own data and are less dependent on procedures of public authorities or educational institutions. At the same time the service level is higher; students with complex problems receive better help from employees within the Service Community who have more time and knowledge to formulate solutions.

2.2. Electronic Tax Declarations in Estonia

The Estonian Tax and Customs Board (Maksuamet) offers tax payers an electronic service with pre-completed electronic tax declarations for private persons and businesses (E-Maksuamet). The service features a functionality whereby tax payers can file a request for a tax refund electronically by simply pushing a button. Then the system starts an electronic risk analysis procedure to assess whether a refund is justified. If it is, a refund payment may be made the same day. E-Maksuamet is a one-stop-shop for both citizens and businesses. As a single point of access, it not only offers an on-line income tax declaration service, but also many other services are available on-line. Communication with Maksuamet can be fully electronic. All tax-related communications are concentrated on one site and are easily accessible.

Goals

Although it did not define specific quantitative objectives for the on-line services, Maksuamet aimed at an increase in on-line private income tax declarations every year and an increase in customer satisfaction. Additional objectives were greater efficiency for tax payers and a reduction of processing time in respect of refunds. Finally, cost reduction and better quality of tax information and risk-analysis were important objectives.

Approach

The main improvement in the tax-declaration procedure is the use of electronic forms and communication with citizens on the one hand and electronic risk analysis and audits on the other. Decision-making regarding refunds is processed automatically and therefore faster. The back-office is more efficient due to automated and centralized procedures. Maksuamet shares its electronic data with other public authorities, which has been an important incentive for intergovernmental cooperation.

Maksuamet followed a distinct step-by-step approach. From the start, the system has been simple but highly functional, and only after it proves to be accepted by customers will it be developed further. Because of the modularity, the development of the system is relatively easy and reasonably priced.

Success and Failure Factors

Since its independence from the Soviet Union in 1991, Estonia has placed particular emphasis on the use of technology to build an efficient administrative structure and deliver high-quality public services.[2] Because there were no significant historical, technical or organizational limitations, Maksuamet could build a new, simple and attractive system making maximum use of already available data.

The fact that the government of Estonia aimed at a modernized image proved to be a strong advantage for the introduction of ICT in public services and has also dissolved many legal barriers that restricted the sharing of information. However, poor legislation has been a major barrier during the development of the service. In addition, the knowledge gap between technical personnel and tax experts has also been problematic.

Results

Efficiency for both customers and Maksuamet has increased, for example due to the fact that e-Maksuamet refunds can be organized within one day instead of six months. In addition, user uptake has increased and Estonia is now widely perceived as being one of the best examples in the area of e-government development in Europe. Maksuamet has reduced the workload by approximately 3.5 months, and the workload is also more evenly spread. At the same time customer satisfaction has increased. Because of the pre-filling system, customers only need to push a single button and besides that, a refund can be given within a day (compared to 6 months previously). Previously, after filling in and signing the declaration, citizens had to bring it to the Maksuamet personally, for which they sometimes had to queue for up to two or three

---

[2] See among others: http://europa.eu.int/idabc/en/document/3192/5580

hours. Maksuamet is also more transparent and offers clear and complete insight into and information about the way it works, and what processes are taking place.

2.3. Environmental Compliance and Electronic Data Interchange in Finland

The Finnish ministry of the Environment has developed a database called VAHTI, in which all relevant environmental information is stored for environmental compliance and monitoring. VAHTI uses the already available TYVI system[3] for electronic data interchange, which is used by several public authorities and was developed by the Ministry of Finance.

Goals

The objective of VAHTI with TYVI was to make reporting easier for customers. Furthermore, the objective was to create an integrated tool for all participating back offices and help regional public authorities with decision making and control.

Approach

With TYVI a new business model has been set up for electronic data interchange, which is highly flexible and uses open standards. The clearing-house concept of TYVI fits like a module into many different systems (cf. RINIS in chapter 5). The business model allows more cooperation between public authorities, and between government and private organizations (operators and banks, among others regarding the authentication procedure). The system is innovative because it integrates many points of contact between customers and public authorities and different communications standards. Furthermore, in order to do this efficiently, these activities are outsourced to private operators.

The Ministry of Finance took the initiative to start with TYVI, and played a coordinating role. The idea was not to involve as many authorities as possible, but rather to develop a business model that would be beneficial to as many authorities as possible. For VAHTI the Ministry of the Environment decided to connect to TYVI after the maintenance of their own systems grew out of proportion.

Success and Failure Factors

In a fast-changing and complex technical environment, the use of an external electronic data transfer service with standard interfaces is a critical success factor. One of the best features of TYVI is that it works with the necessary high number of technical and organizational combinations.

Public authorities that use TYVI do not have to invest in the development of a system for data interchange with customers and they do not have to maintain the system (this is done by the TYVI operators). The service makes it easier to adapt to future complexity.

In the TYVI and VAHTI cases, cooperation at different levels is a critical characteristic of its success. First of all, the cooperation between the authorities regarding TYVI (public authorities and other agencies) is important. Although the

---

[3] TYVI is short for the flow of information from customers to authorities.

Ministry of Finance acts as the coordinating ministry, many other organizations are involved and share services and data. Secondly, there is cooperation between authorities and the operators with respect to the development of the TYVI concept and custom-made services. Thirdly, cooperation with banks regarding the use of an already available authentication method is an important condition and success factor (cf. authentication systems in chapter 12).

Since it is difficult to unite the different interests of the various organizations involved, the Ministry of Finance took the initiative to get started, take some risks and invest. This approach has contributed to the success of TYVI. Although the Finnish government as a whole is relatively structured and small, cooperation regarding this topic was difficult to realize because of the differences in objectives and strategies.

Although few errors have been made in the process, one critical error in judgment was the architecture of VAHTI. Instead of analyzing the desired functionalities in advance, a technical solution had first been developed. This solution did not fit the daily practice.

A barrier has been the lack of coordination between operators and authorities. Since electronic data exchange is not obligatory, operators have no real reason to cooperate with one another yet. Because of this lack of coordination, in case of VATHI, the Ministry of the Environment has chosen to work with a single operator.

Results

Because of TYVI, data have to be reported only once to a single operator, which makes reporting relatively easy. It limits time of contact, and customers do not have to adapt their data to the different reporting standards, file structure and data network interface of several public authorities. However, many organizations have had to update their systems (or manual processes) before being able to work more efficiently. Large companies have been obliged to file electronically, and communication efforts have been made to help meet this obligation in time.

Information supply has improved. Quality of information is higher and customers and public authorities have better management information. They can view historic data and carry out cross data analysis more easily. The system eliminates paperwork. Especially with respect to periodical reports, major savings can be made.

The TYVI service has achieved the main objectives by providing a low cost and simple solution that is easy to implement and easy to adapt to future changes. VAHTI is transferable since it is based on common technology, international classifications and European legislation.

2.4. Online Services in a Public-Private Partnership in Germany

Bremen Online Services (BOS) is a public-private partnership including the city of Bremen and some large local companies. BOS has developed an on-line transaction platform called Governikus, which facilitates fully automatic financial transaction processes for government services in a secure and legally binding way. It uses open standards for achieving platform and application independence.

Goals

BOS aims at reducing transaction costs for customers and reducing workflows and operating budgets of the public administration. The objective is to make the transaction process more efficient and user-friendly for both customers and public authorities. In 2004 more than 120 services were available online. One of these services is the application and payment for birth and marriage certificates.

Approach

A grant of € 10 million from the *Media@Komm* award was an important financial injection to start cooperating.[4] A regional collaborative network of the city, banks and universities has been set up in a public-private partnership structure. The regional orientation and proliferation of private companies made it relatively easy to start consortia. The unique constitutional situation in Bremen – being one of the three relatively autonomous 'city states' of Germany – has further speeded up the policy process.

Because of the operability to other services, the development costs for digitizing processes and for implementing online transactions are relatively low. In addition, the participation of local businesses (mainly banks) offering money and expertise made it possible to develop e-government at relatively low cost. However, some public authorities find the cost for the implementation of an infrastructure for digital signatures expensive. A full integration of back office workflows was only possible with the use of additional secondary services offered by BOS and private companies (for authentication and payments).

Success and Failure Factors

The development and the integration of the online service is complicated because of high costs and legal boundaries. BOS has opted for a complex development approach taking three main aspects into consideration simultaneously: access, applications of public services and infrastructure. This has been a barrier to development. Furthermore, BOS cannot influence the legal aspects and has to take these into consideration during the development of the project. A low uptake for some services has also been a barrier.

Essential for the success of BOS (besides the funding) was the cooperation in the partnership. Private companies, for example, have a long-term vision and did not hold back because the return on investments is still insignificant. Although it was a difficult process, all aspects of e-government are taken into account at the same time.

Results

Administrative burdens and transaction costs for customers have been reduced. Also the personnel costs for agencies involved have been reduced. For a particular service, "Outstanding Liabilities", the online register handled 20,000 requests which led to a one-third reduction in personnel and the service saves roughly €7 per transaction. A positive side effect is the spread of Governikus through Germany. Several cities and governments demonstrated their interest. Perhaps more important is the interest shown

---

[4] Media@Komm stimulates the development of transferable e-Government solutions in Germany.

by federal governments. If the federal governments commit themselves to Governikus as the main open standard transaction platform, the position of BOS becomes stronger.

2.5. Summary

This section examined four cases in which changes have been made to improve public services. In every case ICT has been used and organizational changes have been made. In the Danish case, the emphasis was on the development of a self-service web environment, whereas the Estonian case focused on pro-active services (pre-completed forms) and automatic risk assessment. In the Finnish case a new business model was created to develop a centralized database and an electronic data interchange platform. In the German case, an online transaction platform developed in a public-private partnership improved the possibilities of electronic services. The next sessions will discuss the instrumental and institutional aspects of the changes made.

3. Instrumental Assessment

This section will provide an instrumental assessment of the ICT innovations described in section 2. It will assess the degree to which the use of ICT has been successful and to which the objectives of public service innovation have been accomplished. Furthermore, it will answer the question of whether modernization goals have been achieved.

The four cases share a focus on objectives in terms of efficiency and customer satisfaction, which results mainly in a reduction of process time and costs and an improved service level. These objectives first and foremost stimulate the digitization of existing processes and information flows, which can be regarded as the introduction of the most basic form of process innovation. In most cases, the first step is to optimize current processes in the sense that superfluous or complex steps have been eliminated or simplified. Secondly, these optimized processes are digitized. In most cases this included the possibility of interacting online. These two steps, however, are only part of the innovation.

In many cases limited organizational changes and limited costs have been conditional for the change approach. The fact that in many cases public authorities prefer a gradual step-by-step change approach strengthens the focus on efficiency and customer satisfaction. Modernization has been necessary in order to reach these objectives, but to a lesser extent an objective in itself. At the same time all cases studied show that innovations have more impact when organizational changes are made alongside the process changes. For example, in some cases the centralization of services resulted in a single point of access for customers (the *one-stop-shop* principle), in which case a real integration of processes and back office changes were necessary.

Due to investments in ICT, government becomes more transparent. Citizens can approach public authorities more easily because the service level has increased, for example due to the one-stop-shop principle and more efficient processes. In the case of one-stop shopping, customers do not have to adjust their information to different reporting standards, file structure and data network interfaces.

The improved service level and increased customer satisfaction can contribute to a higher user uptake and an improved image of public authorities. An additional advantage is the higher quality of (management) information, which can be beneficial for both public authorities and customers, for the most part businesses. For example, students in Denmark have easy access to their own data and Finnish companies can run simple queries and management reports can be generated instantly.

The level of returns for government depends on the potential impact of the services on the one hand, and on the level of user uptake on the other hand. The larger the target group of customers for the services and the more frequently services are rendered, the higher the potential returns will be. And, of course, the higher the user uptake, the higher the actual returns for public authorities.

On the basis of the case studies it seems that secondary services that are more or less conditional to improve online services, like authentication and online payments, are very crucial to push usage levels to a maximum (cf. IDM in chapter 12).

We can conclude that objectives regarding the use of ICT are largely accomplished, especially when they are related to targets such as efficiency and customer satisfaction. Objectives regarding modernization of the organization are more difficult to realize and, maybe because of that, more modest. Section 5 will discuss the factors that are critical for success.

4. Institutional Assessment

This section will identify the institutional changes and will provide insight into the extent to which investments in public service innovation and the use of ICT contribute to a modernized government and to what extent existing practices are challenged.

4.1. Distribution of Information

In most cases the distribution of information between organizations changed, which involved a redesign of workflows and more interaction. These changes are not restricted to the distribution of information, but in some cases this has also contributed to a changed division of power. For example, the data input bureau in the Danish case became unnecessary and information flows were revised accordingly. Functions changed from administrative to service-related functions. Work has been decentralized, first to the educational institutions, then to students themselves. Because of these changed tasks and responsibilities, transparency has improved, students are more flexible and have more control over their own data.

In the Finnish case the business model changed more radically in order to improve data interchange. Several public authorities that make use of TYVI now outsource electronic data interchange to private operators. In addition, information can be stored centrally and shared more easily, which ensures that customers provide the same data only once. Because of the more efficient information flows, management information is gathered more easily and public authorities can now focus on content instead of on administrative procedures. Therefore, the position of regional officers (who used to collect the data and have contact with businesses) has changed, their task has shifted from intensive customer contact and checking detailed information such as incoming data to less direct contact, analysis of data, controlling main points and responding to incidents.

Experience from other public service innovations (for instance the cases that have not been described in this chapter) contributes to the conclusion that a centralized distribution of information is a first step to challenge existing procedures and relationships and in some cases it can be the first step towards a more structural cooperation, which will be discussed next. In the Netherlands the Housing Benefits Law has been fundamentally revised (this process started in 1998 following a political target to cut back costs), leading to a more centralized execution of the benefits regarding rent [2]. This example shows that because of the changed distribution of information, responsibilities and the division of power changed accordingly. In the new situation the ministry of Spatial Planning is the centralized back-office organization, instead of local authorities. Work has been centralized and partly automated. Due to the simplified procedure and the sharing of data and services fewer organizations are involved and local authorities no longer have an executing responsibility towards customers. Customers are no longer responsible for collecting already available data at several other organizations. You could say that after the initial application, government now has the duty to gather the information and pay benefits accordingly, whereas in the previous situation customers had to find the requested information and send in the application themselves.

The changed distribution of information contributes to more transparency and efficiency. In general you could say the control over information flows can be centralized or even outsourced and privatized, which means responsibilities and tasks change. Furthermore, cases show a switch in control over information. In complex transaction processes, it is more and more common to take each case individually and take into account customers' points of view. This sometimes means customers themselves control the data (in the students' case) or that government collects already available information (by sharing data and cooperation) and customers no longer have to do this; they only check the information (for example in Estonia and in the Dutch case). This shows that existing practices can be challenged and that relationships between central government, local institutions and customers can change.

4.2. Cooperation

Improved cooperation between both public authorities and public and private partners is more and more common and changes relationships in the public sphere. Public authorities are more sensitive with respect to developments of other organizations and more often coordinate their activities. They cooperate because they see the advantages of sharing data and systems (Germany, Estonia), they carry out activities that affect their shared customer together (Denmark) or even see the possibilities of jointly outsourcing part of their activities (Finland). These forms of cooperation also change the way in which these organizations operate and existing practices are challenged step by step.

Technological solutions can be a driver for the development of cooperation. For example, establishing technical connections to communicate or share data, the use of open standards, and shared authentication methods are being developed or implemented. These ICT applications are practical and free of sensitive (political or organizational) notions and therefore relatively more easy to implement since they do not directly change the way parties involved are organized. Of course, these organizations and their relationships will change eventually. In that sense ICT is used as a carrier for organizational changes.

Cooperation Between Public Authorities

In the Danish case the three ministries involved have learned to focus on customers and have taken the students' point of view as a driver for change. Therefore, each individual ministry's interest was of secondary importance and cooperation was necessary. The organizations involved set up a new structure in which they cooperate, the Service Community, in order to develop joint business models to integrate services across government authorities. Services to students are now a joint responsibility. The relationship between the public authorities and students has also changed in a way: students deliver their data online and receive immediate feedback.

Other cases have also shown cooperation between public authorities. In Finland, for example, TYVI integrates a flexible 'clearing house' solution for a large number of users and at the same time offers great flexibility to authorities. Although many authorities use the TYVI service, it now represents the needs and objectives of the Finnish government as a whole, while the service is centrally steered and maintained by the Ministry of Finance.

Cooperation between public authorities has shown significant returns and can be considered successful, although it is difficult to realize. Estonia seems to be an exception to this: due to the relatively new government, existing structures have hardly been a barrier for successful cooperation and institutional innovation has been easier.

Public-Private Cooperation

The private sector plays an important role in service delivery solutions. Banks and Trusted Third Parties, for example, support fully digital transaction processes. As pioneers in e-banking, banks offer knowledge and tools, sometimes even free of charge. The use of already available authentication infrastructure is also a clear example of cooperation between public and private organizations. But public-private partnerships can be more far-reaching. In the Finnish and Estonian cases, the government adopted the authentication method of banks and consequently the user uptake has been high. In the examples, customer demands have been taken into account as well as already available and proven techniques. This way, development and maintenance costs are limited. These partnerships can change existing relationships in the sense that private partners fulfil a role in the development of e-government and take over some tasks that until recently were restricted to government for reasons such as privacy and security.

In the Finnish case, electronic data interchange between customers and various public authorities is carried out by private service operators. Because of this, public authorities do not have to invest in ICT individually and complicated technical changes in the back offices' information infrastructure are not necessary.

In the German case a public-private partnership was set up to develop electronic public services for intermediaries, businesses and citizens. The city of Bremen owns 51 percent of BOS. The other 49 percent is owned by private partners, primarily Deutsche Telekom, banks and several local ICT companies. Even though they did not expect returns in the short term, these private partners have matched the necessary funds, which has enhanced and stimulated the innovation of digital services. Another important partner for the development of the services was the University of Bremen, since they provided up-to-date knowledge.

Cultural and institutional frameworks are more limiting than technical obstacles. Cultural preconditions and institutional histories, for example regarding privacy, need to be considered when reorganizing public services [3].

As in the case of changed distribution of information, cooperation can also contribute to objectives regarding transparency and efficiency. Furthermore it can contribute to the one-stop-shop principle regarding public services, including authentication and payment. Cooperation means activities are at least coordinated, but in some cases also centralized or even outsourced to private partners. In the latter example institutional changes have been made in the sense that private partners play a role in public services. This changes existing relationships, but only makes initial attempts at developing new practices.

4.3. Legislative Changes

There are examples of changes in legislation that make it obligatory to adapt to electronic services and achieve a higher user uptake. These legislative changes hardly challenge existing practices, but they do enhance the use of the service. Although in the cases discussed here, legislative changes are mostly instrumental, other cases show that changes can also have institutional implications and challenge existing practices. In the Estonian case legislation has been changed to make it easier to share information and the division of power between organizations has changed for that reason. In this case the legislative changes have contributed to new relations, although transparency or the integral approach of public authorities has not been improved. Another more far-reaching example is the Housing Benefits Law in the Dutch case that has been mentioned above. In this case legislative changes have been the guideline for designing a new organizational structure for the execution of the law and centralized processes. In other words, legislation has fundamentally changed the existing practices and positions. This has been a long and difficult process to manage and at the same time legislation on privacy has been a barrier in the design of the process. However, no steps have been taken to alter legislation. These kind of legislative changes are more complex, since decisions have to be made at another level and more organizations are involved. Therefore, public authorities still hesitate to make legislative changes that fundamentally change the organization of public administration.

ICT makes it possible to change the way public authorities are organized and cooperate. In order to realise this, changes in legislation can be necessary. Legislation can also be changed in order to achieve more instrumental goals, such as user uptake by compulsory use of the internet or compulsory sharing of data. Although not every case supports this at the moment, some cases also show that legislative changes can introduce new practices (especially in the Netherlands and to a lesser extent in Estonia).

5. Conclusion

In the cases examined, objectives regarding the use of ICT that have been stated in advance have largely been accomplished. In many cases, these objectives are related to returns in terms of improved levels of transparency, efficiency and customer satisfaction. In other words, changes contribute to a more open government and a more efficient public sector performance. It can be concluded that investments in the use of

ICT lead to modest institutional changes. Cases show that structural organizational changes in the back office are mainly restricted to a changed distribution of information or strengthened cooperation that can lead to shared services, a new business model or public-private partnerships. Especially these different forms of cooperation are becoming more and more common and are developing gradually. Institutional changes that have been made do not drastically change existing relations, but show more modest changes. ICT does challenge the existing responsibilities and tasks, but does not introduce new practices.

In the future however, it seems to be inevitable that the existing relations and processes will be challenged and revised more thoroughly. The increasing possibilities of ICT and changing customer demands will not only change service delivery; in the long run this will also more fundamentally change the relationships and institutions that are in practice now. And in turn, this will contribute to a much higher impact of returns of investments in ICT.

In the future, transparency, efficiency and customer satisfaction will no longer be the only drivers for public service innovation. Government will also have to invest in returns such as the improvement of legitimacy, accountability and the strengthening of democratic values (principles of 'good governance'), which will force public-service providers to expand their objectives and become more responsive towards citizens and businesses. Objectives will no longer impose a narrow, primarily economically based perception of e-government. In this way, more institutional changes must follow [4].

The current phase in which modest changes regarding process innovation are central seems to be necessary since governments in general prefer a step-by-step approach. In the next phase public authorities should be more open to organizational changes that have more impact.

Lessons Learned

Three main critical success factors for modernizing public services can be learned from the cases described in this chapter. First of all, in all cases a clear political or organizational goal has helped the change process by creating or strengthening the sense of urgency to invest in ICT. This is conditional to create the opportunity to bring together the necessary key players and raise funding accordingly. Although these goals may vary in their focus, they have been crucial for success. In the Danish case a target to cut back staff has been essential to develop a web-based system, in Estonia, the political wish to get a more modern image, alongside an efficiency target, has contributed to the success of e-Maksuamet. For the Finnish and German case targets regarding efficiency and user-friendliness have been key. Other research also shows that unless specific political problems or objectives are the driving force behind back-office reorganization, changes are quite smooth in nature [5].

Secondly, cooperation is essential for public service innovation and demand-driven development. In all four cases investments have been made to cooperate. In the German case the €10 million grant has been the main driver to get started and get relevant parties involved in a public-private partnership. In the Finnish and Danish case the coordinating organizations first had to prove the added value of a new way of working to convince others to cooperate or to cooperate more intensively in the future.

Taking the customer demands as the starting point, instead of organizational objectives or technical possibilities, contributes to the shared insight that cooperation is necessary for a more efficient and customer friendly public service. Although the cases presented here now are all successfully cooperating and even expanding this, the process that has preceded the cooperation has often been time consuming and difficult. A difference in interests and organizational goals has a strong impact on the chosen solution and the change approach. It is likely that in many cases the most feasible instead of the best possible solution for the long run will be chosen. The fact that more organizations are involved in order to really modernize processes seems to be an important explanation for the focus on minor or less uncertain changes. The fact that organizations other than the one(s) that invest will also benefit is another important reason for the difficult cooperation processes. Finnish experience shows that one coordinating party that takes the lead and responsibility for the initial investments was crucial.

Thirdly, a combination of a gradual step-by-step approach in combination with strong direction of one party that takes the initiative to get started has been critical for success. Although in some cases this means not all parties are involved from the start. Even in the German case, where finances have not been a barrier, and in the Estonian case, where a long organizational history did not limit possibilities, a step-by-step approach while showing the advantages was most successful. Although it should be emphasized that getting started without striving for comprehensiveness or unanimity is essential. Therefore one party that takes the lead and coordinates the innovation is crucial.

Lack of budget is often mentioned as a barrier to invest in ICT. Although in the German case the grant has unquestionably contributed to the success, this is not a guarantee and not conditional for success. The Estonian case in particular has shown that with a more modest budget even greater successes can be achieved. In that case, the fact that there have hardly been any organizational barriers because of a relative new government have made cooperation and the decision-making process easier.

For the moment public service innovations are focusing on instrumental changes and modest institutional changes. This may be logical, since it fits the step-by-step approach in which first attempts to challenge existing relations are successful. Services and interaction online are examples of process innovation regarding public services and have shown that existing practices can be challenged and that this contributes to a more effective and efficient government. For customers, public administrations should not only be effective and efficient, but also, and maybe primarily, transparent, democratic, legitimate and accountable. In order to realize these objectives too, public administrations need a long-term strategy aiming at both instrumental and institutional changes, involving substantial innovations in back offices and in the organization of public administration. The lessons learned can help to achieve this.

References

[1]   Capgemini and TNO-STB, *Does E-Government Pay Off?*, study under the authority of the Dutch Ministry of the Interior and Kingdom Relations, in preparation of the chairmanship for the European Union of the Netherlands, Utrecht, 2004.

[2]   A. van Venrooij, *Nieuwe vormen van interorganisationele publieke dienstverlening. De ontwikkeling en verkenning van een ontwerpaanpak*, Eburon, Delft, 2002.

[3]   Institut für Informationsmanagement Bremen and Danish Technological Institute, *Reorganisation of Government Back-Offices for Better Electronic Services – European Good Practices*, Brussels, 2004.
[4]   V.J.J.M. Bekkers, *Onttovering van het openbaar bestuur*, Openingsbijeenkomst Center for Public Innovation, Rotterdam, 2005.
[5]   European Institute of Public Administration (EIPA), *Organizational Changes, Skills and the Role of Leadership Required by eGovernment*, Luxembourg, 2005.

Information and Communication Technology and Public Innovation
V.J.J.M. Bekkers et al. (Eds.)
IOS Press, 2006
83

Designing Flexible Information Architectures in Policy Chains and Networks: Some Dutch Experiences

Marcel THAENS [a,1], Victor BEKKERS [b] and Hein van DUIVENBODEN [c]

[a] *Ordina & Erasmus University Rotterdam, Faculty of Social Sciences, the Netherlands*
[b] *Erasmus University Rotterdam, Faculty of Social Sciences, the Netherlands*
[c] *Capgemini & Tilburg University, Tias Business School, the Netherlands*

Abstract. In this chapter, flexibility is presented as an aspect of process innovation in relation to the computerization of policy chains and networks. We present a theoretical framework and two cases from the Netherlands. Based on analysis we conclude that both the cases show that technology itself is not a bottleneck for flexibility. The development and use of standards make it possible to base the design of an architecture on a minimum but robust set of agreements. One case shows that such a design increases the adaptive power of architectures. Another conclusion from the case studies is that a so-called high road or low road approach to information architectures is decisive for the level of its flexibility. In our case studies, the choice of the low or the high road was determined not only by aspects regarding information management or technological aspects, but mainly by the political-administrative setting and by the judicial context.

Keywords. Architectures, policy chains, flexibility, information management, information engineering

1. Introduction

The execution of rules and regulations and the delivery of public services and provisions are processes in which different public, semi-public and private organizations fulfil specific but interrelated tasks for which they have to exchange information. The dependencies between these tasks can be made understandable by using the metaphors of a policy chain and policy network. Although other definitions are possible, we will describe in this study a policy chain and network as semi-permanent collaboration arrangements between organizations, in order to produce - in a rather routinized way - specific outputs, such as the delivery of employment benefits [1]. In a policy chain the working processes between the organizations involved and the dependencies which stem from them have a sequential character, while in a policy network the dependencies have a reciprocal nature [2]. Chain or network

---

[1] Corresponding Author: Ordina & Erasmus University Rotterdam, Faculty of Social Sciences, Public Administration Group, P.O. Box 1738, 3000 DR Rotterdam, The Netherlands, E-mail: Marcel.Thaens@Ordina.nl.

computerization can be understood as the use of information and communication technologies (ICT) to support and/or redesign the working, coordination and information processes between organizations in order to enhance the efficiency and efficacy of implementation and service delivery programmes. ICT makes it easier to share and exchange information across the traditional borders of a fragmented and dispersed government organization, improves cross-organizational communication, increases the transparency of and control over working processes and policy outcomes, and enhances the accessibility of organizations. Simultaneously, there is a shady side. The effective use of ICT presupposes the formalization and standardization of working processes and information exchange relations. Stability and predictability are important conditions for its effective use. ICT may automate the status quo, freezing organizations into patterns of behaviour and operations that are difficult to change, once they have been computerized, and thus contributing to a process of bureaucratization [3]. Hence, flexibility is an important issue in innovative chain and network computerization and in the design of innovative information architectures. Will organizations that collaborate in a policy chain be able to adapt to changing circumstances (such as changing legislation or the inclusion of new partners), once they have computerized cross-organizational working and information processing processes? This dilemma can be illustrated, if we look at the development of information architectures that support the use of ICT in a policy chain. An information architecture consists of agreements and policies that prescribe the exchange of information between organizations as well as the use of ICT.

This article investigates how flexibility as a quality of process innovation has been achieved in the development of information architectures that facilitates the exchange of information and the use of ICT within the Dutch social security domain. What factors account for the flexibility of an information architecture within a policy chain in order to guarantee the innovative exchange of information?

The first step is to explore the notion of an information architecture (section one). The next step is to see how flexible architectures can be designed (section two). These explorations enable us to develop a theoretical framework in order to study the flexibility of information architectures in policy chains (section three). In section four we will describe how flexibility in the design of information architectures has been achieved in the Dutch social security sector. What instrumental and institutional factors have contributed to the adaptivity of the described information architectures? And, did the development of these flexible architectures lead to changing positions and practices in Dutch social security? These last two questions will be addressed in the final section (section five).

2. Designing Information Architectures

From an information management perspective an ICT infrastructure can be defined as the set of information policies and rules that govern an organization's actual and planned arrangements of computers (hardware), data and databases, human resources, network and communication facilities, software and management responsibilities [1: 435, 4: 62]. Sometimes a distinction is made between an ICT infrastructure and an information architecture. An ICT infrastructure refers to the existing or actual set of physical facilities, services and management that support all shared computing services within an organization or between organizations. The information architecture is defined as a conceptual framework for the future organizational ICT infrastructure. It is a plan for the structure and integration of the information resources in or between organizations in order to support the information needs of organizations which are related to the specific processes within the organizations and the tasks and (strategic, tactical and operational) goals of an organization [4: 62-63]. An architecture specifies how and why pieces fit together as they do, where they go, when they are needed and why and how changes will be implemented [3: 435]. The emphasis lies on the information requirements in order to support these processes, tasks and goals. This is the main challenge for professional information engineers and planners, who predominantly define an information architecture as a neutral set of supportive tools [5].

However, one can question the one-dimensionality of this approach. An architecture can also be perceived as a constructed social and political 'artefact', which embodies different interests and values as well presenting a set of different playing rules. Several reasons can be given.

First, information and ICT are powerful resources that actors (i.e. organizations or organizational units) use to protect their domains [6]. This is a unique sphere of influence, ownership and control over information – its specification, format, exploitation and interpretation [7]. The existence of an information domain is signalled by a) a break in flows of information, b) compartmentalization of information resources, c) idiosyncrasy of information specifications, d) the hegemony of specific discourses that shape information and influence its creation and interpretation and e) cultural and professionally accepted procedures that may not be surrendered so easily [8, 9, 10]. The development of a cross-organizational architecture implies that the existing information domains within and between organizations are being challenged, because it touches upon existing interests and practices. However, an essential factor is how organizational stakeholders perceive the nature and degree of the uncertainties and dependencies that result from a more intensive and coordinated exchange of information between them [11]. On the one hand, organizations are rather autonomous and want to protect their interests. On the other hand, organizations are part of the same logistical and administrative chain (or even network) of activities in which each organization fulfils a specific task in the handling of certain cases, requests, assessments etc. While each office controls specific resources - such as information, knowledge experiences, authority, money, competences - it is, simultaneously, also dependent on other resources that are controlled by other offices [12, 11]. There is no organization that is able to unilaterally enforce its will. Organizations are willing to set up an information architecture that crosses organizational boundaries, if they are able to minimize their dependency on other organizations or maximize the dependency of other organizations on them [13]. Therefore, chain and network computerization can be understood in terms of 'information politicking', resulting in conflict, competition, exchange, negotiation and cooperation [14, 15].

Secondly, the development of an information architecture in policy chains can be defined as a governance challenge [7, 16]. Governance can be described as the process of horizontal coordination, in which different actors are involved in creating a shared understanding and definition of the problems they are confronted with and of the measures to be taken [17, 18]. Chain and network computerization can be defined as the co-production of a common information domain through interaction, communication, negotiation and exchange [1]. It is important to define a dynamic balance between (qualitative and quantitative) costs and benefits (in the short run but also in the long run), so that a 'win-win' situation emerges based on the recognition of interdependency [19, 20]. In order to achieve this, it is important to respect core values and vital interests [21, 22, 23, 18]. Trust, reputation and social capital within a policy sector seem also to be important for (re)defining interdependency between the involved organizations in order to achieve productive relationships [24, 20]. Positive collaboration experiences, stemming from the past, influence the degree of trust, which is important to define win-win situations. Experiences with opportunistic behaviour or even 'power play' can enhance distrust [25]. Trust can also be a quality that facilitates the preparedness of an organization to reconsider existing information exchange agreements, thereby contributing to flexibility. Moreover, the degree of specification of the agreements which are laid down in an architecture can also be understood as the expression of trust or even distrust [25].

Thirdly, from a political science perspective, it is important to look at the different values which are embedded in computer-supported policy processes. These values are related to different design rationalities that compete which each other in the drafting of an information architecture. At least four rationalities are important [26]. These rationalities have their own internal logic and legitimacy. They stress specific core values, which have to be balanced. The political rationality deals with the question 'who gets what, when and how' if we look at the political challenges with which a political community is confronted [27, 28]. Information and ICT are important policy instruments that governments use to realize specific political values such as efficiency, security, liberty, equity or accountability. Moreover, they use ICT to deliberately influence the information position of actors and their relationships [29, 30]. The legal rationality stresses the importance of the rule of law, which, for example, implies offering legal security, consistency and legality. The economic rationality focuses on cost-efficiency, due to the scarce amount of resources which are available in order to achieve specific goals (in terms of benefits). The technological rationality emphasizes the question of how to design effective, efficient and trustworthy tools and intervention strategies which are based on the professional knowledge of a specific policy field. In this case of ICT, it refers to professional knowledge concerning the requirements under which ICT can operate effectively and efficiently.

Hence, we conclude that competing design rationalities – and their values – play an important role in the development of information architecture. Moreover, it is important to recognize that an architecture touches upon existing interests, practices and positions of the organizations in a policy chain.

3. Flexible Information Architectures

From an information engineering perspective, the flexibility of an information architecture is addressed in two ways. Allen & Boynton [3] make a distinction between the 'low' and the 'high' road. Following the low road, flexibility is achieved through a highly decentralized approach. Data, computers and networks, applications, programming and all the supporting resources are pushed as far down in the organization as possible. Variety is seen as a precondition for flexibility. Efficiency advantages are achieved through a) the definition of a common but minimal set of standards and definitions for the exchange of information and the building of networks that link dispersed workstations, databases etc; b) ensuring that there is full access to information instead of restricted access, primarily based on trust; c) ensuring the integrity of the data definitions and network standards. Hence, the emphasis is on specification of minimal but critical standards and interfaces that makes it possible to exchange information between rather autonomous organizational units in order to create a minimum of uniformity in the framework of organizational heterogeneity [3, 31]. An information architecture should only regulate those issues which are vital for the functioning of the organization as a whole in order to prevent it breaking down [32, 33].

The 'high road' focuses on creating flexibility and efficiency through uniformity, based on centralization: corporate-wide networks, central data collections, common application systems, standardized hardware, operating systems and databases. Core applications are designed to be organizationally independent, immune to the restructuring of an organization. The development of a central imposed, homogeneous information architecture and infrastructure is seen as the road to meet the changing conditions, without fundamentally changing the systems themselves [3].

At the same time it is important to observe that the nature of the technology itself has fundamentally changed. The technology itself has become more flexible than 20 years ago. A practice has emerged whereby electronic communication is based on open – hence flexible – and internationally accepted standards, such as XML. For instance, the internet and the WWW has provided a basic and publicly available infrastructure which can be used as a hub for the development of cross-organizational information architecture in order to create new strategic alliances and new collaborative arrangements [34].

4. Theoretical Framework and Research Strategy

An information architecture is said to formulate a number of agreements and rules which facilitate the smooth exchange of information and the use of ICT between organizations in a policy chain. These agreements reflect not only information planning and engineering requirements, but also other design rationalities which play an important role if ICT is used to support policy processes. Therefore, we have to address the different kinds of agreements which have been laid down in an architecture. The object and the nature of the agreements which have been made are important in order to make an instrumental assessment of the process innovations to be studied.

First, we will focus on the *object of the agreements* which organizations develop to exchange information within a policy chain or network; agreements that reflect different design rationalities and which add, differently, to the flexibility of the architecture:

- political and administrative agreements, referring to the interests and the information domains that are at stake as well as to the political goals to be achieved. For instance, how to deal with the autonomy of the participating organizations;
- technological agreements, which refer to a) the definition of the (standardized and formalized) information to be exchanged, b) the use of ICT to support this exchange and c) the management and control of the use of ICT;
- economic agreements, which refer to the specification and allocation of costs and benefits, related to the exchange of information and the use of ICT;

- legal arrangements, which refer to specific rights and obligations which are laid down in rules and regulations and to more fundamental rights, such as privacy.

Secondly, it is important to look at the *nature of the agreements* that have been formulated, referring to the degree of specification of the agreements [25]. Are the agreements specified in detail or are they vague? Moreover, the nature of these agreements gives us an indication of the way organizations have perceived flexibility as a relevant attribute of the information architecture. In our view the object and nature of agreements to be studied are rather intertwined and interacting factors that should be taken into consideration.

However, an information architecture does not only consist of technological and operational agreements. The agreements that have been made also show that information and ICT are important powerful resources that organizations use to protect their own interests, domains and positions, although they are dependent on each other. Organizations value differently the use and exchange of information and ICT in a policy chain or network, which can be traced back to the contents of an information architecture. Therefore, and thirdly, it is important to look at the *structure of the policy chain* in which an information architecture is being developed. In particular, it is important to look at the interests, positions of the organizations and the dependency relations between them as well as the resources they can mobilize to protect these interests. An architecture may reflect the power relations and positions within the policy chain or network. However, these relationships are not static, but dynamic due to the interactions between the organizations involved. This implies, fourthly, that the *quality of the collaboration process* between the organizations that have been involved in the development of an architecture should also be considered. Especially the trust in past and present interactions, the way in which a common challenge has been defined, may influence the object and nature of the agreements and the way in which flexibility is perceived as an important characteristic of the architecture [25]. An analysis of the structure of the relationships in the policy chain as well as the quality of the collaboration process can give us information about the institutional factors which have contributed to the process innovation in Dutch social security. Figure 1 outlines the relationships between the relevant variables.

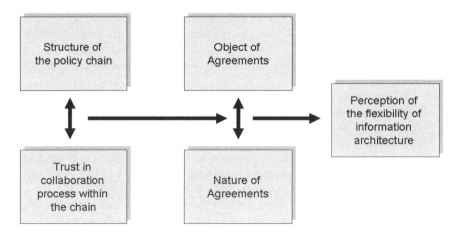

Figure 1. Relevant variables and relationships

The research strategy that we have followed consisted of two critical steps. The first step was to select two cases within one sector, which could be viewed as mirror cases. We have chosen the social security sector, in which two information architectures and exchange infrastructures have been developed. Both vary in terms of the kind of agreements which have been formulated. The RINIS information architecture resembles the low road of architecture design, while the so-called Suwinet architecture resembles the high road. Moreover, the Suwinet architecture was an architecture which has been imposed by law (top-down), while the RINIS architecture has been the result of a bottom-up process. Secondly, we have selected the case study method to describe and analyze the relationships between the variables which have been sketched in figure 1. A case study method is especially helpful in the reconstruction of complex and dynamic interactions between organizations which were involved in the development of an information architecture [35]. This reconstruction has been based on the interpretation of data that have been gathered by studying policy documents and interviewing key figures using in-depth interview techniques ('triangulation'). In order to guarantee a valid comparison, we have used the standardized set of items that was presented in the previous theoretical framework [35]. However, our findings do not pretend to be a statistical generalization, because of the rather unique character of the cases, the limited number of cases and the use of semi-open interview techniques. Our aim is to obtain a better analytical understanding of the multi-dimensionality and dynamics of information architecture development in policy chains and networks.

5. Information Architectures in Dutch Social Security

In the Netherlands the way in which organizations in the policy field of Work and Income have to collaborate is laid down in a specific law (Wet SUWI). This is to enforce the necessary cooperation of the different organizations that are involved in this policy field. The principle is that they link up in chains, steered on the basis of citizen demands. All of the processes in these chains are related to either work or income.

5.1. RINIS

RINIS stands for 'Routeringsinstituut voor (Inter)Nationale Informatiestromen in de Sociale Zekerheid', which can be translated as the Institute for Routing (Inter)National Information Flows within the Social Security Area'. RINIS is an infrastructure that supports the complex administrative exchange of information between different organizations. It also replaces the manual processing of information with automatic processing. Therefore, in addition to more accurate and more reliable information, the use of RINIS also leads to a cost reduction for the participating organizations. In the policy area of social security, RINIS is mainly used to *improve the efficiency of the exchange of information* between the various offices involved within the policy area of Work and Income.

There are several reasons why the cooperation between organizations in this field has increased in recent years. One of the reasons is that the organizations, due to legislation and the need for more efficiency in the execution of tasks, are becoming more and more dependent on each other. Another reason is that the organizations involved face the same challenges, such as an increase in the complexity of laws and rules and an increase in fraud within the social security sector.

In RINIS, different organizations (which are called sectors) share (part of) their information, for example:

- The implementation organization for employee insurances (UWV);
- The organization for Child Benefits and Old Age Pensions (SVB);
- The organization for collecting alimonies (LBIO);
- The office for enquiries in the social policy area (IB);
- The office for granting student loans (IB-groep);
- The association of Care Insurers (ZN);
- The office for Judicial Institutions (DJI);
- The Dutch Tax Department; and
- The association of Bailiffs (SGN).

The structure of the Policy Chain or Network

To carry out their tasks, many organizations collect, store, process and distribute a lot of information. Before the establishment of RINIS, these organizations were sometimes collecting the same information about the same subjects, for example information about citizens who are looking for a job or applying for a grant. Also, the processing of this information was mainly done by hand.

As stated earlier, the main target of RINIS is to improve the efficiency in the exchange of information between organizations. This is done by sharing information between organizations. An important aspect of this sharing is that the concept of original sources of information has been introduced. This concept means that a specific organization (the best-suited one) is responsible for collecting a set of well-defined data. When they need these data, the other organizations will use the original data from the original source. Consequently, they do not collect that information themselves. Within the policy area, different original sources for different kinds of information are developed. Besides sharing information, the organizations involved in RINIS have also developed a format for the (automated) exchange and application of their information. One element of this format is the use of reference indexes that mediate between demand and supply of information within the social security policy area. These reference indexes contain information on where in a sector information about a person or object is stored. The idea behind RINIS is that each sector within the social security area has its own focal point which serves as a 'counter' for this sector. This counter takes care of the exchange of information from their own sector to other sectors, but also of the distribution of information within its own sector. Because of the reference indexes, sectors can ask for information without knowing in advance which organization has that specific information or in which system the information is stored. In 1997, 200,000 messages were exchanged between the different sectors. In 2002, almost 30 million messages were exchanged between 10 different organizations. This number increased in 2004 to almost 56.4 million messages.

A RINIS bureau has been established as an intermediary between the focal points in the different sectors. The bureau can be seen as a kind of Trusted Third Party which oversees compliance with the agreements that are made. It also facilitates the routing of messages, the use of software, standardization, security, protection of privacy, the helpdesk and looks after the general coordination. It is important to note that the RINIS bureau does not store files in a central place. It does, however, gather and store information with regard to the processes of information exchange. To be able to check whether messages have been sent or received, tracking and tracing systems are used. These systems register the kind of information that is sent from one organization to another and the time at which this information is sent.

Objects of Agreements

Within the framework of RINIS, the following agreements were made that are important for the adaptive power of the chain.

Technological agreements are seen as a responsibility of the RINIS bureau. This bureau does not interfere with the organization of the different participating sectors. The technological standards that are agreed upon only concern the information exchange between different sectors, the requirements regarding the organization of a focal point for each sector and the requirements regarding the RINIS server that automatically mediates between the demand and supply of information.

Agreements regarding *information management* concern the definition of the information that is exchanged and the format that is used for the exchange. Within RINIS, some robust agreements are made on the way in which the information is exchanged between sectors and the quality of this exchange. Furthermore, it is also important that all the offices involved agree on only using original sources of information within the policy field. Because of this, an organization within one sector does not have to collect information if this information is already available within another sector. The information management agreements are minimal agreements. This means that agreements are only made on issues that really require agreements.

One of the *ICT management agreements* within RINIS is that the RINIS bureau is responsible for the ICT management and maintenance of the RINIS servers that are located in the different sectors. The sectors themselves are responsible for the ICT management of their own focal points. Agreements are also made concerning the supervision of the way in which questions that are asked in a sector are answered. A contractually guaranteed reply period is agreed. This guarantees the reliability of the information exchange, which is a precondition for robustness. The reliability is further enhanced by agreements on information security.

Legal agreements are laid down in an Interchange Agreement. This agreement contains arrangements on issues such as the purpose for which the information may be used by sectors, agreements on the quality of information and procedures regarding quality assurance, delivery periods for information, procedures to resolve possible inaccuracies in the exchange of information, the way in which consultation between the organizations involved will take place and ways in which future disputes will be settled. It is important to note that these agreements focus only on the process of information exchange and not on the content of the information that is exchanged.

The *financial agreements* concern the initial development costs and the costs associated with the operation and maintenance of RINIS. The initial costs were paid by one organization. These costs were subsequently paid jointly by the organizations involved. For the coverage of the costs associated with operation of RINIS, an arrangement based on tariffs for the use of RINIS was agreed upon between the participating organizations.

An important part of the *political-administrative agreements* is the fact that the autonomy of each organization involved is respected. This implies that each sector is responsible for the development of their own information arrangements. Agreements between organizations focus only on the exchange of information between sectors. These agreements are also expressions of self-regulation and voluntariness.

The Nature of Agreements

Looking at the kind of agreements that are made within the RINIS framework, the conclusion may be that RINIS is about making a minimum of agreements between the organizations involved. However, these minimum agreements are so robust that they enable a reliable and stable exchange of data between the different sectors. If agreements had been made with consequences for the way in which the information arrangements within the sectors is organized, then the mutual dependencies between organizations would have become very strong and complex. This would have had a negative effect on the flexibility of the exchange system of RINIS. The decision to aim for minimum agreements also reduces the coordination costs for the organizations involved.

The Quality of the Collaboration Process

With regard to the nature of the collaboration process, this latter aspect, voluntariness, plays an important role. Due to developments in the environment in which the organizations operate in the nineties (e.g. increasing fraud and a further refinement and sharpening of social security policy), the organizations in the policy area of social security realized that they had a joint interest in working together with regard to the execution of the social security policy in the Netherlands. This understanding was the foundation on which mutual trust started to flourish.

Based on this increasing trust, the organizations began to see the advantages of exchanging information on the basis of a jointly developed infrastructure. A cooperation based on trust and voluntariness means in general that organizations are more prepared to invest in change and in an improvement of quality than in situations where the cooperation is enforced. This is because trust and voluntariness lead to involvement which is often seen as an important condition to be able to react to or anticipate changes within the policy area of social security and its environment. Also, the fact that one organization was willing to cover the initial development costs of RINIS contributed to the trust among the organizations. This is because it prevented a discussion about the detailed division of costs and benefits among the organizations.

5.2. Suwinet

RINIS and Suwinet are both information architectures that are used within the policy area of work and income. In contrast to RINIS, Suwinet is an architecture that can only be used by a limited number of organizations, namely those organizations that share responsibility for the execution of the SUWI law (Wet SUWI). These organizations are:

- The implementation organization for employee insurances (UWV);
- The Centre for Work and Income (CWI);
- The organization for Child Benefits and Old Age Pensions (SVB);
- And local social welfare organizations.

The Structure of the Policy Chain or Network

As stated previously, the cooperation between the different organizations that are involved in the policy field of work and income is defined and enforced by a specific law (Wet Suwi). As a result, an intensive information exchange between the organizations that are involved in Suwinet became necessary. After all, each organization is, by law, responsible for only a part of the service delivery to citizens, while the information that is necessary for this service delivery is spread among the different organizations. So the cooperation between organizations regarding the exchange of information is not triggered by an improvement in efficiency (as in the case of RINIS) but results from an external necessity, which has been imposed on them.

The different organizations make their own records accessible (at least partially) to other organizations in the SUWI chain. These organizations can retrieve the necessary information when they need it. Although information and files are linked through Suwinet, the management of the information and files is centrally organized. Therefore, Suwinet can be described as a private network in which information is exchanged through a central point of exchange in the network. Suwinet is used to support the various chains in this particular policy field. Within the framework of Suwinet, the exchange of information is supported by joint ICT facilities and by a system of arrangements regarding issues such as work processes, definitions and data. The development and use of the shared infrastructure is a joint responsibility of the organizations involved, under the direction of the Minister of Social Affairs and Employment. One of the instruments included in the information architecture is aimed at giving (authorized) employees of the involved organizations direct online access to relevant data for and about clients (even if the information is only available at other involved organizations). This instrument is called Suwinet 'view from the inside' (Suwinet-Inkijk). The data appear as HTML pages which employees can read directly on their browser screen. The data are also suitable for integration in the applications that are used within the different organizations.

So, where RINIS is limited to the back offices of the organizations involved, Suwinet also supports the front office functions. The way in which information is exchanged also differs between the two architectures. In the case of RINIS, there is always one organization that (even though on demand) brings information to another organization (push). Suwinet enables organizations to retrieve the necessary information from the records of other organizations in the chain (pull).

The management of the central facilities of Suwinet is carried out by a separate unit of CWI called BKWI. The position of BKWI in Suwinet is different from that of the RINIS bureau in RINIS. Tracking and tracing systems are not necessary in Suwinet because information is available to employees online (in a visual form or otherwise). In the event that a failure occurs in the retrieval of information, this is noticed immediately, so action can be taken.

Objects of Agreements

Within the framework of Suwinet, the following agreements are made that are important for the adaptive power of the chain.

The *technological agreements* focus mainly on technical details of the exchange of information between the different sectors. One central element, for example, is an agreement on using XML as a standard for this exchange.

The *agreements regarding information management* primarily have to do with the description and definition of the information that is exchanged. The SUWI data registry, containing a data model and an information dictionary, is a product of this kind of agreement.

As an element of the *ICT management agreements,* service level agreements (SLAs) are concluded at different levels. These SLAs cover the performance of the exchange of information. For example, agreements are made on the timeliness and completeness of information and on the technique that is used for exchanging information. ITIL is used as a basis for the ICT management. BKWI, as a central organization, is only responsible for the ICT management of the shared services between the organizations. The organizations themselves are responsible for their own specific ICT management.

The *legal agreements* that are made are much more stringent than in the RINIS case. This is because the exchange of information is based on a law. A regulation from the Ministry defines for each organization the kind of information that should be provided. It also even defines the times at which the exchange of information must take place. Furthermore, the regulation also describes the conditions under which the way the information is exchanged can be revised in the future.

The Ministry of Social Affairs is responsible for the architecture. Therefore, the *financial agreement* stipulates that the costs of the development and operation of the joint architecture that is used by all the involved SUWI chain organizations are paid by the Ministry. Furthermore, each organization meets its own costs associated with participating in this network.

The most important *political-administrative agreements* are laid down in a law (Wet Suwi). The law describes the division and allocation of tasks, responsibilities and competences between the cooperating organizations. All of these organizations, together with the Minister of Social Affairs, consult each other on a regular basis. Agreements that are made are recorded in a working programme for the chain of organizations.

The Nature of Agreements

In comparison with RINIS, the flexibility regarding the content of the exchanged information is limited in the case of Suwinet. This is because a law prescribes what kind of information has to be exchanged between legally defined organizations. The organizations involved in RINIS have a degree of autonomy in making the agreements they consider necessary, while the Suwinet organizations are committed to the frameworks that are described in the law and the regulations. This means, for example, that the number of participating organizations is limited. Although the cooperation between organizations is enforced by law, this does not mean that all the necessary details on the level of the network or infrastructure are settled automatically. Despite the high expectations, it takes time to reach agreements on these details. Robustness of the agreements made with regard to the joint infrastructure or network can be seen as a requirement for reaching the above-mentioned flexibility regarding the content. It is then not sufficient to limit these agreements to 'big' issues such as an information dictionary, but it is also necessary to devote attention to relatively 'small' issues such as sets of characters used in the exchange of information. These smaller issues are important for the infrastructure or network to function in a proper and effective way.

The Quality of the Collaboration Process

The Suwinet example shows that flexibility is hard to achieve in a situation in which organizations are forced to work together. The freedom of action for a further development of Suwinet was limited by law. Additionally, there was a certain amount of distrust between the organizations involved. Flexibility and adjustment to specific situations can only be achieved if this distrust can be turned into trust between the organizations. Within the SUWI policy area, this led to numerous different consultation structures on different levels. These consultation structures did not contribute to the adaptive power of the chain architecture, because consensus reached in one consultation structure was sometimes revoked in another consultation structure. The distrust that was evident at the beginning can be explained by the fact that SUWI started with a redistribution of tasks, responsibilities and competences, while at the same time the organizations involved were supposed to work together. As a result, the question of who was responsible for what seemed to be more important than aspects of the information exchange or the infrastructure itself. This is the reason why the cooperation between the organizations lacked a joint perspective on the advantages and necessity of sharing information. Distrust was the result.

The redistribution of responsibilities also led to changes within the organizations. A redesign of working processes was necessary, which meant that the attention of the organizations was focused more on the internal operations than on the cooperation with other organizations on the level of the chain as such. In the last few years the quality of the collaboration process has increased. The main reason for this is the fact that the focus on the customer has become dominant. This was a trigger that created a more joint frame of reference so that issues such as content and implementation gained greater prominence.

6. An Instrumental and Institutional Assessment of Flexible Information Architectures

In a previous paragraph the notion was put forward that the design of an information architecture is not only a matter for information managers and engineers. Political and social aspects also come into play when such an architecture is designed. By looking at both the cases, the conclusion can be drawn that, at least in the policy area of Work and Income, information politics played an important role in shaping both the RINIS architecture and the Suwinet architecture. In both cases the ultimate goal of a more efficient and effective exchange of information is reached. But more interestingly, the cases also show how the idea of policy chains and the use and development of the supportive architectures are shaped differently in different settings.

In the case of RINIS, organizations work together on a voluntary basis to achieve goals such as a reduction of costs and having access to more appropriate and more reliable information. This respect for the autonomy of the organizations involved is clearly visible in the way in which the architecture is developed. This is illustrated by the use of ideas such as the original source of information, the use of reference indexes and the choice not to store files in a central place. Another indication is the position of the RINIS bureau. It is seen as a kind of Trusted Third Party that 'only' facilitates the use of ICT. In the way RINIS is shaped, the 'low road' approach towards an information architecture from Allen & Boynton [3] can be seen. In developing RINIS, a very decentralized approach is chosen in which the variety (within the low road approach seen as a precondition for flexibility) is guaranteed by giving precedence to the autonomy of the organizations.

In the case of Suwinet, the dependency between the organizations involved was a result of the SUWI law that rearranged the distribution of responsibilities in the policy field. The driving force behind the cooperation was not voluntariness, but an obligation to work together . As a result, the information architecture in the case of Suwinet seems more formalized than in the RINIS case. An example of this is the fact that Service Level Agreements between the organizations involved are made concerning specific details of the information and the way in which the information is exchanged. And although information and files are linked through Suwinet, the management of the information and files is centrally organized. Because of the responsibility for the management of the central facilities, the position of BKWI is very different from the position that the RINIS bureau has within RINIS. Because of the emphasis on uniformity and centralization, the approach taken in developing Suwinet can be labelled as the 'high road' approach to information architectures as identified by Allen & Boynton.

We now turn the focus to the assessment of flexibility as a relevant quality of process innovation. In this book a distinction is made between an instrumental and an institutional assessment of innovations. In an instrumental assessment, the focus is on those factors that have contributed to the development of flexible information architectures. In our conceptual model, two factors have been identified as relevant: a) the object of the agreements which have been made and b) the nature of the agreements. In an institutional assessment, we address the question of which factors referring to the embedded relationships between the organizations involved (such as the nature of the relationships) and the evolved practices (such as the trustfulness of the collaboration process) have contributed to the development of flexible information architectures. Furthermore, we address the question of whether the development of a flexible information architecture has led to a radical or incremental change in the positions and relationships between the organizations involved.

An instrumental assessment of the 'low road' approach to the information architecture in the case of RINIS shows that the emphasis is on the specification of minimal but critical standards necessary for an efficient exchange of information between the organizations involved. The minimum agreements that have been made are so robust that they enable a reliable and stable exchange of data between the different sectors. Because of the voluntariness of the cooperation, the organizations involved can decide themselves what kind of agreements are defined as minimum and robust. The technical agreements are dominated by political-administrative agreements (taking voluntariness as the starting point).

In the 'high road' approach in the case of Suwinet, flexibility is achieved by using standards, service level agreements, a data model and an information dictionary that are centrally imposed and the development of a homogeneous information architecture and infrastructure. The Suwinet organizations are committed to the implementation of frameworks that are described in the law and the regulations. So, these frameworks determine what kind of agreements have to be made. Therefore, judicial agreements are dominant over other kinds of agreements. As a result, the agreements in the Suwinet case have a more detailed character than the agreements in the RINIS case. The necessity to make formalized agreements and to focus on details has a negative effect on the flexibility in the case of Suwinet.

In an *institutional assessment* of flexibility, a comparison of both case studies shows that the structure of the policy chain and the quality of the collaboration process are also important for the adaptive power of architectures. In the case of Suwinet, the enforced structure of the policy chain caused some degree of distrust among the organizations involved. This led to a high density of all kinds of consultation structures on the political-administrative, operational and information management level. Because this consultation is so structured, only limited space for adjustments and adaptations remains, which therefore has a negative effect on flexibility. It can also be pointed out that robust agreements that were made (for example in the RINIS case) are often the result of trust between organizations, an acknowledgement of mutual dependencies and the ability to formulate a joint goal for the cooperation. An important aspect of the structure of the policy chain in the case of RINIS is voluntariness. The organizations themselves (and not a third party such as a ministry) were convinced that they could all benefit from working together on exchanging information. If trust exists between organizations, it provides a basis on which to change earlier agreements or make new agreements if this is necessary due to changing circumstances.

When it comes to the participation of new organizations in the architecture or rapid adaptation to new emerging circumstances, the flexibility in the decentralized and less formalized approach of RINIS seems to be greater than in the centralized and formalized approach of Suwinet. But if we look more closely at Suwinet, we can see that there is no need for such flexibility. Because of the dominant role of the law, new participants are not expected, and the adaptation to changing circumstances will always be a long-term process because it will often require an adjustment of the law. This echoes the earlier statement that looking at information politics is important for understanding the flexibility of information architectures and the way in which this flexibility is approached.

In this chapter, flexibility is presented as an aspect of process innovation in relation to the computerization of policy chains and networks. In line with our theoretical framework, we can conclude that both the cases show that technology itself is not a bottleneck for flexibility. The development and use of standards make it possible to base the design of an architecture on a minimum but robust set of agreements. The RINIS case shows that such a design increases the adaptive power of architectures. Another conclusion from the case studies is that a high road or low road approach to information architectures is decisive for the level of its flexibility. In our case studies, the choice of the low or the high road was determined not only by aspects regarding information management or technological aspects, but mainly by the political-administrative setting (RINIS) and by the judicial context (Suwinet).

References

[1]   R. Rhodes, *Understanding Governance*, Open University, Maidenhead, 1997.
[2]   J. Thompson, *Organizations in Action*, McGraw Hill, New York, 1967.
[3]   B.R. Allen and A. Boynton, Information Architecture: In Search of Efficient Flexibility, *MIS Quarterly* **15**(4) (1991), 435-445.
[4]   E. Turban, E. McLean and J. W. Wetherbe, *Information Technology for Management*, Wiley, New York, 2002 (3rd ed.).
[5]   J. Martin and J. Leben, *Strategic Information Planning Methodologies*, Prentice Hall, Englewood Cliffs, 1989 (2nd ed.).
[6]   T. Davenport, R. Eccles and L. Prusak, Information Politics*, Sloan Management Review* **34**(1) (1992), 53-65.
[7]   C. Bellamy and J. Taylor, *Governing in the Information Age*, Open University Press, Buckingham, 1998.
[8]   K. Kumar and H. van Dissel, Sustainable Collaboration: Managing Conflict and Collaboration in Interorganizational Information Systems, *MIS Quarterly* **20**(3) (1996), 279-300.
[9]   S. Dawes, Interagency Information Sharing: Expected Benefits, Manageable Risks, *Journal of Policy Analysis and Management* **15**(3) (1996), 121-147.
[10] Ch. Bellamy, ICTs and Governance. Beyond Policy Networks? The Case of the Criminal Justice System, in: *Public Administration in the Information Age*, I. Snellen and W. van de Donk (eds.), IOS Press, Amsterdam/Berlin/Oxford/Tokyo/Washington, 1998, 293-306.
[11] J. Pfeffer and G.R. Salancik, *The External Control of Organizations*, Harper & Row, New York, 1978.
[12] A van de Ven, On the Nature, Formation and Maintenance of Relations among Organizations, *Academy of Management Review* (1976), 24-36.
[13] P. Beynon-Davies, Information Management in the British National Health Service: The Pragmatics of Strategic Data Planning, *International Journal of Information Management* **14**(2) (1994), 84-94.
[14] D. Knights and F. Murray , Politics and Pain in Managing Information Technology: A Case Study in Insurance, *Organization Studies* **13**(2) (1992), 211-228.
[15] V. Homburg, *The Political Economy of Information Management*, SOM, Groningen, 1999.
[16] V.J.J.M. Bekkers, The Governance of Back Office Integration: Some Dutch Experiences, in: *E-government*, A. Wimmer, R. Traunmüller, Å. Grönlund and K. Andersen, (eds.), Springer, Berlin/Heidelberg, 2005, 12-25.
[17] J. Kooiman, (ed.), *Modern Governance*, Sage, London, 1993.
[18] J. Koppenjan and E-H. Klijn, *Managing Uncertainties in Networks*, Routledge, London, 2004.
[19] J. Baron, *Thinking and Deciding*, University Press, Cambridge, 1994.
[20] B. Uzzi, Social Structure and Competition in Interfirm Networks: The Paradox of Embeddedness, *Administrative Science Quarterly* **42**(4) (1997), 35-68.
[21] W. Orlikowski, The Duality of Technology: Rethinking the Concept of Technology in Organizations, *Organization Science* **3**(3) (1991), 398-427.
[22] W. Orlikowski, Using Technology and Constituting Structures, *Organizational Science* **11**(4) (2000), 404-428.
[23] H. de Bruijn, E. ten Heuvelhof and R.J. In 't Veld, *Process Management (Why Project Management Fails in Complex Decision Making Processes)*, Kluwer, Boston, 2002.
[24] J. Butler and S. Cantrell, Communication Factors and Trust: An Explanatory Study, *Psychological Reports* **74** (1994), 33-34.
[25] O.E. Williamson, *The Economic Institutions of Capitalism*, Free Press, New York, 1985.
[26] I. Snellen, *Boeiend en geboeid*, Samson, Alphen, 1987.
[27] H. Laswell, *Politics: Who Gets What When and How?*, World Publ., Cleveland, 1958.
[28] D. Stone, *The Policy Paradox*, Norton, New York/London, 2002.
[29] Ch. Hood, *The Tools of Government*, MacMillan, London, 1983.
[30] H. Margetts, Computerising the Tools of Government, in: *Public Administration in the Information Age*, I. Snellen and W. van de Donk (eds.), IOS Press, Amsterdam/Berlin/Oxford/Tokyo/Washington, 1998, 441-460.

[31] A. Mowshowitz,, Virtual Organization: A Vision of Management in the Information Age, *The Information Society* **10** (1994), 267-288.

[32] G. Morgan, *Riding the Waves of Change*, Jossey-Bas, San Francisco/Oxford, 1990.

[33] C. Hastings, *The New Organization*, McGraw Hill, London, 1993.

[34] P. Monge and J. Fulk, Communication Technology for Global Network Organizations, in: *Shaping Organizational Form*, G. DeSanctis and J. Fulk (eds.), Sage, Thousand Oaks, 1999, 71-100.

[35] R.K. Yin, *Case Study Research: Design and Methods*, Sage, London/Thousand Oaks/New Delhi, 1989.

Part 3

Product and Technological Innovation

Information and Communication Technology and Public Innovation
V.J.J.M. Bekkers et al. (Eds.)
IOS Press, 2006

Geographical Information Systems and the Policy Formulation Process: The Emergence of a Reversed Mixed Scanning Mode?

Victor BEKKERS[1] and Rebecca MOODY

Erasmus University Rotterdam, Faculty of Social Sciences, the Netherlands

Abstract. In this chapter we have looked at the potential of GIS for the policy formulation process in public administration as well at the factors that influence the actual use of GIS. The potential is related to get a better insight in the complexity of wicked policy problems and the possibility to visualize effects. Through a literature scan we have listed a number of relevant instrumental and institutional factors that account for the successful use of GIS. Furthermore we have studied the use of GIS in a regional development practice. The possible contribution of GIS to institutional renewal is that it may facilitate a process of reversed mixed scanning.

Keywords. Geographical Information Systems (GIS), regional development, policy formulation, rationalization, mixed scanning, Blue City Project

1. Introduction

In December 2005 the American City of New Orleans was hit by a devastating hurricane, named Katrina. Pictures of its devastating power circled over the world. Houses were scattered into pieces; neighbourhoods were flooded through the rise of the water level by more than two meters; bodies were floating through the streets; and thousands of injured people were sitting on the roofs of their houses. Could this have been prevented? This was one of the questions which were raised in the political and public debate that followed the disaster. Although the power of the hurricane was gigantic, specialists and politicians have pointed out the fact that information and knowledge about the effects of such a hurricane had been available. However, no measures were taken, like the heightening of the dikes around the New Orleans' delta. Different agencies, like the FEMA – the Federal Emergency Management Agency – did possess advanced data models and computer simulations, which were used to develop different scenario's predicting these horrifying effects. In the drafting of these

---

[1] Corresponding Author: Erasmus University Rotterdam, Faculty of Social Sciences, Public Administration Group, P.O. Box 1738, 3000 DR Rotterdam, the Netherlands; E-mail: bekkers@fsw.eur.nl.

scenario's geo-graphical information and geographical information systems (GIS) played an important role, although history has proven that they did not lead to all kinds of preventive actions due to all kinds of political considerations.

Hence, the potential of GIS – as a technological innovation – can have profound implications for the way in which issues can be put on the political and public agenda (agenda building) as well for the development of policy programs. Two advantages of GIS can be put forward. First, GIS make it possible to enhance the transparency of rather 'wicked policy problems' through the combination of different data and data models with location based information. The second advantage is that GIS can help to visualize the 'state of the art' of specific problems as well as to visualize the effects of specific developments (like the effects of hurricane) or measures (like the effects of higher dikes).

In this chapter we want to look at the potential of GIS for the policy formulation process in public administration as well as to explore which factors influence the actual use of GIS[2]. In order to do so we will explore the nature of GIS and the policy potential of GIS (section two). Next we will demonstrate how GIS has been used in different policy (formulation) processes in different countries. Some best practices will be presented (section three). Although the potential of GIS may be to some extent revolutionary, in the practice of public administration we may observe that this potential is not always used. What are the relevant factors that influence the usage of GIS in policy development practices? In section four we address a number of instrumental and institutional factors as they have been described in literature. In section five a small case study will be presented, in which the use of GIS in relation to the development of rural plan in a Dutch region has been investigated. In section six some conclusions will be formulated.

2. The Nature of GIS and its Policy Potential

2.1. The Nature of GIS

Geographic information systems (GIS) are computerized systems that can order, manage and integrate large quantities of spatial data. They can also analyze this data and present it, mostly in the form of a map [1]. GIS can help in supporting policy-making and decision-making since it can combine different data and demonstrate different alternatives, because many digital records or digital objects contain an identified geographical location. By integrating maps with spatially oriented (geographical location) databases (called geocoding) and other databases, users can generate information that enhance the quality of their planning, problem-solving and decision-making process [2]. Some relevant qualities can be mentioned [3].

In the first place, GIS holds the quality of calculation, this means that GIS can calculate different algorithms and so make a possible cost-benefit analysis a lot easier. Through GIS it becomes easier to develop a more sophisticated 'if …then' reasoning. For instance, in the case of the Katrina hurricane it was possible to generate rather

---

[2] This chapter has been based on the combination of two research projects that have been carried out for two Dutch ICES/KIS Innovation Programs, the so-called BSIK programs on 'multiple use of space' and on 'the establishment of nation-wide geographical information infrastructure.'

complex (taken into account numerous factors and aspects) estimations of the possible damage.

GIS can also link different data sets, which share a geographical component, to one another and thus produce a new data set in which information is shown that was not visible before. The combination of existing data creates new information which enhances the transparency of the policy problem which is at stake, but also the transparency of different kind of policy processes. We can demonstrate the power of GIS by quoting Hamilton [4: 12]: "I can put 80 page spreadsheets with thousands of rows into a single map. It would take a couple of weeks to comprehend all of the information from the spreadsheet, but in a map, the story can be told in seconds". For instance, GIS make it possible to generate a integrated picture of the degree and nature of the environmental quality of specific region, because different kind of pollutions (water, air, noise, soil) can be linked with the other urban and rural qualities of a region (like the number of houses, industrial activities, roads etc.). The multi-dimensionality of problems and possible solutions become evident, while at the same time it is possible to view and analyze a specific problem from different perspectives. This could facilitate the way in which the environmental quality of such a region is being put on the agenda of local and regional authorities facilitate a more sophisticated mix of measures to be taken, but also facilitate a more integrated monitoring of the measures and its effects.

Another important quality of GIS is the ability to visualize problems and effects. At this moment we observe that advanced visualization (three dimensional graphics), multi media and simulation tools are integrated within GIS capabilities which improve their 'look' and 'feel'. The result is that plans become more visible. In this way people do not have to look at a plan on paper anymore but can actually 'see' the plan. This virtual world may help choosing between alternatives in the policy process. Moreover, these qualities make it also possible to allow users to generate their own 'maps' and visualizations which correspond with their own interests, wishes and ideas.

Hence, we may conclude that GIS could enhance the rationality of problem-solving and decision-making processes within public administration. However, in order to asses the possible contribution of GIS, it is important to obtain a better understanding of the nature of the policy formulation process within public administration.

2.2. The Nature of the Policy-Making Process

Several theories exist on the nature of policy formulation. In most cases these theories can be seen as a reaction to the shortcomings of the rational-comprehensive model of policy formulation and decision-making, which in essence is an ideal type. In the rational decision model the starting point is a policy problem (like e.g. air pollution or the social quality of neighbourhoods) which presents a choice to a political actor (e.g. a municipality). This actor is someone who must choose a course of action in order to attain a desired end. The actor then goes through a sequence of mental operations leading to a decision. These steps are: 1) defining goals, 2) imagining alternative means for attaining them, 3) evaluating the consequences of taking each course of action in terms of costs and benefits and 4) choosing the alternative most likely to attain the goal. In the most extreme case, the ideal of perfect rationality would require an actor to consider all possible alternatives (an infinite number), and evaluate all possible consequences of each [5: 233].

Simon, with his 'satisficing model' or 'bounded model of rationality' was one of the first reacting to the rational actor model. In Simon's model it is believed that actors do act goal-oriented but Simon acknowledges the cognitive limits to the degree of rationality humans can demonstrate. The idea is that policy-makers consider only some alternatives, have limited information, and as soon as an alternative is found that proves to be satisfactory, and thus fits the criteria that are set up in advance, it is carried out. A policy-maker then stops searching for other solutions [6]. He does not look for optimal solutions but for satisfying solutions.

In 1959 Lindblom developed a model named 'successive limited comparisons', better known as incrementalism. In this model it is believed that actors cannot act as rational as in the rational actor model. It is also believed that values, contrary to the rational actor model, can not be clarified in advance, since often the values involved in a policy problem are conflicting, a logical means-end reasoning becomes impossible. In this approach a few alternatives are listed for a problem and the alternative that is chosen is the alternative with which all involved actors agree, regardless of the values included; this makes the successive limited comparisons approach very fit for pluralistic societies. Additionally, the chosen alternative must not differ significantly from past policies, this because in this way the prediction of consequences becomes easier. A succession of these incremental changes in the end then result to a larger change [7].

Dror developed the normative optimum model; here in this model factors of extrarationality are included, like intuition, experience and creativity. Besides this the limits in the degree of rationality humans can demonstrate are acknowledged. The model exists of four stages and every stage is sub-divided into phases. In the model it becomes clear that policy-making involves dealing with a large amount of different values, and that these values are not static but change constantly, the priority of the values can not be determined through a rational process but needs to be determined by value judgment. Additionally the model deals with the processing of reality, since perception of reality depends on different individual values. In this model there is a lot of emphasis on the understanding of the problem. An alternative is chosen on the basis of whether the means, listed in this alternative, are available and if the cost benefit analysis demonstrates that this alternative is optimal, again various analysts must agree on the chosen policy [8].

Etzioni developed the model of mixed scanning as a middle road to the rational actor model and incrementalism; here the core of the model is that policy-makers look at alternatives at two levels. First they scan all alternatives that come to mind, like in the rational actor model but with the exception that they are analyzed very generally, all alternatives that reveal a serious objection, in, for example, availability of means, values etc., are rejected. That is where the successive limited comparisons approach comes in, by rejecting all alternatives in advance that pose objectives; the unrealistic aspects of the rational actor model are reduced. In the second stage the remaining alternatives are analyzed in full detail, like in the rational actor model, until one alternative stays put and is the only option; the shortcomings of the successive limited comparisons approach are reduced here by letting go of its conservative slant and exploring alternatives aimed at the longer run that might differ from existing policy more fundamentally [9].

2.3. The Potential of GIS for Policy Formulation

In the models demonstrated above it can become clear that GIS has an interesting potential for policy formulation. First of all, in all models, which challenge the rational comprehensive model, it is shown that the degree of rationality one can demonstrate is limited. However, GIS has the potential to strengthen the degree of rationality in the policy formulation process, thereby overcoming the limits of rationality. While the multidimensionality of processes and problems become more transparent, while alternatives can be visualized in virtual reality programs or on a map, while cost and benefits can be easier calculated and while new information is generated by the linking of data sets, rationality might increase. Policy-makers can make a more rational choice of alternatives because consequences of alternatives are clearer to them.

In the satisficing model it can be said that the use of GIS can either be limited or increased. This is dependent on the criteria for a satisficing policy set up in advance. If GIS is incorporated into these criteria, the usage of GIS, naturally, increases and would be mandatory for a satisficing policy. If not, the usage of GIS would only lead to optimality and would thus be useless and overdone. In this model the criteria for a satisfactory solution thus determine whether GIS is used or not. Additionally, the model deals with bounded rationality, it is acknowledged that actors do not have all information, cannot analyze all alternatives and are not able to predict all consequences of every possible alternative. GIS here could help increase the capability to analyze, calculate and predict for each alternative. Provided that the usage of GIS is part of a satisficing policy, GIS could increase the rationality within the model, although the limits to rationality as set still exist, maybe to a lesser degree.

For the model of successive limited comparisons the usage of GIS could, but definitely not necessarily would, create a problem since there could be no past policies to fall back on since GIS is fairly new. A policy alternative only incrementally different from past policy would logically not include a large deal of new means, like GIS. GIS would thus slowly have to find its way into the policy-making process since there are few precedents of using it. The potential of GIS then might not fully be used, especially when just recently using it; GIS might not be explored to its full contents. Although GIS could help making predictions and analysis of alternatives easier, the model of successive limited comparisons does not allow policy to differ fundamentally from existing policy.

The normative optimum model deals with the same contradiction, the extrarational components in the model could either get practitioners excited about the usage of GIS but on the other hand they could also feel very uncomfortable with an unfamiliar system. This could lead to a usage of GIS that does not meet its full potential. Additionally the emphasis on the problem of conflicting values in this model could not be reduced by the usage of GIS. On the other hand, within the model the choice for an alternative is partly based on the cost-benefit analysis, something that by the usage of GIS could become a lot more comprehensive. For this model the same goes as for the satisficing model, while limits to rationality still play a part, the usage of GIS with its effects and qualities could increase the degree of rationality in policy-making.

Mixed-scanning is the model that could change in the largest degree by the usage of GIS. In the first stage, more alternatives could be scanned due to the more time efficient dealings with them by the usage of GIS; it becomes possible to look at more alternatives or alternatives could be looked at more in dept in the same time as before. While the first stage was originally fairly incremental in nature now the aspects of the rational actor model here could significantly increase, by either looking at more alternatives or analyzing the alternatives in more detail. In the second stage originally alternatives were looked at through a rational actor mode of policy-making, now due to GIS predicting consequences and effects more sophisticated, this stage could become even more rationalist. From being the middle ground between the rational actor model and the successive limited comparisons approach, mixed-scanning could move towards the rational actor side of the spectrum, while still remaining to have its incremental components. In this way GIS can very well serve the model of mixed scanning and even reverse it to some degree.

3. The Use of GIS in Policy Formulation: An International Overview

When looking at the use of GIS in policy and policy formulation from an international, comparative point of view, one can find a wide variety of examples. Internationally, GIS is used in many countries and is not only used in the obvious sectors, like urban and rural planning and environmental protection, but also in a large variety of other areas. Below some examples are listed that demonstrate the usage of GIS in different countries.

Thailand provides for a very fair case of the use of GIS in policy formulation regarding avian influenza. In 2003 and 2004 Thailand was the country hardest hit by the avian influenza. At the time, the Thai government used a GIS application to generate information and to support decision-making for the responsible agencies. The information on the outbreak areas of the Ministry of Agriculture and Cooperative were matched with the information of geo-databases such as the Administrative layer and the Transportation layer. In this way an analysis could be made of the trend and direction the avian influenza followed. Next these maps were converted so identification with the 50 km buffer zone was made possible, this to prevent further spreading. An analysis was made of high-risk farms, areas with densely clustered farms, and thus a potential for rapid spreading of the influenza and farms close to the outbreak area. All this information had been placed on the internet map server; all relevant agencies thus could use the same system for deciding how to deal with their part of the avian influenza. With this information national and regional government could set up a barricade plan for areas with densely clustered farms, pre-emptive slaughter and restriction and surveillance measures. Using GIS in this case made possible that different measures were taken, fit for different areas. Instead of formulating a nation wide policy, with the area-specific information GIS provided, several policies were formulated matching the problems and potential risks for each area [10].

In Russia all land used to be held in public property, when in the beginning of the 1990's this system disappeared, Russia found itself the task to restructure land ownership. This was not an easy task to fulfil since farmland played a major role in social life, these farms provided next to farm commodities, also for social infrastructure, public transport and other utilities. An economic market for agricultural land had to be established, this was done by the Law on Turnover of Agricultural Land, here a policy had to be formulated to redistribute the land to private individuals or enterprises. In this policy other interests, like forest, irrigation, road planning and environmental protection, had to be incorporated. Since a lot of information had been undocumented, active involvement of local authorities was needed in order to formulate an accurate policy. GIS was used here to document the parcels for farming but also to incorporate all legal documents concerning individual parcels. The quality of the land also needed to be taken into consideration, GIS made sure that parcels could be weighed on this quality. These GIS applications together formed the basis of the draft redistribution plan. The end result was that the plan was implemented, due to the use of GIS the plan was performed with fairly low costs and in a relatively short time, otherwise, a nationwide plan for reallocation would not have been possible [11].

In Belo Horizonte, the fourth largest city of Brazil, an initiative was taken up by local authorities to restructure the public transportation system. The transportation system was to be set up so that people could travel in the most efficient, cheapest and safest route through the city. GIS was used to simulate all alternative plans. A GIS application was made by combining all information listing every traffic sign, every legal turn, every bus stop, all one-way roads and all existing bus routes. Together with this the routes were identified that were used most frequently. In this map simulations were made of a variety of possible alternatives for the new public transportation system. Cost-benefits analyses of the alternatives were made and finally an alternative was chosen and implemented. GIS here made possible that policy-makers could compare the different alternatives in a visible, integrated way. Policy-making became a lot easier [12].

In Fresno County, California GIS is helping to make sure federal funds are fairly distributed among different schools. Under the provisions of the Improving America's Schools Act schools with a large number of children of low-income families receive extra federal funding. The idea, naturally, to implement this was to link the children of low-income families to individual schools to calculate which school should receive extra money and how much. This proved to be a problem, the information on low-income families was listed in one database and the school district information in another, and additionally the maps of the school attendance zones were aged and not well kept. GIS provided for a solution here, first files of school districts were made, schools were placed within it, and attendance zones were added. The files containing all streets and addresses, as a layer, were place on top of the map. Next the files on low-income families with children were incorporated in this map. This provided for a clear view and GIS was able to calculate how many children of low-income families were attending each individual school. The process now takes 200 hours, instead of the original 750 hours and the costs decreased from $30.000 to $8.000. GIS here made possible that policy was executed accurately and properly [13].

GIS is also used in health care policy, as was the case in Yakima County, Washington State. Because of the high infant mortality rate a program was designed called 'First Steps' to make sure that infants of low-income mothers received extra care additional to the care provided by Medicaid, while mothers were also given prenatal care. In 1998 policy makers discovered that twenty five percent of the woman entitled to the extra's provided by 'First Steps' were not making use of it. The question was, who are these woman and why are they not using this? It was needed that this question was answered in order to launch a campaign directed at these women making sure their children received a healthier start in life. GIS was used to answer this question, first all birth records were linked to addresses and placed on a map. All Medicaid births were identified by census block and made visible on that map. By census block average age and education level of mothers was mapped as well. It then became very easily to identify who was not making use of 'First Steps', by putting the census blocks with Medicaid births together with the woman using 'First Steps'. It became clear that not, as expected originally, the young, low educated, non-American born woman were not making usage of 'First Steps' but the older, slightly better educated, American born woman, were not making use of the program. GIS made sure here, that a policy could be formulated for a campaign directed at the right group of woman [13].

4. The Actual of Use of GIS: A Literature Review

Although GIS could potentially account for radical changes, and in theory has a very large potential to change policy and the way policy is made, in practice this is not always the case. There are several factors that influence the usage of GIS, these individual factors account for several hurdles that prevent the use of GIS to an optimal degree. We can distinguish between instrumental factors and institutional factors that have been mentioned in the literature on the use of GIS.

4.1. Instrumental Factors

One of the main factors influencing the use of GIS is the possibility of sharing data between departments and agencies. If this proves to be not a large issue GIS can be used fairly easy but this sharing of information does not always occur. A reason for this is different priorities within organizations. One organization might be willing to share information for a specific purpose; if the other organization does not believe this purpose to be a priority it will not be willing to put the manpower, nor the costs, into this. This issue becomes even larger when organizations do not only differ in their priority listing of certain interests, but when these interests are conflicting. Sharing then becomes extremely undesirable for the organization since it will counter serve their interests [14]. Another issue in sharing information is not having suitable contacts within the organization one would want to share with. A lack of connection can make sure that the sharing of information between organizations is not possible. Resource constrains naturally, also prevent the sharing of information as well as privacy concerns [23]. Another observation is that organizational stability is needed in order to generate trust and commitment to sharing. When an organization is not perceived as stable by others, they will not be willing to share with this specific organization since there are concerns about whether integrity of data use can be guaranteed [15, 14]. Another problem in sharing information is the quality of the data, this quality of data often proves to be poor, and sharing then becomes useless [15].

A second factor is the technical knowledge needed in order to work with GIS. When people, departments and agencies either own or obtain the technical knowledge GIS has a large potential to be used very effectively in policy-making. But a lack of technical knowledge can prove to be a problem in two ways. In the first place when GIS is used in matters of public participation: not everybody has access to the internet where a public participation GIS could be used and not everybody has the technical knowledge to deal with the program. In this way, public participation through GIS is seriously hindered and will not prove to have the democratization effects originally aimed for, since certain groups are excluded by means of technical knowledge [16, 17]. Second the constraint accounted for by technical knowledge does not limit itself to applications of public participation GIS but also applies for government agencies or departments. Policy-makers are used to traditional systems and are often not able to work with GIS, the result might be that extra money for training should be made available in the best case and in the worst case, misinterpretation of data or the rejection to use GIS as a whole [18].

Another problem seen in literature on GIS is that while mostly data is provided by governments, NGO's and citizens mistrust the data and refuse to work with the GIS application set up with this data, the original aim of the application might not be realized here because of the rejection of the data by others [19].

Availability of data also seems to be a problem; some data are simply not available. And thus a policy aiming to use this data cannot be made using GIS. Additionally the price of data proves to be a problem. The pricing of data is often not regulated and for local governments far too expensive to buy. This proves to constitute a divide between the providers of data and the users of data; this also undermines the consensus on the policy to be made as a whole. In countries where there is a market for data, data proves to be cheaper and more available for use; this proves to be a factor in the usage of GIS in policy formulation. The factor of data availability proves to be very important, where in western countries data seems very available, in developing countries and Eastern Europe this seems not to be the case. It is thus seen here that GIS is used in a lesser degree [12, 15, 18].

4.2. Institutional Factors

One of the institutional factors limiting the optimal use of GIS is to be found in the field of public participation. In some cases it is seen that in a centralized system authorities mitigate against local empowerment. Increased public involvement is sometimes seen as undermining current positions of power, local authorities may feel very threatened by this, this is seen especially in countries with little history of public participation like the United Kingdom [14, 19]. Another point in public participation is that in several countries there is no free access of data, which means that only people who can afford it can join in the public participation aimed for originally. In the United States this seems less of a problem since local authorities stimulate local empowerment initiatives and data access is free or available for a lower price. This stimulates the use of GIS in public participation on policy [14]. For example, in Minneapolis the Powderhorn Park Neighborhood Association started a project using GIS which provided the neighbourhood with data on housing with the purpose of having the community provide for input in order to address critical housing issues to improve housing conditions. Not only, due to a large number of people joining in this project, progress was noted in housing conditions but also the power relations within the community organization had altered. This would not be possible if data would not have been made available [17].

A major factor that withholds GIS to be optimally used is the incompatibility of data sets; data can only be shared with great difficultly especially when there are no standardized systems available for this. This is linked to the notion of an information domain; an information domain is a sphere of influence, ownership, power and control over information, unique to an organization or groups of organizations. Additionally it so that together with the control over the information the specification and the format of information are also established. In order for information to be standardized these information domains need to be altered and the control that comes with them must partly be given out of hands [20]. Efforts are being made to achieve national standardizations but the effects are still limited [15]. In order to achieve standardization, as stated above, often restructuring of an organization is needed. Not everyone in an organization proves to be ready for or positive about change. It shows that this is a large obstacle for fully implementing GIS. For a large deal, successful implementation of GIS and accurate use of GIS for policy formulation depends on the possibility of integrating data. A national standard for GIS would very much stimulate the use of GIS in policy formulation and make GIS a more accurate tool in this [21].

Intellectual property rights and privacy issues also prove to be a factor in the sharing of information and the usage of GIS in policy formulation. Privacy regulations might in some cases make it impossible to use certain data, or make those data public. This proves to be a large constraint on the diffusion of GIS applications. For example, the GIS application containing the data on Medicaid in the United States are confidential, they could thus not be used in the First Steps program described above, this was the reason analysis was done by census block and not by address. The Medicaid application proved to be useless because of privacy laws and thus could not be used a way that would support public policy best [13]. Intellectual property rights make the data more expensive than they originally were and make it hard to publish data publicly. The usage of GIS and the degree in which GIS is used in this matter is thus very much dependent on the legal framework for privacy and intellectual property rights. Legal systems that are very rigid on these matters will see the usage of GIS in a lesser degree than legal systems that are not [14, 19].

Another important factor is that authorities are not willing to lose power to new or other agencies. In the using of GIS for policy these authorities prove to defend their share of power and thus direct policy and the usage of GIS in another direction The main fear of authorities is that decisions on their territory are not made by them anymore and that they are placed for an established fact once the decision is made. Authorities are thus reluctant to cooperate in a GIS application for policy and might be unwilling to share certain information. This is what happened in a project in the Amsterdam region in the Netherlands in which a GIS application fostering an interactive public service counter with fully integrated real estate information on a regional level was being established. An intermediary organization was set up in order to decide on issues related to the GIS application; the organization had the authority to decide over individual local governments. This met a great deal of resistance by these local governments because they perceived themselves powerless in the decision-making process. As a result the decision-making arrangement had to be altered drastically. This hinders the expected effect of GIS of deterritorialization. When authorities are secured that they will remain power over their territory or when GIS initiatives are organized more decentralized the usage of GIS will increase and thus play a larger part in policy formulation [21].

Related to this is the notion that GIS can serve as a power source, like all information, those who own it tend to have power over those who do not. GIS especially is seen as the liberator of socially and politically marginalized groups, since GIS can, through public participation, be at the basis of collective action for those who otherwise did not have a voice. On the other hand, authorities might restrict this for the reasons mentioned above, since GIS and the access to GIS means power and the potential of control. It is thus very well possible that GIS is not used to its full potential since the ruling elite would want to keep this kind of power in its own hands to serve its own interests and is not willing to share this power [22].

As mentioned, GIS can provide for more transparency in public policy. Where this at first glance seems to be positive, it also proves to have some downfalls, organization fear that when more transparency is achieved, comparisons are possible between organizations this could lead to more demands of harmonization of policy and thus taken power out of the hands of these organizations [21].

While these hurdles and constraints to the optimal use of GIS prove to pose problems for basically all countries, the developing countries have and extra hurdle. Namely: mostly GIS programs are financed by international aid programs and planned for two to three years. As soon as the money dries up the GIS application is neglected and not further used. Additionally, mostly the international aid programs send their own experts over to the developing countries, when the program ends they leave; locally there is nobody to operate the GIS application. Another problem is that these experts do not have a lot of local knowledge and try to place western standards in the GIS application; locals here then might be very unwilling to cooperate [12].

Although we have listed a number of instrumental and institutional factors which account for the success of the use of GIS in policy formulation, it is interesting to see, how GIS has been used in an actual policy development practice. In the next section a minor case study will be presented.

5. GIS and Integrated Regional Development: A Case Study

5.1. Developments in Urban and Rural Planning

If one looks at the Dutch theory and practice of urban and rural planning, one can observe a shift from a rather restrictive planning practice – based on command and control – towards a planning practice in which stakeholders through communication, negotiation and exchange develop a common planning practice. This can also be understood in terms of a shift from 'top down' towards a more 'bottom-up' approach of urban and region policy development.

The Netherlands traditionally has an urban and rural planning system, in which each of the formally involved and responsible government layers develop a plan within the framework of conditions which have been laid down in a prior and super-ordinated planning document. On a central level, it is the Ministry of Housing, Urban Planning and Environmental Affairs, that defines the assumptions and headlines regarding how to use the available space in the Netherlands, which kinds of spatial, traffic, economic, leisure and other functions should be realized, and under which conditions. The general specifications are laid down in a central planning document (the so-called *Planologische Kernbeslissing*). Following this document, the provinces develop a regional planning document (the so-called S*treekplan*), while the municipalities develop their own plan, based on the conditions which are set in the regional planning document (the so-called *Bestemmingsplan*). This local urban and rural planning document plays an important role in the allowance of local building permits. This planning practice can be defined as hierarchical way of imposing a cascade of restrictions, in which each restriction is based on and derived from other restrictions, which in the end lead to the acceptance of the proposed building practice.

At the same time there is a growing tension between the vertical, restrictive, quite static and rather one-dimensional (functional) planning approach of the way land should be used and the dynamic, multi-dimensional needs of citizens, companies, local and regional public authorities and real estate developers. The contents of these urban and regional plans do often not match the actual developments that take place in specific urban and rural environments [23, 24, 25]. This has led to another planning approach, which tries to anticipate on the multi-dimensional and dynamic nature of urban and rural development. The main challenge is to produce a common policy practice in which relevant actors (stakeholders) are able to create a shared understanding about the necessity of integrated regional development as well as the content of the development. These actors do not only represent different interests and frames of references, but they also operate within several (public, private or semi-public) domains and within different functional and territorial layers of government. In this, more developmental planning approach, it is important that stakeholders substantially participate in the development and implementation of plans and that arrangements for cooperation and negotiation are being established. Looking at the practice of this approach, five characteristics can be distinguished:

- the need for a rather robust planning concept, which sets a horizon for the desired development of an area, but at the same time is flexible enough to react and anticipate on all kinds of economic, social, demographic developments and their spatial effects;
- many developments take place at regional level, which is a scale that can be located between the level of the municipalities and the level of the provinces. That's why a regional focus should prevail in rural planning which actually takes into account the specific regional conditions and developments. Up till now the regional level has a independent level has not been recognized in the formal practice of Dutch rural planning;
- it has an open character, which implies that a lot of discretion has been given to the participating actors in order to give them actually influence in the way a region should be developed;
- this open character also implies room for innovation through competing design perspectives, which can be seen as the expression and recognition of the multiple meanings which different actors with different interests and frame of reference attach to the a region should be the developed;
- a strong focus on implementation, because implementation conditions (in terms of investments, allocation of costs and benefits in relation to the provision of a business case) play an important role in the definition of successful regional projects.

One vital issue in this new planning approach is the sharing of information and knowledge between the stakeholders which are involved in these open planning processes and in the negotiation, communication and cooperation processes which take place between them. How did GIS play a role in the exchange, sharing and use of information?

5.2. The Blue City Project

In this section we will describe how the world of developmental regional planning (the world of policy-makers), in which concerted and tailor-made solutions have to be explored through communication, negotiation and exchange, has been able to meet the world of information analysts and computer scientists which try to produce standardized computer-based geographical information. These two worlds meet during the economic development process of a specific region in the Groningen, one of the provinces in the North of the Netherlands: the development of the Blue City.

First, we will describe the main characteristics of the Blue City Project. Second, we will describe how the main actors that were involved in this project, assessed the role and meaning of geographical information, produced by GIS.

Project Content

In the north of Groningen lies the territory of the so-called Blue City which covers about 40.000 ha. In this territory a lake should be excavated of 8 km². Surrounding this lake new nature reserves, recreation areas and housing locations should be realized. The building of these houses should generate the money for the development of the lake and the nature reserves. The economic and social problems of the region, with fallow agricultural areas, high unemployment, a low average income, the migration of younger people to the city, a strong growing number of elderly people, decline of shops and other private and public facilities (like public traffic provisions) were an important reason to revitalize the region. In order to do so an integrated approach of the regional problems has been proposed. The idea was that a large lake, surrounded by nature and housing areas, could attract new people and business. Since 1992 several sketches, based on analysis of the area, have been made. This idea has been worked out in all kinds of imaginative sketches. On the basis of the combination of these sketches, a developmental plan was drafted which was worked out in more detailed projects. In essence, this elaboration process resembles and can be perceived as an interactive process of mixed-scanning [9] in which global ideas have been worked out in competitive, more detailed plans – based on different perspectives and views on the desired development of the region and specific areas in this region. These plans were subjected to an open debate with relevant stakeholders that also lead to a number of adjustments. Those plans which actually had gained support were integrated in the regional plan of the province of Groningen and in local urban and rural plans of the municipalities which were involved in the Blue City Project.

Use of GIS

If we look at the role of geographical information and GIS in this project some interesting observations can be made. Geographical information in combination with other policy information (like economic prognoses and residence information) has played an important role in the development of the plan. In the beginning of the project, there was a rather broad and generic need for information about the different kinds of existing economic activities, economic prognoses, specific characteristics of the parcels involved, resident and income distribution information, soil and water information and information about altitudes. The combination of this information was needed to get a better insight in the specific conditions of the region. GIS has been an important instrument to combine these relevant information sources and datasets, because it provided a common background.

Later on, during the design and the planning of concrete facilities, geo-information and GIS have played a limited role. Primarily geo-information and GIS were used to test and to legitimize afterwards the design decisions which have been made, and to assess the (intended and unintended) effects which stem from concrete planning decisions. Geographical information has primarily not been used as input for the design process. One reason was that a too detailed image of the region, based on geographical information, was perceived by town and country planners as a possible threat to their creativity, because it would impose all kinds of limitations. Due to this attitude, town and country planners did sometimes present sketches which were not always realistic. In one case a planner has not been aware of the presence of a number of ecological limitations, laid down in specific legalisation, which was aimed at protecting the specific ecological characteristics of an area in which he wanted to locate a new housing complex. Moreover, these planning professionals have used all different meanings to the destinations which were presented on different digital maps. However, it is important that all these parties use the same definitions of specific urban and rural destinations. For instance, uniformity in the colour which is given to a specific destination on the map, uniformity in the name-giving of the destination and the planning code which relates to a specific destination, and uniformity in the way these destinations should be graphically being presented, is essential to create a shared understanding about the development of a region. If destinations are multi-interpretable, maps are difficult to read by the involved local and regional planning authorities and architectural firms. However, especially the relation between a specific colour and a specific destination is being perceived as a rather sensitive issue, because it touches upon the proclaimed discretion of the parties involved. One the hand the actors that were involved in the development process did recognize the need to standardize geo-graphical information between them, because this would facilitate the quality of the process; on the other hand they were afraid to make these specific agreements, because they would diminish their discretion.

Moreover, the absence of a nation wide geographical information infrastructure has not stimulated the smooth exchange of information in these integrated regional planning projects, like the Blue City Project. Up till now the Dutch world of geo-graphical information and GIS can be seen as an archipelago of different approaches, definitions and systems, which frustrated the exchange and sharing of information and knowledge in specific projects.

Furthermore, during the development process parties did not consciously consider what kind of information they need to have. To some extent this is rather difficult, due to the developmental and goal-searching character of the planning practice. However, it is possible to define some basic needs which suits all the parties involved of specific groups of parties. There was no systematic and intended information searching process to support the planning process. An emergent and incremental information search strategy prevailed, that was based on 'trial and error', following the contents of the negotiations between parties involved. Another problem has been the difficulty to find specific information. And, if relevant information was found, it was not always accessible, which made it difficult to exchange it or combine it with other information, using a GIS underground. In the end, the process of gathering and processing reliable information was perceived as a rather time-consuming process, with and without using the potential of GIS.

However, there is one example in which geographical information has played an important role as intended input resource for the design process. One part of the region is protected by the so-called Ecological Structure Plan. Town and country planners, civil engineers, representatives and experts of the Regional Water Board, the province of Groningen and the municipalities in this area as well the National Forest Agency had to develop a plan for this area which could respect the ecological importance of the area as well as to combine it with other relevant economic and social activities and interests. In advance a common information set was provided to all parties involved (like information about altitudes, about the composition of the soil and water management information). This contributed to the quality and the speed of the design process, because realistic design alternatives could be taken into consideration. The emerging debate was more focussed on the assessment of effects of possible design alternatives, which improved the quality of the feedback of the design process and the supplementary dialogue between the parties involved.

Another important observation is that in order to work out a specific, more detailed project plan it was necessary to look whether this plan was in accordance with specific, location based administrative and legal requirements and obligations. Therefore, the need to have more detailed information grew exponentially. However, the information which had to be provided by the databases which were used for the drafting of the broad sketches for the development of the region, could not be used. In many cases additional research have to take place in order to present a very detailed and integrated picture of a specific parcel within an area, containing micro-level information. For instance, in order to comply with environmental legislation ('the so-called MER-obligation'), it is necessary to make an integrated assessment of possible intended and unintended effects of the proposed measures and plans. To assess the hydrological effects of specific interventions in the landscape, it was necessary to have very detailed soil profiles as well as to assess what kind of water management measures should be taken to handle possible unwanted effects effectively. However, the gathering of this additional and detailed information was a time-consuming process. The existing geo-information databases and processing devices were not able to provide the necessary information at the desired level.

5.3. An Instrumental and Institutional Assessment

If we look at this case, and want to assess the innovative potential of GIS two perspectives can be used. First, from an instrumental perspective we could ask ourselves the following questions. Did GIS contributed to a more rational development process, due to the information which was generated through the use of this technology? And, what factors did influence the use of GIS? From a more institutional perspective we will ask other questions? Did the use of GIS contributed to the emergence of new practices and did it challenge the established interests and positions of the parties involved?

An Instrumental Assessment

The case shows that GIS has enhanced the 'rationality' of the policy development process, because GIS makes it possible to create new information out of old existing information. Using GIS makes it possible to combine databases and datasets which provides a more detailed, integrated and sophisticated picture of the existing conditions of a region. Moreover, GIS makes it possible to assess and to visualize the intended and unintended effects of the measures to be taken. The added value of GIS was especially demonstrated during the development of the first drafts of the design process. GIS added to the provision of a rather broad and generic view. However, the case shows that the contribution of GIS in the development of more detailed plans and projects is ambiguous. For example, whenever rather detailed plans have to be developed, it shows that the existing GIS databases and applications are not able to provide a very detailed plan of the characteristics of a parcel. However, one reason could be the absence of nation wide, and thus standardized, geo-graphical infrastructure.

The case study also shows that the use of GIS has also been frustrated by the fact that the stakeholders involved did not define their information needs at forehand. No translation has been made of the general goals of the plan for regional development in information and ICT requirements and needs. The absence of such strategy can also be explained by referring to the fact the Blue City Project can be characterized as a goal-searching process, in which 'trial and error' plays an important role; as well as the fact that information and ICT are important powerful resources that are used in negotiation processes.

An Institutional Assessment

From an institutional perspective the case study reveals a number of interesting issues. First, GIS can only operate rather smoothly if potential users are willing to comply with general standards. The case study shows that GIS has been perceived as a possible threat to the existing professional working practices and routines. The use of data standards and formats as well as the fact that GIS can provide detailed pictures are apparently been defined as a threat to the creativity of the professional architects and planners which have been involved in the drafting of the sketches and plans. Moreover, we observe that GIS is also being used strategically. Due to the complex bargaining processes which emerge when more detailed plans have to be elaborated, GIS has primarily been applied as an instrument to produce information that can be used to legitimize afterwards the decisions that have been made.

However, one example has been put forward, in which a glance of the potential of GIS can be seen in terms of institutional renewal. GIS facilitates the creation of a common data set, which stakeholders and designers use as a common frame of reference or as a common knowledge infrastructure in order to draft, through interaction and communication, a specific plan.

Furthermore, we see the emergence of a new policy development mode. Although this mode has been described in literature in terms of 'mixed scanning', we define the mode which can be derived from this case study as a 'reversed mode of mixed scanning'. As mentioned earlier, Etzioni has tried to combine rationality and incrementalism in his planning system. Originally Etzioni has aimed to make sure that in each stage of the process the downfalls of the rational actor model and the successive limited comparisons approach are reduced by incorporating the desirable elements of each approach and leaving out the unrealistic or undesirable elements. With the usage of GIS it seems like the successive limited comparisons approach loses ground and that in the first stage, where it was dominant before; the aspects of the rational actor model now become more dominant, changing the model into a more rationalist approach. The Blue City Project has shown us that the first stage of developing plans rather did resemble the rational model of policy formulation, in which GIS have been used to gather additional information about the nature of the region. Later on, when more detailed plans were needed to be developed, the political clash between interests and values became more evident, which has led to a more incremental policy formulation process. Therefore in the near future, we want to do more research into question if GIS, and under what conditions, leads to the emergence of a mixed or a reversed mixed scanning mode.

6. General Conclusions

In this chapter we have made an assessment of the innovative potential of GIS in policy development processes. First we have looked at the possible benefits of GIS. A number of striking examples, based on a limited international comparison, have been presented, that show us something of the added value of GIS. At the same time it important to look at a number of instrumental and institutional factors which account for the success and failure of GIS applications in policy development processes. In order to reveal these factors we used a double empirical strategy. First, we have looked at the literature on the use of GIS. What factors have been presented in literature? Second, we have presented a small case study in which GIS has been used in order to draft an integrated regional plan for the development of region in the North of the Netherlands.

The innovation potential of GIS is especially been based on the quality to enhance the transparency of rather wicked, multidimensional policy problems as well as to enhance the transparency of possible effects and side-effects (wanted and unwanted) of the measures to be taken. Furthermore, the possibility to visualize the effects makes GIS a very powerful instrument. We could say that GIS enhances the rationality of policy formulation process, but this does not imply that the outcomes of the policy formulation process have become more rational. Other factors also influence the way in which GIS can be used. From a more instrumental perspective we see that GIS depends on the ability and willingness to share data, which is not self-evident, due to different priorities and interests, mistrust or lacking resources. Moreover, working with GIS requires sophisticated knowledge, which is also not always available. Another factor is that some data is not always present and cannot be acquired, due to the fact that in some countries geographical information is rather expensive to buy. From a more institutional point of view our research review has listed several factors. The most important factor is that GIS can only work effectively and efficient if there exist a nation wide geographical information infrastructure (in which privacy and intellectual property rights are also dealt with) which facilitates the sharing of information. However, this presupposes standardization, but standardization is very often perceived as a threat to the existing (multiple) information domains of all kinds of public and private organizations within the geo domain, which implies the loss of power.

The case study on the regional development of the Blue City Project in the Netherlands confirms a number of factors which have been mentioned. From an instrumental point of view it is reported that GIS has contributed to the rationality of the policy formulation process, but that the possible advantages of GIS were not fully used because of: a) the lack of nation wide geographical infrastructure, b) the lack of a systematic information strategy in which basic geographical needs were explicitly addressed and c) the fact that geo-information and GIS are important powerful resources in negotiation processes. From an institutional point of view we have observed some contradictionary results. First, we witness that GIS provoke resistance and may frustrate innovation, because they touch upon the existing working practices and routines of the involved professionals, like architects and town planners. GIS presuppose standardization which is perceived as a threat to the discretion of these planning professionals. Secondly, GIS has been strategically used to generate information which is used to legitimize the decisions that have been made afterwards. Thirdly, and perhaps this is the most interesting observation, GIS could contribute to a policy formulation mode that can be described as 'reversed mixed scanning'. However, our research material is too limited to strengthen this claim. Further research should demonstrate if this is a valid claim.

References

[1]   A. Meijer, Geographical Information Systems and Public Accountability, *Information Polity* **7** (2002), 39-47.
[2]   E. Turban, E. McLean and J. Wetherbee, *Information Technology for Management*, Wiley, New York, 2002.
[3]   V. Bekkers and V. Homburg, Innovatie in tweevoud, *Rooilijn. Tijdschrift voor Wetenschap en Beleid in de Ruimtelijke Ordening* **35** (2002), 506-511.
[4]   J.M. Hamilton, A Mapping Feast, *CIO* (1996), March.
[5]   D. Stone, *The Policy Paradox*, Norton, New York,/London, 2002.
[6]   H.A. Simon, *Administrative Behavior. A Study of Decision-Making Processes in Administrative Organizations*, John Wiley & Sons, New York, 1976.
[7]   C.E. Lindblom, The Science of 'Muddling Through', *Public Administration Review* **19** (1959), 79-88.
[8]   Y. Dror, *Public Policy-Making Reexamined*, Chandler Publishing Company, Scranton, 1968.
[9]   A. Etzioni, Mixed-Scanning: A 'Third Approach' to Decision-Making, *Public Administration Review* **27** (1967), 385-392.
[10] S. Moukomia, *Rapid Response Spatial Information Systems: Avian Influenza in Thailand*, Geo-Informatics and Space Technology Development Agency, Bangkok, 2004.
[11] A.L. Overchuk, L. Hansen and N.H. Hansen, *Developing a Farm Land Distribution Model in Russia, Cadastre*, Federal Agency for the Immovable Property, Russia, 2004.
[12] K.A. De V. Borges and S. Sahay, GIS for the Public Sector: Experiences from the City of Belo Horizonte, Brazil, *Information Infrastructure and Policy* **6** (2000), 139-155.
[13] R.W. Greene, *GIS in Public Policy. Using Geographic Information for More Effective Government*, SRI Press, Redlands, 2000.
[14] P. Turner and G. Higgs, The Use and Management of Geographic Information in Local e-Government in the UK, *Information Polity* **8** (2003), 151-165.
[15] P. Pollard, Geographical Information Services: A UK Perspective on the Development of Interorganizational Information Services, *Information Infrastructure and Policy* **6** (2000), 185-195.
[16] S. Carver, *Participation and Geographical Information: A Position Paper*, Paper prepared for Spoleto Workshop on Access to Geographic Information and Participatory Approaches Using Geographic Information, Italy, 2001.
[17] D. Weiner, T.M. Harris and W.J. Craig, *Community Participation and Geographic Information Systems*, Paper prepared for Spoleto Workshop on Access to Geographic Information and Participatory Approaches Using Geographic Information, Italy, 2001.
[18] A. Pawlowska, *GIS as a Tool in Local Policy-Making*, Sklodowska University, Lublin, 2001.
[19] S. Carver, A. Evans, R. Kingston and I. Turton, Accessing Geographical Information Systems over the World Wide Web: Improving Public Participation in Environmental Decision Making, *Information Infrastructure and Policy* **6** (2000), 157-170.
[20] V. Bellamy and J. Taylor, *Governing in the Information Age*, Open University Press, Buckingham, 1998.
[21] M. Lips, M. Boogers and R. Weterings, Reinventing Territory in Dutch Local Government: Experiences with the Development and Implementation of GIS in the Amsterdam Region, *Information Infrastructure and Policy* **6** (2000), 171-183.
[22] A. Haque, GIS Public Service, and the Issue of Democratic Governance, *Public Administration Review* **61** (2001), 259-265.
[23] D. Dammers, F. Verwest, B. Staffhorst and W. Verschoor, *Ontwikkelingsplanologie. Lessen uit de praktijk voor de praktijk*, Ruimtelijk Planbureau, Den Haag, 2004.
[24] P. van Rooy. L. Sterrenberg and A. van Luin, *Ontwikkelingsplanologie als sociaal-culturele opgave*, Den Haag, 2004.
[25] WRR, *Ruimtelijke ontwikkelingspolitiek*, Den Haag, 1998.

Information and Communication Technology and Public Innovation
V.J.J.M. Bekkers et al. (Eds.)
IOS Press, 2006

Interactive Digital Television and the 'New' Citizen

Colin SMITH [a] and C. William R. WEBSTER [b,1]

a School of Computing, Napier University, Edinburgh, Scotland, UK
b Department of Management & Organization, University of Stirling, Stirling, Scotland, UK

Abstract. This chapter presents a case study of the use of interactive digital television (iDTV) to deliver electronic public services in the UK. It reviews a number of innovative iDTV initiatives which have sought to test the feasibility of using iDTV technology to deliver 'interactive' electronic services directly to citizens and service users homes, thereby potentially making public services more accessible, universally available and cheaper to administer. The introduction of these new service delivery arrangements, based on the capabilities of new information and communication technologies, present a challenge to established organizational structures and ways of working. In particular, the emergence of iDTV as an electronic service delivery channel is forging a new citizens-state relationship, based around the transformed role of the television, a medium typically associated with entertainment. In this chapter the authors argue, that although the iDTV initiatives demonstrate that it is possible do deliver electronic services via iDTV, and although there is evidence that citizens are interested in using IDTV to access public services, the current provision of IDTV is not yet sufficiently advanced to support widespread provision and use. Despite this, the rapid take-up of digital television and the emergence of iDTV services suggests that iDTV will be an important complementary medium for the future delivery of electronic government and public services.

Keywords. Interactive Digital Television, iDTV, Digital television, DTV, electronic public services, e-government services

1. Introduction

This chapter presents a case study of the use of interactive digital television (iDTV) to deliver electronic public services. It is based on research into the planning, implementation and evaluation of a number of innovative pilot initiatives in the UK, including; 'INtouch kirklees', 'DigiTV' and the 'Scottish iDTV Pilot'. These initiatives have set out to test the potential of iDTV and to explore the possibility of delivering electronic digital services directly to citizens and service users' homes, thereby making public services more accessible, universally available, and potentially cheaper to administer. As such, these initiatives have sought to harness the innovative potential of

---

[1] Corresponding Author: Department of Management & Organization, University of Stirling, Stirling, FK9 4LA, Scotland, UK, E-mail: c.w.r.webster@stir.ac.uk.

new information and communication technologies (ICTs) to modernize public service administration and provision by organizing and delivering services in a revolutionary new way. Not only have these initiatives posed a challenge to existing organizational arrangements, but also to the traditional processes and procedures embedded in relations between service providers and service users. In the case of iDTV, the potential for the modernization of services is predicated on the emergence of a new citizen-state relationship, where services are accessible across a range of electronic channels complementing established channels of citizen-state interaction.

This chapter explores the ways in which the innovative and organizational potential of ICTs, in the form of new iDTV services, have been applied to the modernization of public administration in the UK. In doing so, it seeks to critically assess existing iDTV initiatives and to examine the institutional meaning of iDTV. The chapter utilizes empirical research conducted by the authors as part of a number of commissioned research projects examining and evaluating the use of iDTV for the provision of public services in the UK[2]. This unique research has provided the authors with unrivalled insights into the patterns of iDTV use, service providers and users experiences of iDTV, and of the institutional and organizational impacts of the technology.

Following this introduction, the remainder of the chapter is split into the following sections. Sections 2 and 3 provide a brief overview of iDTV technology, relevant UK Government policy in this area, and the main UK iDTV initiatives. In particular, section 3 presents an overview of three of the main UK iDTV initiatives, namely; 'INtouch kirklees', 'DigiTV' and 'The Scottish iDTV Pilot'. Section 4 considers the aspirations, purposes and intended outcomes of these initiatives, and section 5, the role played by new ICT's in delivering new iDTV services. Sections 6 and 7 critically assess the instrumental and institutional arrangements and effects of iDTV provision, including a critical assessment of its potential. Finally, section 8 offers some concluding comments, including a number of critical success factors.

2. iDTV Technology and Policy

The background to the emergence of iDTV is the development of new ICTs and the subsequent convergence of different technologies, including; telephony, computing, photography and television. Developments in new ICTs have transformed the way government, public and democratic services are delivered and consumed, they have enhanced existing services and led to the introduction of innovative new electronic services [1]. A central plank of this information age 'revolution' has been the emergence of the Internet, as the main channel for delivering electronic information and services. However, despite its popularity, household access to the Internet remains restricted to about 53% of UK households [15: 2], making the desire for universal household access to electronic public services via the Internet unobtainable. Television is distinct from the Internet in that it is ubiquitous, popular and convenient, and is used by the vast majority of people on a daily basis. Furthermore, the technological shift from analogue to digital television, which has brought interactivity to television, has resulted in iDTV being recognized as medium with great potential for the delivery of electronic public services directly to all citizens' homes [20, 23].

---

[2] Much of the empirical evidence presented in this chapter derives from research commissioned by Kirklees Metropolitan Council in 2002 [21, 22] and the Scottish Executive in 2005 [19].

2.1. iDTV Technology and Services

The terms 'iDTV' and 'digital television' are often used interchangeably to describe the digitization of television services, yet they refer to different aspects of the modernization of television. Digital television, or DTV, refers simply to the digital broadcast and reception of digital television signals, as distinct from the traditional analogue method of transmission. Digital signals are more efficient than analogue signals because more services can be broadcast using less bandwidth capacity, and because digital broadcast offers improvements in terms of picture and sound quality. *Interactive* digital television (iDTV), on the other hand, involves the transmission of digital signals together with a capacity for 'interaction' between the service users and the service providers. Some of this interaction relies upon the existence of a 'return path', or two-way signal, which enables a two-way communication between broadcaster and viewer, or service provider and service users. So where DTV relates to the broadcast of digital programs, iDTV additionally supports for the transmission of interactive information and services. By 2012, current UK Government policy states that the analogue broadcast of TV and radio signals will be completely replaced by digital transmission, in a process commonly referred to as the digital 'switchover' [6]. After the switchover all UK households with a television will have access to digital and interactive television services, making iDTV the most pervasive of all electronic service delivery channels.

The UK is considered to be the world leader in the diffusion of digital television. In just over five years since the launch of the technology, 62% of UK homes, which is more than 15 million households, are receiving and have access to digital services [14: 16]. In the UK there are three main digital television platforms, satellite, terrestrial and cable, each providing access to digital television services. The main digital television broadcasters are; SKY Digital, providing digital satellite services, FreeView, providing digital terrestrial services, and NTL and Telewest, both providing digital cable services. Each platform employs different broadcasting infrastructure, and consequently different equipment requirements for receiving services. Digital satellite services are received through a satellite dish, digital terrestrial services through a conventional television aerial, and digital cable services through the network operator's fibre optic cable network. All the broadcasters, except FreeView, provide a return path to support interactive communications. None of the networks offer total UK coverage. Following the digital switchover access to television programmes and services, including interactive services, will be possible through either a new digital television set, or through an old analogue television combined with a digital set-top-box, which coverts the digital television signal into a format suitable for analogue televisions. Such set-top-boxes are currently provided by all digital television broadcasters.

A range of public services can be delivered electronically using digital television. Elsewhere we have classified these as either: 'information', 'interaction' or 'transaction' services [23]. For the purposes of this chapter we prefer to offer a typology based upon the extent to which the services exploit the technological capabilities of iDTV, by distinguishing between 'basic', 'extended' and 'interactive' services. This typology is presented in Table 1, and highlights the extent of interactivity supported by each 'type' of service. The typology demonstrates that there is a step change in the levels of interactivity embedded in each type of service, from basic to enhanced services and from enhanced to interactive services, with interactive services offering the greatest capacity for interactive exchanges. Basic services are usually associated with digital broadcasting and DTV, and interactive services with iDTV. This distinction is subtle, and after the digital switchover, all households with digital television, except those with FreeView, will have access to all the types of service discussed here.

Type of Service	Description of Service	Public Digital Television Service Example	Extent of Interactivity
Basic Services	The broadcast of digital programmes.	The Local Government TV Channel.	User selects programme to view from the different channels available. No additional capability than that offered by analogue TV, except in the range and quality of channels available.
Enhanced Services	Digital broadcasts with additional programme content. Viewers may select from a range of additional text, programme information, and viewing streams. Additional services often accessed via the 'red button' on the remote control and usually relate directly to the programme being broadcast.	'Red Button' services providing additional pages of information, possibly including; the location, opening times and contact details of service providers, and possibly more information about services available.	Enhanced services offer the user greater control over programme content, but are 'one-way' services in that the user selects additional services from content already being delivered to the set-top-box.
Interactive Services	Interactive services combine digital broadcast with interactive two-way communication between the service user (viewer) and service provider (broadcaster). Interaction is supported by a two-way communication channel known as the 'return-path'. Users interact by; completing forms, sending email, or making selections via their remote control.	Beyond the digital broadcast of programmes and information, interactive services may allow users to; submit a form to apply for a particular service or to make an appointment, send an email to a local representative or service provider, conduct a personalised post-code search of local services, make payments, and vote on issues of public concern.	Interactive services offer the user digital broadcasts, enhanced service content and the capability to electronically interact with service providers. Interaction may take a variety of forms including access to information and services, and the ability to make service transactions.

Tabel 1. A Typology of Electronic Public Digital Television Services

Basic Services involve the digital broadcast of TV programmes and the digital broadcast of public service information from service provider to service user, or broadcaster to viewer. In accessing basic services, the user can select the programme or service which they wish to view, but cannot use the system to request particular information streams associated with that service or to make any input to the content provider. The extent of interactivity supported is therefore limited to the viewer selecting a particular programme over an alternative. An example of a basic iDTV service is the 'Local Government TV Channel', which was launched on the SKY Digital platform in September 2005. The channel features news, interviews, case studies and live coverage of relevant local government events [11]. Basic services accessible via iDTV involve the one-way provision of electronic public information, which the viewer can choose to look at or not. They are therefore not truly interactive.

Enhanced Services are those programmes or services accessible over iDTV that make use of embedded technical capabilities to deliver enhanced or personalized information or content. While enhanced services are commonly thought of as an expression of the interactive abilities of iDTV, they are actually still 'one-way' rather than truly interactive services. This is because the data streams that users access when selecting such services are already being supplied to the users' equipment, whether the user chooses to access them or not. In the UK, enhanced services are often associated with the 'red button' on the iDTV remote control, which provides access to the range of services available for a specific programme, with such services commonly referred to as 'red button services'. Certain television programmes broadcast over iDTV regularly provide viewers with an on-screen prompt to 'press the red button' in order to access further information or alternative broadcast streams within that programme. For example, a broadcast news bulletin may prompt the viewer to select further information on a particular news story, information which is then delivered within a text box on the screen, or alternatively, to allow the viewer to select other news stories of more interest to them than the one being currently featured in the programme. The viewer is always given the choice to return to the mainstream content of the programme at any time. These capabilities are often utilized in broadcasts of sporting events, by offering the viewer a choice of camera angles to watch the sport in progress. In terms of 'enhanced' public services, enhanced iDTV services enable the user to select particular information areas from within the service, allowing a degree of personalization in their use of the service. For example, a traditional broadcast advert about the dangers of smoking could be supported by a red button link to extra information, including contact details of advice and support groups. Enhanced iDTV public services enable the user to interact with broadcast information by allowing them greater personalized control of broadcast content.

Finally, *Interactive Services* allow the user to interact with the service provider in a much more specific and meaningful way. Beyond the selection of digital broadcasts and red button services, interactive services allow the user to communicate - interact - with the service provider by inputting information or making requests for information. This could happen via an on-screen form, email or a keyed selection via a remote control or keyboard. Popular interactive services include; online shopping, banking and gambling. Shopping channels, for example, allow the user to purchase a product being demonstrated on-screen, by supporting the actual transaction process, from making the selection through to inputting payment details. Interactive services are dependant on the ability of the user's equipment to communicate with the service provider via a 'return path'. For digital cable users the return path is supported by the cable network, while for digital satellite and digital terrestrial users a telephone line can be used to create the link between the user's set-top-box and the service provider. In terms of public services, all the iDTV initiatives discussed in this chapter use on-screen forms to allow users to submit information, for example, to apply for a service or to complete a transaction. Other interactive features supported by iDTV include; the possibility to vote on certain public service issues, to search for information by location or postcode, and to complete payments or bookings for certain services. For public services delivered via iDTV, interactivity refers to the ability of a user to make an 'input' in order to receive a specific requested 'output', where the interaction may involve; contacting an official, requesting information, or completing a transaction. Of the three types of iDTV services brought forward here, interactive services offer the greatest capacity for innovative interactions.

2.2. iDTV Policy in the UK

In 1999, the UK Government's White Paper 'Modernising Government' [4] identified electronic service delivery as a key feature of the 'renewal' and 'reform' of public services, and stated that all 'dealings with government' should be capable of being delivered 'electronically' by 2008 - since revised to 2005. The vision for information age services is further expanded in the Performance and Innovation Unit's report 'e-Gov: Electronic Services for the 21st Century' [13]. This report agues that electronic service delivery will transform the way public services are provided, by allowing service users to choose when and where they interact with government, by delivering services through multiple channels, and by reorganizing government to deliver services that are customer focused. In 2000, the Central Information Technology Unit (CITU) published the consultation document 'Digital TV: Framework for Information and Government' [5], and in 2003, the Office of the e-Envoy published a policy framework setting out the potential future for iDTV and e-government services [2]. This framework outlined the government's vision for iDTV and sets out a range of policies for a coordinated way forward. Key developments included establishing a central iDTV presence, in the form of UK Online, now Directgov, setting up the Digital Television Project to manage the digital switchover, and encouraging service providers to experiment with iDTV technology. The most important of these 'experiments' are discussed in section 3 below.

The Government's vision for iDTV, as set out in these policy documents, is based on a desire to make public services more efficient and more inclusive, and by being able to reach all citizens and service users - "*the Government's vision that DTV becomes a means to provide all citizens with access to e-government services*" [2: 3]. More than 97% of households possess at least one television set [5], making it one of the most pervasive, familiar and accepted technologies in the home. iDTV therefore provides the potential for government and public service providers to reach virtually the whole population, giving people a new way to access and consume public services. Furthermore, when the 'digital switchover' takes place all televisions will be digital, making iDTV the most pervasive government-to-citizen channel. An important driving force behind the emergence of the iDTV platform is the belief it can help overcome social inclusion, by bringing e-government services to people who currently may be reluctant or unable to use them via personal computers. At the moment digital television has a higher household penetration rate than the Internet, especially in the homes of lower income groups, groups who traditionally are intensive public service users. Central to the Government's vision for iDTV is increasing the take-up of e-government services. However, iDTV is not indented to achieve this alone, but is one of a several channels designed to deliver complimentary e-services, in what is commonly referred to as a 'multi channel strategy' [3]. Possible 'electronic' channels include; the Internet, mobile telephony, call centres and electronic kiosks. For Government, iDTV contributes to the objective of making all services available electronically by 2005 and to offer multiple access routes to all services.

3. The iDTV Initiatives

Over the last few years there has been a number of iDTV initiatives involving a range of public service providers designed to experiment with and test iDTV technology [20, 23]. Typically, these initiatives are intended to identify optimal delivery arrangements, gain experience of using the technology, and assess the organizational implications of using iDTV technology. Some of the most significant initiatives include; 'INtouch kirklees', 'DigiTV', and the 'Scottish iDTV Pilot', each is discussed in more details below. At the local level a number of local authorities have experimented with innovative iDTV services. Prominent here are Knowsley Council, Newcastle City Council, Kirklees Council, Plymouth Council, the London Borough of Newham and Hertfordshire County Council. Typically these authorities are using digital television to provide information about council services and perceive iDTV as a useful mechanism for enhancing citizen engagement and social inclusion. The more innovative services provide opportunities to; make payments, submit online application forms, book facilities and services, vote, and send email. Arguably the most ambitious service was INtouch kirlees, which in addition to providing a range of services electronically also provided service users with a degree of influence and control over service content.

3.1. INtouch kirklees

The INtouch kirklees[3] digital television project, led by Kirklees Metropolitan Council, in partnership with Calderdale and Huddersfield Community Health Trust, Artimedia, and ntl, was established to deliver electronic services, via ntl cable infrastructure, to disadvantaged communities in the Kirklees area [21, 22]. This project was particularly innovative, because it utilized iDTV to provide electronic public information and services, and because it sought to give service users the opportunity to shape and influence the content of the service, thereby making it more relevant to their everyday lives. Households taking part in the project were provided with access to digital television and a network of 'community consultants' to ensure they had the necessary skills and motivation to allow them to access, use and shape a range of public services and information available.

The provision of information and services on INtouch was organized around the main service areas, such as; 'housing', 'crime', 'transport' and 'employment'. In addition to the provision of electronic information there was a range of 'interactive' services, such as an 'A to Z' search of services, email, and onscreen forms. There were also sections specifically designed to allow service users to shape the online content. A 'have your say' section allowed users to offer their views on a current topic, a

---

[3] http://www.kirklees.gov.uk/community/intouch/intouch.shtml

'neighborhood guides' section allowed users to publish information about local events and attractions, the 'speak to' section, allowed users to submit questions to a senior council employee or politician, the 'making choices' section, allowed them to 'vote' on the issue of the day, and a 'reading circle' allowed them to exchange views on books with other iDTV service users. The intention behind arranging the service in this way was to; provide a platform for delivering services directly to service users' homes, to design a service relevant to disadvantaged communities, and to identify which iDTV services would actually be used.

3.2. The National Project – DigiTV

At the national level the Office of the Deputy Prime Minister (ODPM) supported the development of iDTV by financing trial 'pathfinder' projects in Suffolk and Somerset and by making iDTV one of its 'national projects' in its Local Government Online Strategy [16]. The ODPM National Project on iDTV, known as 'DigiTV'[4], is being developed by the team that introduced INtouch kirklees, and is using the knowledge gained from the pathfinder trials to help local authorities get a presence on digital television and to disseminate best practice through the creation of and diffusion of an iDTV 'starter kit' [9]. The starter kit allows public sector agencies to upload their content onto digital television through as series of genetic templates, including one that can be used to create forms. The use of general templates reduces the need for time-consuming tests. There is also a DigiTV 'plug-in', which allows service providers to integrate iDTV services with the back-office systems. Examples of interactive features supported by DigiTV include; the 'Jobs Hotline' in South Yorkshire, that allows service users to make appointments with Job Centre Consultants, the 'Report It' forms in the Plymouth, that allow service users to report noise nuisance, abandoned cars, fly tipping and graffiti (etc), and the Library book reservation and renewal service in Kirklees.

The DigiTV starter kit allows local authorities and other service providers to develop, publish and maintain an iDTV service on all the digital platforms. It provides a technical platform for delivering iDTV services, as well as the information and training required to get an iDTV service established. It was designed and tested between 2003 and 2004, and so far 68 local authorities have established a DigiTV presence [9: 13]. The service is managed centrally and local authorities are encouraged to group themselves into 'clusters' in order to share the significant platform access costs, which can be as much as £60,000 per local authority per annum [9: 20]. Each local authority provides content on its own 'microsite', which through the DigiTV interface is then broadcast over the different digital television platforms. In this way contributors do not have to deal with the digital television broadcasters themselves, nor do they have to design their own templates and navigation systems. The main downside for service providers is that they are locked-in to the DigiTV templates, which govern the scope and format of content, and which discourages the development of innovative new iDTV service applications.

---

[4] http://www.digitv.org.uk/

3.3. The Scottish iDTV Pilot

The Scottish iDTV Pilot[5] provided access to electronic public information and services on the SKY Digital platform between May 2004 and April 2005 [19]. It was initiated and led by the Scottish Executive's 21st Century Government Unit, as part of its 'Digital Inclusion' program [18]. The pilot involved a partnership between six partner organizations; The Scottish Executive, Dumfries and Galloway Council, NHS Scotland (Health Scotland), StartHere, West Lothian Council and Young Scot. Each partner provided informational and interactive content and participated in project management.

Service content was designed around a set of generic templates, with each service provider providing the relevant content for their section. The different interactive features of iDTV were 'shared' between the different content sections. For example, Dumfries and Galloway Council provided tourist information about the region and an interactive form to enter a competition, and NHS Scotland (Health Scotland) provided information about the dangers of smoking and access to a 'smoking calculator', to estimate the annual cost of smoking. Other interactive features incorporated into the service included; the opportunity to vote on local environmental issues in West Lothian, online applications for a Young Scot card, and requests for a 'call-back' from NHS Scotland or a West Lothian Neighbourhood Response Team, and the opportunity for young people to identify local entertainment and product savings via a postcode search.

The Scottish iDTV pilot was intended to test the feasibility of delivering public services electronically through iDTV. An important part of this experiment was to capture service users and service providers experiences of and attitudes towards the technology. This, it was hoped, would provide some early indicators as to the likely future use of iDTV. In particular, for service users, the pilot hoped to identify which interactive features of iDTV were most useful, which content was popular, how easy was it to use, and whether users found iDTV to be a realistic or preferable alternative to existing electronic and traditional service mechanisms. For the service providers, it was hoped that the pilot would offer useful insights into; providing an electronic service in a partnership arrangement, what providing an iDTV service involved, and whether the service could successfully be integrated into existing technological and organizational arrangements and service delivery procedures.

4. Aims, Orientation and Innovation

The aim of these initiatives is to test the feasibility of iDTV for delivering a range of electronic public information and services. Typically, these projects are orientated towards certain groups within a designated pilot area, such as the disadvantaged in Kirklees, and are focused on particular service areas or user needs. They are innovative because they are intended to explore new ways of engaging with local communities and service users, and because they are explicitly testing a new technological platform, to see if it can be used to provide services [20]. As such, these services are forging new relations with service users, with the emergent relationships based on the informational and interactive capabilities embedded in the new ICT systems. Their innovative nature also stems from their potential to offer new and complementary mechanisms for the

---

[5] http://www.scotland.gov.uk/Topics/Government/Open-scotland/17820/idtvpilot

delivery of focused, personalized information and transactional services to recipients, while also supporting varying degrees of interactivity. Beyond technological innovation, the iDTV initiatives discussed here are also innovative in the way they are organized and management, and potentially in the way they are integrated into existing organizational arrangements. All of the initiatives discussed here are delivered via collaborative partnership arrangements, with the explicit intention being to expose as many service providers as possible to the possibilities offered by iDTV, to encourage shared learning experiences and to assess which services are actually best suited to iDTV. Such arrangements necessarily involve the introduction of new working procedures and organizational routines, such as, weekly cross-organization team meetings, whilst at the same time exposing the introduction of iDTV services to existing organizational routines, structures and institutional norms. The extent to which these innovations interact with and reflect the institutional norms of public administration and public service delivery is the core focus of this book.

5. The Role of Technology

A discourse centered on the capabilities of iDTV has been at the heart of the modernization initiatives discussed in this chapter. iDTV has been seen as a means to provide all citizens with access to e-government and public services, regardless of their socio-economic status or their orientation towards new technologies. The perceived potential of iDTV is based upon its technological capability to support interactive services directly to households, using a medium - television - that has high penetration rates, a high degree of familiarity, and is easy to use. Significantly, for the initiatives discussed here, household digital television penetration rates are highest for those socio-economic groups that are traditionally intensive public service users, but low personal computer users. For these households, iDTV offers a viable alternative access point to services and information delivered via the Internet. In the case of iDTV, new ICTs are facilitating new ways of organizing the primary process of public administration, by acting as a mechanism for integrating service areas around one common delivery platform, and a new electronic service interface between service providers and service users. In so doing, the technology is demanding new organizational arrangements and working procedures, and is forging new electronic citizen-state relations.

The aspiration for iDTV, is that it will ultimately become the most pervasive of all electronic service delivery channels. However, the current approach taken by Government focuses on the need for a range of complementary service delivery channels, including traditional channels and new innovative electronic channels, of which iDTV is just one [3]. Such an approach is driven by the convergence of electronic media realized by the digitization of services. This has enabled service providers to share information across electronic service delivery platforms, whilst at the same time delivering closely targeted content which utilizes the particular strengths of the different platforms. In this respect the aspiration for iDTV is not just to deliver electronic information and services directly to citizens' homes, but also to integrate it with existing service delivery channels.

The role of technology is clearly central to the iDTV initiatives discussed in this chapter. It represents a revolutionary new way to deliver electronic services, and instigates a new interface between service providers and service users. Consequently, the introduction of iDTV technology is responsible for forging new relations between citizens, service users and public service providers, where these new relations are embedded in the technological capabilities of iDTV systems and services. Beyond the creation of a new channel for delivering service, iDTV also initiates the modernization of public services by encouraging the convergence of ICTs and the sharing of information across organizational boundaries, in a way that supports the delivery of e-services. In this way, and along with other ICT systems and e-service channels, iDTV is also a driving force for organizational change.

6. An Instrumental Assessment of iDTV

An instrumental assessment of public service iDTV initiatives would focus on whether the services 'worked' and whether they delivered the expected service outcomes. However, the iDTV initiatives discussed in this chapter were explicitly or implicitly informed by an 'action research' approach where one of the primary goals was to develop organizational learning about exactly what constitutes possible and acceptable public service applications of iDTV technology. The initiatives are therefore best assessed according to the extent of information produced and knowledge created about the utilization of the technology, rather than on narrow definitions of success or failure. Critical success factors determining the extent of organizational learning from the initiatives included; extent of user uptake and use, extent of organizational commitment, quality and reach of the service, and service integration with other service delivery channels.

The existence of innovative iDTV initiatives has led to a growing evidence base of service providers' and service users' views and experiences of using iDTV. Usually in the form of public attitude surveys and in-depth evaluations, this evidence base is being used to inform the development of iDTV in the UK. Some of the most important evidence derives from; research into public attitudes towards digital television conducted for the Department of Trade and Industry [8], the detailed evaluations of INtouch kirklees [21, 22] and the Scottish iDTV pilot [10, 19], case studies and public attitude surveys conducted by the DigiTV National Project [17], public attitude research into the diffusion of digital television conducted for the Department of Culture, Media and Sport [7], and qualitative research into public attitudes towards digital television services conducted by a number of service providers, for example, Suffolk County Council [24] and West Lothian Council [25].

6.1. Using iDTV to Access Public Information and Services

Access to iDTV services is rapidly increasing. There are currently over 15 million UK households [14: 16] with access to digital television services, including the iDTV services discussed here. Although each of the initiatives is not universally available across all platforms, each is available to all subscribers on the platform on which it is delivered. So, all SKY Digital subscribers had access to the Scottish iDTV Pilot, and all ntl subscribers had access to INtouch kirklees. However, despite the increase in access to iDTV services, the emerging evidence base shows that there is currently low awareness and low use of public iDTV services [17]. All the iDTV initiatives discussed here have reported disappointing usage data. For example, the INtouch kirklees service had on average 222 visits per week and 32 per day [22: 27], the Scottish iDTV pilot recorded only 43 visits per week and 6 visits per day [19: 33], while DigiTV claim that *"between 20 and 400 people are using the service a day"* [9: 3]. Furthermore, it is also evident, that after an initial surge in use, both services experienced a gradual decline in use over time. There are a number of factors that might have deterred use, including; speed of access, difficulty in finding the service, cost of access, limited awareness of service, and the scope of service content. Despite low levels of use, the usage data does highlight a number of trends; firstly that service use was highest in the early evening, and secondly, that a typical visit lasted just under 30 minutes. This was the case for INtouch kirklees, [22], the Scottish iDTV Pilot [19], and the Suffolk iDTV Pathfinder Initiative [24]. Additionally, the evaluation of INtouch found that although a wide variety of people used the service, there tended to be a dominant user in each household, who used the service once a week for approximately 30 minutes [22: 28-30].

Despite the low levels of use research suggests that citizens and service users are interested in using iDTV to access public information and services, and that there is an underlying desire to be able to undertake certain transactions via iDTV, particularly; making appointments, submitting applications, requesting information, making payments and voting [8, 10, 17, 24, 25]. This research also shows that the desire to use iDTV stems from its perceived convenience, ease of use, and it's perception as a viable alternative point of contact. The evaluation of INtouch kirklees showed that the most popular iDTV content is local and community information and that service use was highest when service users had a clear reason, or purpose, for using iDTV, and where content is relevant to their lives and up-to-date [21, 22]. However, although most users found INtouch 'easy to use and useful' [22: 19], they also reported; that the service required greater 'depth', that it should be updated more regularly, that it occasionally suffered from technical difficulties, and that there should be more opportunities for interactivity [22: 23].

Central to the instrumental approached to assessing iDTV is whether these initiatives actually deliver electronic services directly to citizen and service users' homes, thereby making public services more accessible and available. Here the research evidence is inconclusive, mainly because of the low levels of service use. Despite this, the evaluation of INtouch found that "the significance of INtouch for the disadvantaged communities targeted by the project is highlighted by the service users positive response to the technology…the majority of service users agreed that technology like INtouch makes it easier to access public services… (makes them) more likely to use public services…(and)…more aware of (the) public services available" [22: 6]. Whilst research conducted for the DiTV National Project Board found that there was a substantial 'business case' for delivering services through iDTV and that public iDTV services were 'inevitable' despite current low levels of use and awareness [17].

6.2. Organizational Learning

A key feature of all the iDTV initiatives discussed here is the explicit or implicit intention to learn about the capabilities and impacts of the technology by testing it in real 'live' settings. In this way service providers hoped to gather knowledge about which services were most popular and how the services could be integrated alongside existing technological and organizational arrangements. Organizational learning is therefore both instrumental and institutional. It is instrumental in that it gathers information about what the technology can do and how it is used, and it is institutional, because by testing the technology, the organizations involved are able to assess the extent to which the technology compliments existing institutional patterns and ways of working.

The importance of the learning process for an innovative new technology like iDTV should not be underestimated. Prior to the initiatives discussed here, very few public service providers in the UK had experimented with iDTV technology, so the introduction of new iDTV services, by definition, involved new activities and relationships between service providers, service users and new iDTV technologies. The extent of organizational learning is demonstrated by the significant differences between the initial intended iDTV services and the services that were actually delivered. Both INtouch kirklees and the Scottish iDTV Pilot were intended to offer comprehensive information about a range of public services and a series of frequently used interactive features. In practice, both services were scaled down when the speed of iDTV and the quantity of information that could be displayed became known. For both these initiatives, the capabilities of the technology only became apparent through the processes of design and testing. Also, difficulties associated with integrating iDTV services with existing technological and organizational networks only became apparent once the service providers started to build the systems. For example, although it was initially hoped that iDTV could 'share' information with Internet services, in practice, the ways in which iDTV information is displayed, formatted and transmitted, made convergence very difficult. Consequently, INtouch kirklees and the Scottish iDTV Pilot, both of which were initially intended to be integrated alongside existing information systems, were actually 'stand-alone' services with specialized dedicated information and information systems.

Although the limited number of service users and the failure to integrate iDTV technology suggests that instrumentally these initiatives have failed to test the feasibility and potential of the technology, the development of new iDTV services has underpinned significant organizational learning and led to a deeper understanding of the complexities in developing and delivering appropriate user-friendly public services via iDTV. In this sense all the initiatives discussed here can be considered successful.

7. An Institutional Assessment of iDTV

The institutional perspective addresses the ways in which existing institutions respond to, and are shaped by, the use of new technology [12]. The iDTV initiatives examined here pose a significant challenge to established approaches and procedures for developing and delivering services, and assessing and responding to user needs. This is because they encourage new relations with service users, new organizational forms, and the introduction of new working practices and procedures. However, in the case of iDTV, although the technology was initially intended to challenge established administrative procedures, in practice they changed very little, and in many cases they actually reinforced existing established approaches.

Issues about the integration of iDTV with other ICT systems raise important questions about the extent to which the characteristics of the technologies were fully utilized and therefore fully tested. Although iDTV technology has the capacity to support interactivity, few elements of the initiatives discussed here provide good examples of the use of interactivity in ways that were organizationally and institutionally embedded. Procedures for developing and delivering content were put in place, but were typically ad hoc, labour intensive, inefficient, costly, and un-related to the standard operating rules and procedures of those organizations. Fundamentally, the nature of the iDTV services actually delivered – services that were limited in scope and depth, and not fully exploiting the interactive potential - reflected the institutional shaping of those services. To some extent this was due to the experimental nature of the projects, which saw iDTV services rolled out as stand-alone bespoke services that were not properly integrated with back-end content management systems and with other e-services. Ultimately, this lack of integration prevents a proper assessment of a technology that was intended to be one of a variety of integrated complimentary electronic service channels. The limited nature of the iDTV initiatives has meant that the potential for such cross-channel integration has not been robustly tested.

These limitations have also meant that services provided for iDTV have not always been designed solely for the iDTV platform and with its strengths, limitations and capabilities in mind. Typically, public service providers, most of which have established a digital presence through an Internet site, prefer to utilize this investment when extending their digital channel portfolio. Consequently, much of the content delivered through iDTV has its origins in content previously supplied for the Internet. This would include text and graphics designed for the Internet and not alternative audio-visual materials, which might be better suited to the television medium. The 'republishing' of material across multiple delivery platforms has been seen as a necessary compromise arising from the lack of integration achieved in the pilots, and between the iDTV platform and the 'back end' content management database systems. Such integration depends not only upon the seamless flow of data from back-end systems towards the 'citizen facing' systems, such as iDTV and the Internet, but also the automatic 're-purposing' of that content into a format suitable for the capabilities of each particular platform. The repurposing of content is important because it tailors content, in terms of the size, font, and colour of text and graphics, into a format suitable for each medium, and acknowledges that service users use the mediums in different ways. For example, iDTV service uses typically use their remote control to navigate the service and sit some distance from the screen, unlike personal computer users who typically use a keyboard and sit very near to the monitor. The different nature of these human-technology interfaces suggests service content is provided in different ways.

The process of actually developing and delivering new iDTV services has brought the limitations of iDTV technology to the fore. In terms of service content new iDTV services have presented service providers with a number of difficulties in developing content suitable for television screen formats and resolutions. Techniques for user navigation have had to be developed reflecting the norms of iDTV user-technology interaction - typically with a user sitting some distance from the television, and reliant on a basic remote control handset and on-screen prompts to navigate around the service. Also, the processing power contained in the set-top-box in the users homes, which handles digital information for their televisions, has proved to be inadequate for supporting the delivery of data rich graphic materials. Compounding these problems are the raised expectations of service users who are familiar with the scope, speed and interactivity of service delivered via the Internet.

The lack of integration with traditional institutional activities and other e-services, as well as the problems and limitations of the technology, raise concerns about the sustainability of iDTV as a customer-facing e-service delivery platform. However, despite these concerns, and despite doubts about whether the initiatives represent a thorough test of iDTV technology, their development has provided a thorough learning opportunity about the limitations of the technology and the pitfalls associated with developing an iDTV service.

8. Conclusions

The iDTV projects discussed in this chapter explored the feasibility of providing electronic public services using the iDTV platform. These innovative projects should be regarded at 'pilots', designed to test the technology and to see if there is any user demand for services over this medium. An initial assessment of their success shows mixed results. On the one hand, the development of iDTV initiatives has demonstrated that it is possible to deliver, directly to service users homes, electronic interactive public services via the television, while on the other hand, the current provision of iDTV is not yet sufficiently advanced to support widespread provision and use. The evidence base emerging around existing iDTV initiatives suggests that citizens and service users are interested in using iDTV to access e-government services, in particular, when there is a clear reason, or purpose, for using iDTV, and where content is relevant and up to date. The emergent evidence base also suggests that the most popular iDTV content is local and community information and the ability to undertake certain transactions, particularly; making appointments, submitting applications, requesting information, making payments and voting.

The rapid increase in the number of households with access to digital television represents a unique opportunity to deliver electronic services directly into citizens and service users' homes. The take up of digital television, the forthcoming digital switchover, the development of government policy and services in this area, and the emerging evidence base from a number of iDTV initiatives, points to iDTV being an important complimentary medium for the future delivery of electronic government and public services. However, the provision of public services via iDTV is still in its infancy, but can reasonably be expected to expand rapidly over the next decade as more service users have access to and experience of digital services - though future services will probably will look very different to the initiatives discussed here.

Evidence from existing iDTV initiatives suggests that there will be three critical success factors influencing its future development. Firstly, ICT projects like iDTV, must focus on a grounded assessment of user needs and organizational capacity rather than upon the capabilities of the technology to support particular modes of operation and interaction. So service content must be relevant to peoples' lives, whether it is to enable them to make a service transaction or access a specific piece of information.

The second critical success factor relates to the role played by governments in raising awareness of the technology and providing support for those who wish to utilize the technology. This applies to both potential service providers and users. Thirdly, the extent to which new iDTV technologies are integrated with other access channels is likely to be a key determinant of success. It is clear from these initiatives that the iDTV platform is sufficiently different to the Internet, in terms of technological capability, content and patterns of use, and therefore iDTV services should not seek to replicate Internet provision, but should tailor content specifically for the medium of television. Moreover, for iDTV to be cost effective it has to be able to share information and content with other electronic service channels and be able to compliment existing organizational practices and procedures. This is crucial if cost-benefits are to be realized and if iDTV is to be a viable access point for public services.

References

[1]   C. Bellamy and J. Taylor, *Governing in the Information Age*, Open University Press, Buckingham, 1998.
[2]   Cabinet Office, *Digital Television: A Policy Framework for Accessing E-Government Services*, Office of the e-Envoy, Cabinet Office, London, December 2003.
[3]   Cabinet Office, *Channels Framework: Delivering Government Services in the New Economy*, Office of the e-Envoy, Cabinet Office, London, September 2002.
[4]   Cabinet Office, *Modernising Government*, Cm 4310, Cabinet Office, London, 1999.
[5]   Central Information Technology Unit (CITU), *Digital TV: Framework for Information Age Government*, Cabinet Office, London, 2000.
[6]   Department of Media, Culture and Sport (DCMS), *A Guide to Digital Television and Digital Switchover*, 1 June. DCMS, London, Available at URL: http://www.digitaltelevision.gov.uk/pdf_documents/publications/guide_dtvswitchover_june05.pdf, Accessed on 23 August 2005.
[7]   Department of Media, Culture and Sport (DCMS), *Digital Television 2001: Final Report*, MORI, DCMS, London, June 2001.
[8]   Department of Trade and Industry (DTI), *Attitudes to Digital Television: Preliminary Findings on Consumer Adoption of Digital Television*, The Generics Group, DTI, London, January 2004.
[9]   DigiTV, *DigiTV - The New Citizen Channel for the Digital Age: Delivering Local Government Services on Digital Interactive TV*, Local e-gov, National Projects, Available at URL: http://www.digitv.org.uk/content_images/Digitv_finaldoc_tcm2-568.pdf, Accessed on 9 November 2005.
[10] J. Gilliatt and J. Brogden, *21st Century Government: Interactive Digital Television (iDTV) Pilot*, Lambda Research and Consultancy, The Scottish Executive, Edinburgh, 2004.
[11] Information TV, *Information TV and the Local Government Channel*, 26 September, Available at URL: http://www.information.tv/News/?id+19, Accessed on 20 October 2005. Local Government TV Channel URL: www.thelocalgovernmentchannel.com .
[12] D. MacKenzie, *Knowing Machines: Essays on Technical Change*, MIT Press, London, 1996.
[13] Performance and Innovation Unit (PIU), *e-gov: Electronic Government Services for the 21st Century*, Cabinet Office, London, 2000.
[14] Office of Communications (Ofcom), *The Communications Market 2005 – Overview*, Ofcom, London, Available at URL: http://www.ofcom.org.uk/research/cm/cm05/overview.pdf. Accessed on 8 November 2005.
[15] Office of Communications (Ofcom), *The Ofcom Internet and Broadband Update*, Ofcom, London, Available at URL: http://www.ofcom.org.uk/research/telecoms/reports/bbresearch/int_bband_updt/may2004/#content Accessed on 8 November 2005.
[16] Office of the Deputy Prime Minister (ODPM), *National Projects: At the Heart of Excellent Services, Local e-Gov*, ODPM, London, Available at URL: http://www.localegovnp.org.uk/default.asp?sID=1 Accessed on 9 November 2005.
[17] RBA Research., *Evaluating DiTV: Interim Report From Research Carried Out on Behalf of the DiTV National Project Board*, RBA Research, Leeds, May-June 2004.
[18] Scottish Executive, *Digital Inclusion: Connecting Scotland's People*, 21st Century Government Unit, Scottish Executive; Edinburgh., September 2001.
[19] C. Smith and C. Webster, Final *Report: Review of interactive Digital Television Pilot*, The Scottish Executive (Finance and Central Services Department), Edinburgh., 2005.
[20] C.F. Smith and C.W.R. Webster, *What's on the Box? Electronic Public Services and the Future of Television*, Paper presented at the European Group of Public Administration (EGPA) Annual Conference, Oeiras, Portugal, 3-6 September 2003.
[21] C.F. Smith and C.W.R. Webster, *Final Report on the INtouch kirklees Digital Television Project*, Kirklees Metropolitan Council, August 2003.
[22] C.F. Smith and C.W.R. Webster, Initial *Report on the INtouch kirklees Digital Television Project*, Kirklees Metropolitan Council., April 2003.

[23] C.F. Smith and C.W.R. Webster, Delivering Public Services Through Digital Television, *Public Money and Management* **22**(4) (2002), 25-32.
[24] Suffolk County Council, *Attitudes to Digital Interactive Services – Qualitative Research: Key Findings*, Research study conducted for Suffolk County Council, Ipswich Borough Council and Babergh District Council, MORI, June 2002.
[25] West Lothian Council, *Interactive Digital TV Pilot Project: Feedback from Focus Group Consultation*, Cunningham, L., West Lothian Council, October 2001.

Part 4

Organizational Innovation

Information and Communication Technology and Public Innovation
J.J.J.M. Bekkers et al. (Eds.)
IOS Press, 2006

Implementation of Shared Service Centers in Public Administration: Dilemmas and Trade-offs

René WAGENAAR [a,1], René MATTHIJSSE [b], Hans de BRUIJN [a],
Haiko van der VOORT [a] and Ruben van WENDEL DE JOODE [a,2]

[a] *Delft University of Technology,Faculty of Technology, Policy and Management,*
the Netherlands
[b] *Verdonck, Klooster & Associates, the Netherlands*

Abstract. Governments are seeking ways to improve the service provisioning to their citizens by using the Internet, whilst at the same time reducing the operational costs in their back-office and IT. The implementation of shared service centers (SSCs) is claimed to be a valuable organizational redesign that will lead to less redundancy in operations, less staff and more concentrated knowledge accumulation. However, the decision-making and subsequent implementation of such SSCs is a complex task full of risks of failure. This is partly due to diverse expectations and interests among the actors involved. Triggered by the failure of a major shared service center for Human Resource Management within the Dutch central government (P-Direct), this chapter discusses in depth the risks involved and the dilemmas faced in the design and implementation of SSCs. There are various scenarios which can be thought of for decision-making on and implementation of SSCs. They lie in the spectrum from central top-down steering to bottom-up emergent process growth. The authors propose a framework for strategic choice that may be of guidance in the search for a successful implementation strategy, and that may help future empirical research in developing 'best practices'.

Keywords. e-Government, Shared Service Centers, Public Administration, Process Innovation, Organizational Design, Design and Implementation Dilemmas

1. Introduction

Governments in the industrialized world are seeking ways to improve the service provision to their citizens by using the Internet, whilst at the same time reducing the operational costs in their back-office and IT. Politicians and managers of public administrations are becoming increasingly dissatisfied with the returns obtained from

---

[1] Corresponding Author: Faculty of Technology, Policy and Management, Delft University of Technology, P.O. Box 5015, 2600 GA Delft, The Netherlands; E-mail: renew@tbm.tudelft.nl.
[2] Van der Voort and Wendel de Joode made substantive contributions to the interviews and the reporting underlying the research for this chapter.

public sector investments in ICT, costs are rising too rapidly and technology seems to be changing so quickly that departments can hardly keep up with the latest developments. Enabled by IT, new organizational arrangements into shared services centers (SSCs) have become feasible. The SSC is a business model in which selected government functions are concentrated in a semi-autonomous business unit with management structures that promote efficiency, value generation, and cost savings in a manner akin to companies competing in an open market [1, 2]. New developments in ICT, notably the proliferation of Intranet and Web service technologies based on commonly accepted standards, allow for sharing of a wide variety of IT functionality with efficient and reliable coordination mechanisms. SSCs have been advocated to achieve operational efficiency and have gained considerable attention from politicians and other government representatives [3, 4, 5]. They can thus be considered as important potential drivers towards innovation within the public sector.

SSCs make it possible to *focus on core tasks*. A government that delegates tasks which are not policy-related to SSCs will be able to concentrate on its core tasks. Consequently, it creates room to focus more clearly on the development, implementation and enforcement of policy. SSCs contribute to *transparency*. The use of an SSC creates distance between the client and the provider. Distance always forces explicitness about orders, prices, delivery conditions, account identification, etc. SSCs make it possible to *build up and share expertise*. Because an SSC is dedicated to the design of a single or a few functions at most, it gathers all expertise on these functions. This compilation of expertise allows faster and better use of new developments on the function concerned. In this way, one prevents the continuous reinvention of the wheel within each individual unit of public administration. SSCs increase *strategic flexibility*. Shared services make it possible to distinguish between core activities and supporting activities which are adaptable, independently of one another, to strategic, organizational, political, economic or technological changes. The ability to adapt to dynamics and specific changes increases. SSCs will *reduce costs*, since economies of scale can be reaped and processes and tasks further standardized.

As with many other organizational change processes, the realization of the claimed benefits that SSCs may yield do require careful management and clear leadership in order to convince stakeholders to participate and commit themselves to consume the shared services [6]. The introduction of a SSC is a critical decision on a strategic level. It implies a long-term decision between the SSC and clients with considerable complexity and risks. The SSC can be viewed as a particular kind of outsourcing arrangement between many clients and one vendor, whilst classical outsourcing often concerns the relationship between one client and one or more vendors. Much can be learned from existing literature on outsourcing [7, 8, 9] and experiences from existing SSCs [2].

SSCs have been implemented successfully by multiple large organizations in the private sector, and many government bodies are now customizing the concept to their own organization. Although not all SSC implementations are driven and facilitated by IT, it appears that the mainstream of them are justified for reasons of IT cost savings and knowledge concentration. However, public administration has several unique features which distinguishes it from the business community and which prevents exact replication of successful private sector SSCs. SSCs are a promising concept that can lead to better and cheaper service-rendering and more effective knowledge management. Their implementation has many more effects: government processes and information management become the subject of a systematic policy, the division of power and roles will shift, internal and external information relations and organization structures will change, and specific knowledge and experience will accumulate within the organization.

It is because of the strong potential impacts on the existing organizational governance structures that the public sector lags behind the private sector in the implementation of SSCs. It appears that the views and opinions of those who are directly involved in the decision-making vary greatly regarding the need for and claimed benefits of SSCs in the public sector. These views however, are often not explicitly articulated, which may be part of the reason why the decision-making concerning SSCs is progressing so slowly within the public sector [10, 11]. Unfortunately, the number of documented cases regarding SSCs in public administration is very limited. It is therefore still too early to empirically test their actual impacts in terms of instrumental and institutional assessments on public sector innovation. Nevertheless, experiences obtained so far concerning the implementation of SSCs, notably failures, are of great political interest and, as such, are a valuable contribution to the theme of this book.

The authors therefore conducted a broad exploratory study among a large group of key public officials at departmental level in order to reveal their opinions, perceptions and expectations of the success or failure of SSCs in terms of organizational and managerial dilemmas, potential resistance to change among the involved departmental units, and other hurdles. These opinions and lessons learned from similar outsourcing projects were then used by the authors to create a set of possible scenarios and strategies for the implementation of SSCs. An example case study of a SSC for central government-broad HRM will show why a chosen strategy in a large modernization SSC project failed. Disagreements on the functionality to be shared and specific vendor to be selected for the IT system were largely responsible for its failure. Future research should reveal empirically and contextually which "best practices" regarding management issues can be distilled from successful implementations of SSCs.

This chapter has been structured as follows. The next section will first introduce an example case of a failed SSC project within the Dutch central government. It will be used as reference case for the construction of a set of risks and sources of resistance, that may prevent a successful SSC implementation and that should be seriously considered in the decision-making phase. In section 3, an institutional assessment is given in terms of a systematic overview of aspects that key stakeholders confirmed as being critical in the governance of a SSC implementation project. Section 4 highlights a number of instrumental issues in terms of design choices that should be taken into account for an SSC, and the trade-offs between various implementation strategies that can be pursued for SSCs. Finally, section 5 gives the major conclusions.

2. The P-Direct Case: Risk Factors Regarding SSCs

Along the policy guidelines as set out in the document "Renewal HRM systems and procedures central government", at the beginning of 2003 the Dutch Cabinet charged a committee with the task of making the business case for a go/no-go decision in the summer for a SSC HRM with all central government departments as clients. Costs savings were estimated to be as high as 40 million euros per year. In the summer of 2003 the Cabinet and Parliament agreed with the plans and assigned the Dutch Ministry of the Interior and Kingdom Relations the ownership of the SSC, which was from then on named, "P-Direct". The ministry installed a project organization with the vice directors of all of the involved ministries as members. Remarkably, no P&O director was appointed as a member of the project organization, nor project manager of any of the subprojects. In the blueprint design of the SSC HRM, a division was made between the administrative processes such as salary processing on one hand and, the personnel management processes at the other. Although this division seemed reasonable to reduce complexity, it completely neglected existing relationships and interoperability issues between personnel data and HRM related processes. Prior to the green light decision for P-Direct, four departments had already decided to cooperate on a joint salary processing system on the basis of the installed SAP systems. The P-Direct project organization embraced this concept ("proven working solution"), and included the embedding of this SAP system as a requirement in the tender procedure for the SSC HRM. The interested system vendors were far from happy with this because it left very little room for modifications. Those responsible for the P-Direct project organization considered themselves to be the central coordinators who unilaterally had to decide which services should be offered by the SSC. No clear migration strategy was developed, nor a roadmap as to how the departmental systems in due time had to be replaced by P-Direct. Given the variety of the HRM systems and procedures in place, it was no surprise that the departments as intended clients felt alienated and lost their trust in the SSC. The project's organization clearly lacked sufficient knowledge of the various non-SAP based HRM systems in place, and the interworking of those systems with departmental specific processes. As a result, many administrative tasks would remain within the local departments for the manual support of these specific data couplings, thereby violating the projected costs savings in the business case. At the beginning of 2005, the Dutch Ministry of Interior and Kingdom Relations – which has so far not manifested strong leadership – installed a new project program office with the task of coming up with a new design and list of ICT system requirements. It soon became clear, that this second design did not meet the demands of the client organizations either. The result was that IBM – as the only system vendor left in the tender process – decided to withdraw. In October 2005, the responsible minister of Interior and Kingdom Relations admitted in parliament that the P-Direct project had failed.

Shared service center projects can differ in scope, in terms of (a) the type and number of processes that the SSC will support and/or realize, and (b) the organization(s) to which the services will be provided. Figure 1 shows this variety. For example, an SSC may restrict its activities to the provision and support of secondary and/or supporting processes to a single department. But another option may be an SSC designed and implemented to provide primary, policy-making processes for several departments within a single sector (e.g. education) or within several sectors (e.g. education and health care). The P-Direct project falls into the category interdepartmental and secondary process support.

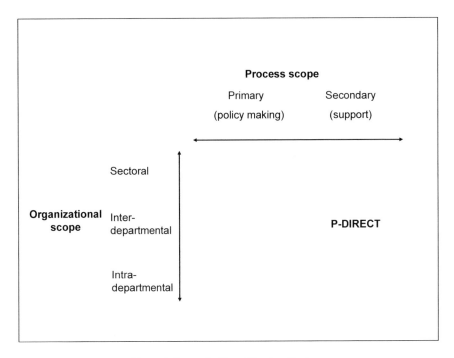

Figure 1. Scope of a Shared Services Center

In order to reveal the factors more in-depth that may explain success or failure of SSCs, and P-Direct in particular, we held semi-structured face-to-face interviews with over 60 top and line managers of the Dutch ministries, directors of specific e-Government task forces and selected experts on e-Government. In those interviews, we probed their opinions, views and perceptions on SSCs by submitting them a set of statements ranging from organizational to technological issues and challenges.

Although there was a broad consensus among the interviewees on some of the potential advantages of SSCs for public services as set out in the introduction, quite a number of them did recognize significant potential setbacks. Not all decision makers in public services are convinced of the necessity of SSCs and there is therefore a risk that the sense of urgency gets lost if some successes are not achieved soon. As a result, the initial support for SSCs can also disappear quite quickly in the case of bad news. The considerations that play a part in the decision-making process in favour of SSCs vary from the risk that intended objectives will not be achieved to the professionalization of the position of the client, from demand steering to transparency and from service rates to the services catalogue. From the interviews, we could deduce the following list of considerations that should be taken seriously to ensure that the implementation scenario subsequently chosen for an SSC will do justice to the complexity of this organizational change.

Resistance Against "One Fits All"

In the P-Direct case the "one fits all' syndrome dominated the decision making and subsequent implementation phase of the project. Contrary to what the top of the departments and the central government assumed, there appeared to be quite a number of differences among the P&O departments and their prevailing reward and incentives schemes. Roughly stated: 'a public officer in the department of external affairs does not resemble those in for example the Dutch Ministry of Health.' Apart from many commonalities, career profiles and incentives deviated greatly. From the beginning, many felt that a government wide HRM SSC would lead to an inflexible, standard information system that would frustrate customization in dealing with departmental specific P&O rules. This concern was the more justified, since the departmental ERP HRM systems in place were incompatible with each other and no consensus could be reached to select one of these for the intended central SSC. The project proved to be a clear example of lack of managerial consensus on the project definition and scope. Functional specifications were not agreed upon, even when the process of tendering for system development with external suppliers had started.

Resistance Against Power Concentrations During Implementation

The implementation of an SSC affects the organization as a whole, from the boardroom to the work floor. Often during such large-scale processes as in the P-Direct case it becomes clear how the dependency relations are actually structured. They may turn out to be completely different from the formal responsibility structure. For that reason, many fear a hardly predictable concentration of power in the hands of a single group which resorts to obstruction and blocking. Resistance will further grow when objectives and consequences remain unclear and top management allows a coincidental, trial-and-error process or an all too participatory style. However, there will be a point in time when consequences become evident and a more precise cost benefit analysis can be made. This often occurs in the tail of the process. This point in time entails a risk, for resistance may then even further intensify and continue until the SSC actually enters the operational phase or is dissolved as in the P-Direct case.

Resistance Influencing Implementation Costs

Cutting costs is an important reason to introduce an SSC. However, there are frequent warnings against high implementation costs. The question is whether the benefits will balance these costs. Implementation costs not only pertain to the project costs themselves but also to the necessary conditions preceding a project, for example the costs of reorganizations. Moreover, resistance may imply that a less beneficial model will be chosen resulting in an actual reduction in costs which will also in the long-term, be less than expected. The P-Direct case suffered from such indirect cost overruns due to organizational resistance and disagreement on the scope of the HRM SSC.

Knowledge Drain

Any reorganization leads to an outflow of staff. The people concerned often feel that their interests are harmed beyond reason. As a rule, these are not the people who perform poorly; indeed, those who are valuable to the organization often have a strong position on the labour market. The outflow of such employees poses a risk, for it implies a drain of essential knowledge.

Environment: the Friction of Time

Many large-scale projects in public services are time-consuming and encounter an impatient environment. It is difficult to satisfy the environment with a long-term project that, moreover, does not appeal to the imagination. If, as in the P-Direct case, the project route is not properly explained, the impression may be created that the project is failing. This negative perception by the environment can adversely affect the implementation and may be detrimental.

3. Institutional Assessment: Governance Aspects of SSCs

During the interviews the respondents mentioned many governance issues which, in their view, required attention but which had not been sufficiently addressed by the P-Direct project. The selection given below is not exhaustive yet provides a proper overview of the broad range of aspects that can make the difference between success and failure. The governance aspects relate primarily to decision-making but also to organization and change management. Figure 2 displays the major impact areas, with ICT as central lever.

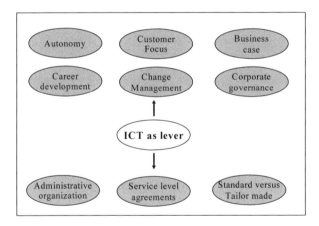

Figure 2. Aspects of Governance of Shared Service Centers

ICT as a Lever

It is important to recognize the role of ICT as a lever for major organizational changes but, at the same time, as a major challenger of existing positions and practices within the public administration. By definition, a fully fledged ICT based SSC like the P-Direct Human Resource Management SSC has to affect existing practices in order to pay off. The previous section dealt with the risks involved when the impact of the implementation of a large scale SSC will have on the current organization is underestimated . It is therefore essential to anticipate such changes right from the start of the project. The ICT industry is moving towards modularization of large information systems; instead of one integrated software package we see that applications are more often developed as separate modules that can be 'clicked' together with the help of standardized interfaces. More specifically, it promises to mitigate the fear of 'one size fits all', by allowing customized functionalities to be included in addition to a common ICT infrastructure base. However, we see a rather slow adoption of this trend by the major ERP systems vendors in their products, let alone their installed base. Since the central governmental departments were using different ERP systems, this created the need for a new system that would allow migration of the existing HRM systems to one centralized system. The scale and scope of the shared functionality of this new system to be built triggered much discussion and resulted in changing specifications. This was the reason why the single remaining vendor in the tendering process finally decided to withdraw. The P-Direct case clearly demonstrates that care should be taken to choose the right ambition in scope and scale. This will be further discussed in section 4.

Autonomy

SSCs have great consequences for the autonomy of departments, since dependency relationships will arise between them and a new SSC. There may be valid arguments for resistance, and opposition from the organizations that give up tasks so these must therefore be taken seriously. This was a major stumbling block with the P-Direct case, triggered by the fear for an imposed 'one fits all' HRM ICT system.

Customer Focus

Shared services presuppose a shift from supply-orientation to demand-orientation and client-oriented thinking. Changes in management must explicitly pay attention to this cultural shift in terms of relation management, client-oriented thinking, handling complaints, etc. This aspect is closely related to the previous one.

Business Cases: Success Stories Matter Greatly

Although business cases should not serve as the sole basis for strategic policy-making, they do need to be worked out. Not everyone is a believer and it is important to induce the unconcerned and the cynics to collaborate. This makes success stories important, for they may make costs and benefits transparent and win the unconcerned and the cynics over. Since the P-Direct case was intended to become the first large-scale SSC of its kind within public administration, no benchmark for a business case of similar projects could be found, with as a result fierce debates concerning the expected returns.

Human Resources: Career Development

There are still some delicate human resources management problems to tackle, since the existing job specifications and salary scales had been developed by the departments themselves, but the new jobs in the SSC may look quite different. Harmonization is a time-consuming and delicate process. This also applies to the career development for staff who will work for the SSC. This aspect was taken seriously in the P-Direct case , but due to its scale and intended overall staff size reduction, it was insufficiently marketed internally.

Change Management

The implementation of an SSC is not just a once-only decision, for resistance can change in the course of the change process. For this reason, making transparent and explicit the possible added value of SSCs is an important factor for success. This is an ongoing process. It should be constantly made clear that further efficiency gain is possible, that the possible threat of bureaucratization can be fought and, that the SSC makes efficient use of innovations, etc. Since change management was not fully mobilized in the P-Direct case, and was instead dominated by a central top-down approach, the project failed to pass the implementation stage.

Corporate Governance

A transparent executive board at corporate level, common in the business community, does not exist in public administration. The thirteen departments of the Dutch government can be looked upon as separate groups with partly conflicting and overlapping objectives. SSCs, on the other hand, will benefit from an unequivocal group steering. This requires the development of a new organization model, in which the property of the SSC is undivided yet in which users can exercise enough influence on the SSC [12]. Since both the implementation and the functioning of an SSC are hedged against uncertainty, a permanent political and administrative commitment to SSCs is necessary. If such commitments do not exist and the support for SSCs were to vanish, they are deemed to fail as manifested by P-Direct.

Administrative Organization: a Shared Information Infrastructure

Efficiency and professionalization are frustrated by the fact that each customer maintains his own information. This makes it difficult to achieve scale benefits and to exchange knowledge. A shared information infrastructure is a prerequisite for efficient provision of services, with or without SSCs. The parties should indeed be willing to finetune data structures unequivocally. This does not mean that autonomy of decision-making on the basis of shared data sources needs to be sacrificed.

Service Level Agreements

Some potential threats from SSCs, like monopolization and bureaucratization, can be overcome by making proper arrangements and recording these in Service Level Agreements. These agreements need to be evaluated and adjusted frequently.

Standardization and Tailor-Made Services

Efficiency can be gained through standardization. A uniform supply to all departments can save costs. However, departments will ask for tailor-made services. Without the supply of tailor-made services the staff of the departments will perhaps scarcely decrease, as a result the efficiency advantages become negligible , as in the case of P-Direct. The costs of tailor-made services should be made transparent.

4. Instrumental Assessment

The views and opinions put forward in the interviews with key stakeholders were abundant, but also ambiguous. Moreover, interviewees disagreed about a number of essential choices to be made in the design phase and during the process of change. These choices may influence the rate of success or failure of a SSC. We chose to represent these choices in the form of dilemmas.

4.1. Dilemmas Regarding the Design of SSCs

Organizational Scope: Maximal or Optimal Size?

The first design choice to be made is about the size in terms of scope to be covered by the SSC. Efficiency gain is the result of economies of scale, which pleads for the largest possible SSCs. The hypothesis here is that efficiency gains and scope are directly proportional, as represented in the left diagram of figure 3.

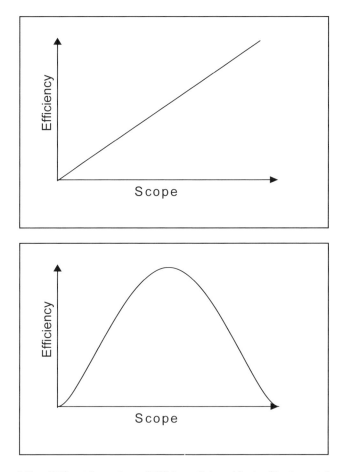

Figure 3. Two Different Perceptions of Efficiency Gain and Scale of Implementation

For some straightforward functions, like lease car management or salary processing, the relation between organizational scope and efficiency will indeed be directly proportional. But for other support functions a continuous increase in scope may eventually lead to loss of efficiency, due to more staff, higher coordination burdens, less transparency, etc. The right-hand diagram of figure 3 reflects this idea, which shows that an SSC has an optimal scope. Once it has passed the optimum point, a larger scope will give loss of efficiency; in that case it may be preferred to have the same function shared by a number of SSCs. As an additional advantage, a shared management function offers prospects for mutual benchmarking and thus (mild) competition. In this respect, the P-Direct project underestimated the existing large differences in HRM systems in place and chose for a too large organizational scope.

Process Scope: Range of Tasks, Limited or Comprehensive?

The second design choice concerns the question of which tasks should be transferred to an SSC. Some interviewees suggested transferring only completely standardized tasks that are policy-neutral and unrelated to departments. A classic example is the salary payment processing. Other interviewees held the opinion that the ambition should be higher; there are tasks that are less policy-neutral, less standardized and more department-specific, but whose performance could be more efficient and perhaps more substantive. For example, legal research efforts could be shared by several departments.

Geographical Location: Concentration or Deconcentration?

SSCs can be physically concentrated whereby SSCs' staff are separated from departments and accommodated in another location away from the client departments. Physical concentration improves the identity of SSCs and prevents old routines from dominating the SSC. Another option is to formally organize a SSC as a separate virtual entity, but to deconcentrate its staff: they remain at the department as an SSC outpost. The advantage thereof is that the SSC employees may become more sensitive to the client's needs; but the risk here is that loyalty will not be with the SSC, but with the client department. The ICT architecture is also more complicated in the latter case.

Relations Between SSC and Client: Professional or Involved?

Closely connected with the previous issue is the question of how to shape the relations between the SSC and the client. Some respondents advocated strictly professional relations. There must be distance between the SSC and the client and an SSC must be strictly impartial towards its clients. This will provide transparency and therefore comparability and manageability. These plead for uniformity in supply, where differentiation between clients should not be permitted. Uniformity is essential since standardization must be realized to get the benefits of scale required to cut costs. However, others were in favour of a close involvement between client and SSC, thus allowing differentiation in supply.

Clients may and will have distinct preferences or distinct cultures and they may attribute a different role to management. This all requires an intensive interaction between SSC and client. Relations that are too formal or too professional are counterproductive in such situations, as was the case of P-Direct.

Service Levels for an SSC: Narrow or Broad?

A first option is to choose for a product orientation in delivering services. This would be entirely in line with the rise of performance measurement in the public sector. Here a shared service center defines its products unequivocally and fixes a price per product. This allows for clear agreements on the products and their costs and provides a benchmark against different SSCs. However, a product orientation in itself is insufficient to form an opinion about the performance of a shared service center. Especially when a SSC supplies more than just standard products, the quality of services delivered (such as research) or the satisfaction of key stakeholders (including senior public management) are important additional criteria.

4.2. Dilemmas Regarding Implementation Strategies for SSCs

Decision-Making: Central versus Decentral

The majority of interviewees prefer central decision-making and gave a number of reasons why. First of all, complex projects like SSCs' require a certain amount of central coordination. A process like the realization of a common ICT infrastructure will be hampered without central orchestration. Another reason is that the development of central directives makes commitment of the top visible.

The need for support of the stakeholder organizations favours decentralization.. Without this support, the implementation process may drag on and the result will be disappointing. Support can be gained by making decision-making participatory. Another argument for decentralization is central management's impossibility of overseeing the whole organization, including all the different contexts and environments. Therefore, a certain degree of decentralization is necessary to adapt the SSC concept to the conditions to a lower level.

Of course, the choice between centralization and decentralization does not need to be made permanently. One of the possibilities is to vary between the different decision moments, such as (a) the decision about the use and necessity of SSCs, (b) the decision about the scale and scope of the SSC to be implemented and (c) the specification of this choice. In the P-Direct case, it would have been better to choose for less central control, given the existing differences in HRM systems.

Implementation: Radical or Gradual?

The second dilemma concerns the pace of implementation. Where some interviewees advocated a one-time, dramatic change, others favoured a gradual introduction. Usually, the one-time strategy of change is goal-oriented; the ideal SSC is delineated on paper and implemented as quickly as possible. The advantage of this radical change is that those concerned get a clear picture of the form and way of implementation. The second strategy is a gradual implementation which allows parties to regularly adjust the design to the specific organization. The advantage is that objections can be handled and overcome during all stages of the implementation project, with room for negotiation and accommodation.

Respondents mentioned various forms of gradual implementation: 1) start with assigning a number of activities, especially policy-neutral activities, to a SSC and subsequently extend the package of activities, i.e. process scope, 2) start with a flexible interpretation of principles and subsequently tighten the rules, (for example, initially voluntary usage of the SSC services can be allowed based on a tariff stimulus, followed later by a mandatory supply in favour of the SSC) 3) start by giving the Service Level Agreements (SLA) a 'soft status', using an SLA as a guideline and giving it more binding force in the course of time.

The challenge for the change manager is to determine in which aspects, and to what extent, a gradual strategy is advisable and where a radical implementation is to be preferred.

Timing: 'Putting One's House in Order First' or 'Over the Wall-Engineering'?

A number of respondents reasoned that 'the house must be in order' before a SSC can be successfully implemented. Processes must first be mapped out and the ICT infrastructure must be standardized. However, others held a different opinion such as not to wait until such complex standardization processes have taken place. They believe that standardization can be a result of the implementation of a SSC. Only when a SSC has been initialized will it be in the interest of many parties to finetune processes and therefore the process of change will encounter less resistance and take place more quickly and smoothly.

The crucial decision about timing is therefore, to determine the moment of abandoning the ambition to 'have the house in order' and to start the actual implementation. In the P-Direct case it would have been better to lower the original ambition in terms of scope and to opt for a more gradual approach.

Management of Expectations: Open or Closed Attitude?

The key question here is, what kind of expectations must the project management create towards its environment? High expectations require high commitments from the clients and an open attitude towards them to contribute to valuable knowledge and ideas. Yet an open attitude also carries risks, such as media exposure and government interventions. The fear of running such risks can easily lead to the decision to adopt a less open approach, thus to keep a low-profile on implementation instead. However, combinations are also possible too; differentiation can be made according to projects or subprojects. In this context, many respondents often attached great value to pilot projects. Pilot projects can be executed in 'openness' and communicated to the environment in order to raise commitment for a subsequent scaling up effort. The expectations in the P-Direct case were raised too high towards the politicians in terms of staff reduction and gave no clear view of the complexity of the systems in use. The project lacked a solid representation of P&O directors and specialists in the steering committee.

Project Management: By the Owner or By the Clients?

When implementing SSCs, a decision should be made about its ownership. At least two roles can be distinguished, that of the clients or the SSC itself. In the P-Direct case, the decision was made very early to assign the Dutch Ministry of the Interior and Kingdom Relations as owner of the SSC HRM. This was by no means a straightforward decision, the choice of owner and client roles both carry risks. If an SSC is mainly seen as the owner's organization, clients may adopt a reactionary approach and feel insufficiently committed to the SSC. If an SSC is mainly seen as the client's organization, then it may suffer from multiple identities as there are clients who have specific wishes about services and judgments on the functioning of the SSC. This tension requires the explicit attention of an 'orchestrator's role' who could balance the interests of the owner and the clients. At first , it may seem unattractive to assign a separate management role beside that of the clients and the SSC because this will increase the complexity of the SSCs governance structure. On the other hand, not having such an intermediary role may cause tension between the roles of client and owner and thus become harmful for the SSCs sustainability. Table 1 summarizes the dilemmas about decision-making and implementation and are grouped as two yet distinctly consistent approaches.

	As a project	As a process
Decision-making	Central	Decentral
Implementation	Radical	Gradual
Timing	'Over the wall engineering'	'Having the house in order first'
Management of expectations	Closed	Open
Project management	Owner of the SSC	Clients of the SSC

Table 1. Decision-Making and Implementation Choices

We may so distinguish two schools of thought. The first advocates implementation of a SSC *as a project.* The rationale behind this approach is that *now* is the right time to introduce a SSC and that when not promptly implemented, the opportunity is lost. And since efficiency dictates that a SSC should have broad enough scope and that there should be sufficient standardization, a *blueprint* is required. The reasoning is that possible negative side effects of a SSC, like bureaucratization and monopolization, should be solved after implementation. To ensure consistency with the blueprint, leadership in both decision-making and project management must be centralized and in the hands of the designated owner. Many respondents liked this idea of a top-down approach: 'maintain the stated objectives and make as few concessions as possible'. They prefer 'a tough approach from the very highest level', following the example of the British cabinet's office. They fear that implementation *as a process* will give potential opponents far too much opportunity to frustrate implementation.

The second school adheres to a *process-oriented* approach. Here the idea is that implementation should follow a more gradual pattern, with the participation of as many stakeholders as possible. Since the process is incremental, shortcomings will be recognized during the process, and the stakeholders can be invited to bring in suggestions how to eliminate these. In a sense, the 'order in the house' will get more attention. A 'point of no return', such as an irrevocable administrative decision, is not created. This 'organic process of organization development' may receive more support from the clients than the top-down approach because there is a feeling of a shared problem.

Table 1 allows us to compile a number of scenarios regarding the decision-making, timing, organization and the implementation of a SSC in government agencies. By contrasting these scenarios, each with their own pros and cons, two main implementation strategies can be formulated: the *Big Bang* (a 'magnificent and compelling' SSC implemented as a project) and the *Soft Pressure* (a small and flexible SSC implemented as a process).

Strategy 1: Big Bang (a Large and Rigid Organization; Implementation As a Project)

A large-scale SSC is set up top-down and in a short time frame. This prevents resistance from getting a chance as it creates an accomplished fact. Departments will then admit that the SSC is a fact of life. As it was created as an impressive organization with many departments as clients, there is an incentive for these departments to commit themselves to the SSC and to make it a success. Hence, a large SSC creates its own 'countervailing powers'. Evidently, this strategy also carries a great risk factor. As the SSC is realized in a short time, problems become evident only afterwards and have to be solved at the expense of a high commitment and costs by the owner.

Strategy 2: Soft Pressure (a Small and Flexible Organization; Implementation As a Process)

With this strategy, a process approach is chosen and support of the departments for the SSC is considered essential for its quality. During the process, there is the opportunity to learn (for example about the optimal arrangement or the degree of standardization) and the involved departments will experience this as if they are the owners of the SSC. This ownership is essential for potential problems are then shared problems. But this strategy also carries the risk of underperformance. The process may proceed too slowly which will increase the chance of resistance and the change process becomes blocked.

These two strategies can be viewed as extremes. The central question is. How to use the potential advantages of these strategies and minimize the risks of underperformance at the same time? The answer lies in the capability to cleverly combine both strategies. The manner in which this combination is to be realized depends strongly on the circumstances of the project, such as, the stage it is in, relevant power centers, and the administrative context. Below we describe 4 of these combinations.

Combination 1: Decision-Making as Soft Pressure, Realization As a Big Bang

Decision-making is designed as a process and realization takes place as a project. Decision-making will start as an incremental process with the scope and ownership of the SSC still uncertain. When the SSC begins to take shape, the time for substantive central steering will come. Consensus on (parts of) the SSCs' final scope is materialized in a centrally drawn-up blueprint, and subsequently imposed and implemented as a centrally orchestrated project. A 'point of no return' is therefore created, with more chance of support than the Big Bang strategy in its original form. Yet the moment of central intervention is the critical point. An interactive process creates many expectations, all of which can never be met. The risk here is that if too few expectations are met, this combination may raise serious resistance instead of taking it away.

Combination 2: Decision-Making As a Big Bang; Realization As Soft Pressure

The SSCs' blueprint is designed and imposed centrally. Moreover, it is a 'grand and compelling' SSC. Yet the realized principles are initially not strictly enforced; the departments and the SSC are given some room to bend the design to their will. For instance, the SSC can slightly adjust its own organization and procedures, and can further determine its range of services in consultation with departments. The advantage of this combination is the ability to convert resistance into action during the realization. The precondition is that the shared goal remains more attractive than individual goals. However, there is a difficult question about process management. What degree of liberty can be permitted without seriously affecting the SSCs' blueprint?

Combination 3: Big Bang As the Story, Soft Pressure As the Practice

Officially, the SSC is designed and imposed centrally. Once again it is a 'magnificent and compelling' SSC, but in practice, the design is the result of finetuning to and between departments. Moreover, there is room to readjust the design during implementation. This combination is useful in a dynamic environment. In politics and media, the 'Big Bang-language' is better understood than the language of long-term processes. It is, after all, a clear design and a decisive realization. Thus, Big Bang as a story lends legitimacy to the processes that actually take place.

Combination 4: A Momentum for a Big Bang

This combination is a supplement to the strategy of soft pressure, but it puts more emphasis on the temporal component. The possibility of central intervention is deliberately kept open, in case the decision-making process drags on for too long (the process as a reason) or when SSCs threaten to disintegrate (a substantive reason). Hence the strategy of soft pressure is used 'in the shadow of hierarchy'; all parties realize that central intervention is one of the possibilities. Making use of a momentum for central intervention requires commitment. Indeed, exact knowledge of the course of the process and of the interests currently at stake is indispensable for determining this momentum.

Overlooking these scenarios, it is tempting to conclude that the P-Direct project may have had greater chances of success if a 'Big Bang as the story had been chosen, soft pressure as the practice' scenario than a pure Big Bang strategy, and for a lower ambition in process and organizational scope.

5. Conclusions

The governance and implementation of ICT enabled shared service centers can be considered as complicated organizational and technical interventions. A deep understanding of the administrative and organizational processes involved is a pre-condition for developing effective policies and for assessing the impact that the introduction of SSCs will have on the stakeholders' organizations. As we found in our exploratory study, SSCs confront the decision makers and project managers with a large number of management aspects and options to choose from for their design. The specific context of the environment in which the SSC should operate determine which design trade-offs to make. Currently, empirical evidence for 'best practice' implementation strategies is still lacking, as most public administrations are just starting their first initiatives. Our findings indicate, that the views and opinions among key public managers as to whether, and how to introduce SSCs, appear to vary greatly. The problematic decision and implementation processes involved with the central governmental wide P-Direct HRM system show the risks when choosing for a Big Bang strategy. A far larger differentiation among the various HRM systems appeared to exist in the ministries involved than anticipated. This led to a level of resistance that seriously threatened a further go/no-go and deterred software vendors from tendering.

For the coming 4 year period, the Dutch government has recently set clear objectives towards a leaner and more effective public service system, and has taken a number of initiatives to build authentic data resources that have to be shared among all public agencies that deal with those data. The intention is to ask citizens and private companies to only once deliver their data therefore imposing public administrations to share these data as a common resource. This requirement will turn out to be an essential driver for the further interoperability of public services and will remove a large technological and semantic barrier that impedes the implementation of SSCs. For, the diversity of interests and actors involved in a SSC demands normalization and standardization notably on the level of electronic data exchange.

However, the main problem with many governments remains their lack of central authority and control. There is no simple equivalent which has the hierarchical steering exerted by a president and a board of directors of private companies. Nevertheless, we believe that by choosing first for a limited number of basic services within a SSC which are in the interest of all actors involved, a common platform can be built for a further dynamic growth model in scope. In our opinion, the ' *momentum for a Big Bang* ' or the *'Big Bang as the story, soft pressure as the practice'* strategies offer, in this early stage, the best chances for a successful introduction of SSCs within public administration.

References

[1]   B.P. Bergeron, *Essentials of Shared Services*, John Wiley & Sons Inc., New Jersey, 2003.
[2]   H. Strikwerda, *Shared Service Centers: van kostenbesparing naar waardecreatie*, Van Gorcum, Assen, 2003.
[3]   M. Borgers, Het bestaansrecht van het IT-servicecenter, *Informatie* 3 (2003), 14-19.
[4]   Het Expertise Centrum, *Het heft in Eigen Handen*, Report for the Association of Dutch Municipalities, HEC, The Hague, 2002.
[5]   G. Kreizman, *E-Government: Hype and Reality*, Garter Group, available at: http://www3.gartner.com/init, 2002.
[6]   M. Janssen, *Managing the Development of Shared Service Centers: Stakeholder Considerations*, Seventh International Conference on Electronic Commerce (ICEC2005), Xi'an, China, 2005, 496-504.
[7]   R. Hirschheim and M. Lacity, The Myths and Realities of Information Technology Insourcing, *Communications of the ACM* **43**(2) (2000), 99-107.
[8]   M.C. Lacity and L.P Willcocks, An Empirical Investigation of Information Technology Sourcing Practices: Lessons from Experience, *MIS Quarterly* **22**(3) (1998), 363-308.

[9] J.N. Lee, M.Q. Huynh, R.C.H. Kwok and S.M. Pi, IT Outsourcing Evolution. Past, Present, and Future, *Communications of the ACM* **46**(3) (2003), 84-89.
[10] R. Matthijsse and R. Wagenaar, Shared Services in de overheid: samenwerking tussen beleidspartners, *Overheidsmanagement* **10** (2004).
[11] R. Matthijsse and R. Wagenaar, Shared Services: synergie tussen organisatie en informatie, *Overheidsmanagement* **1** (2005), 8-10.
[12] E. Maat, M. Tuinder, S. de Wit and B. Pilon, *Verdeeld sturen of gestuurd delen: 'governance' van SSC's bij de rijksoverheid*, NSOB, The Hague, 2004.

Information and Communication Technology and Public Innovation
V.J.J.M. Bekkers et al. (Eds.)
IOS Press, 2006

Informatization as a Catalyst to Horizontalization in the Dutch Police System

Stefan SOEPARMAN [a,1] and Pieter WAGENAAR [b]

[a] Tias Business School and Tilburg School of Politics and Public Administration, the Netherlands
[b] Vrije Universiteit Amsterdam, Department of Public Administration and Organization Sciences, the Netherlands

Abstract. In some other chapters of this book we have seen ICTs acting as innovations in the public sphere themselves. Yet, the introduction of ICTs can also have indirect effects. ICTs and informatization can act as catalysts spurring all kinds of innovations. In this chapter we show how ICTs and informatization have acted as catalysts to organizational innovation in the Dutch police system. Informatization challenged the dominant vertical logic of the Dutch police system through the use of a novel, horizontally oriented, form of collaboration between police forces. With it an alternative to hierarchical coordination and control has been introduced which has led to recent changes in the 1993 Police Act that provide a legal basis for interregional collaboration between police forces for the first time in Dutch history.

Keywords. Police Informatization, Police System, Horizontalism, Utility Cooperatives

1. Introduction

The Dutch police system appears to be the subject of continuous debate. The question of how best to organize the police force in order for it to be effective and efficient, has kept Dutch policymakers and scholars busy since the end of World War Two. Traditionally, this question has been framed almost exclusively in terms of the need for more or less centralized forms of coordination. Even today, the ongoing debate centers around the question of whether to reduce the number of police forces or to increase central supervision by central government over the different forces. In the past decades the dominant logic underlying the organization of the Dutch police has therefore been a vertical one. A logic that echoes through recent cabinet proposals to replace the 26 existing police forces by a single new legal entity under the direct control of central government.

---

[1] Corresponding Author: Tias Business School and Tilburg School of Politics and Public Administration, P.O. Box 90153, 5000 LE Tilburg, The Netherlands; E-mail: s.soeparman@tias.edu.

Horizontal alternatives to vertical forms of coordination and control do not seem to have been given much attention in the debate although they have been emerging in the field for some time now. This chapter explores the first of these in detail: the efforts to create a countrywide homogeneous information-infrastructure for the Dutch police. Because of its strong horizontal traits, the governance structure associated with this form of interregional collaboration can be considered as a type of organizational innovation. On the basis of our assessments we argue that informatization has challenged the existing vertically oriented institutional framework and has acted as a catalyst to horizontalization. Informatization has paved the way for the emergence of new collaborative practices between Dutch police forces that rely more on horizontal, deliberative mechanisms for coordination and less on vertical, hierarchical mechanisms.

As previously mentioned, organizational innovation within the Dutch police system resulted from efforts to create a countrywide homogenous information infrastructure. In this particular case it is not so much this single information infrastructure itself that merits attention, but the governance structure surrounding it. In the efforts to create a single homogenous information infrastructure, the 26 police forces collectively joined forces with the departments of the Interior and Justice, using a non-hierarchical but deliberative collaborative mechanism. Through these efforts the dominant vertical orientation in the Dutch police forces' organization gave way for the first time in Dutch history to a more horizontal orientation.

Before the innovative organizational effects of informatization can be discussed, it is necessary to understand the dominant logic in the Dutch police force system. In 2005, the Dutch cabinet commissioned an evaluation of the organization of the police [1]. This evaluation highlighted a number of problems relating to a supposed lack of collaboration between the 26 Dutch police forces and a lack of consistency in the way the police forces themselves and the services they provide are organized. Besides these problems the evaluation pointed to a lack of coherence in the formulation, coordination and execution of policies between the departments of the Interior and of Justice in the Hague on the one hand and the 26 police forces on the other.

On the basis of the 2005, evaluation the cabinet recently proposed by law to reorganize the Dutch police force. In this proposal, which from a legal point of view will end the existence of the 26 separate and by law largely autonomous police forces. In the eyes of the cabinet, these should eventually be replaced by a single legal entity headed by a national police board under the direct control of central government. In the future, the rationale behind the existence of 26 forces will be purely operational.

It should be noted that the cabinet's proposal only relates to the administrative management of the police force. In the Netherlands a sharp distinction is made between the authority and administrative management over the police. By and large only one form of police force is known in the Netherlands although the authority over it is in several hands. Authority over judicial police duties – criminal law enforcement and rendering assistance to the judiciary – is in the hands of public prosecutors. Authority over administrative police duties – enforcement of public order and the provision of emergency aid to citizens – is firmly embedded locally and lies with the mayors of roughly 450 municipalities in the Netherlands.

Administrative management of the police force – budgeting, planning, personnel management, etcetera – lies not with individual mayors, public prosecutors or even the departments in the Hague, but with regional boards made up of all of the mayors in a region, headed by a police administrator, who is frequently the mayor of the largest municipality within a police region. Although final accountability for the administrative management lies with the regional board, the police administrator is by far the most influential actor in the political arena, dealing on a daily basis directly with the chief constable and (chief) public prosecutor. Administrative clarity would be greatly furthered by bringing authority and administrative management under one roof. However, the division of authority between individual mayors and public prosecutors requires them to be separated [2].

As indicated previously, the cabinet's proposal only relates to the administrative management of the 26 police forces. Nevertheless it represents a drastic change in the legal basis underlying the organization of the Dutch police forces. Not in the least because administrative management involves the drafting and the approval of long-term policy plans for each police region and control over the budgeting process.

Figure 1. The 26 Dutch Police Forces

The cabinet's plan was proposed only 12 years after the current system came into being. The current debate on perceived problems and proposed solutions closely mirrors the debate that preceded the 1994 reorganization of the Dutch police force; a reorganization that is often considered to be one of the most drastic and complicated governmental reorganizations in Dutch history.

In the 1994 reorganization that was the result of the 1993 Police Act, the existing 148 local municipal police forces were merged into 25 regional, largely autonomous, police regions: all of which were larger than the old municipal forces but most of them considerably smaller than the 12 Dutch provinces. A 26th force called the National Police Services Agency (*Korps landelijke politiediensten* or *KLPD*), was created to provide specialized services countrywide [3]. The 1993 reorganization can therefore be considered a fragile compromise between opponents and supporters of centralization [4].

The 1994 reorganization surprised many. Its introduction ended a stalemate between opponents and supporters of centralization that had lasted more than 30 years. During the 1989 parliamentary elections a policy window suddenly opened. Growing feelings of insecurity among the public acted as a catalyst to the reorganization of Dutch police force. A reorganization of the police force had been under discussion since the beginning of the sixties, but had never actually materialized. At the end of the eighties, several issues called for a thorough rethinking of the way in which the provision of police services was organized. The most notable of these issues were rising crime rates, public concern for social problems occurring especially in metropolitan areas and the notion that crime had become much more organized than in the past. Clever entrepreneurship by the cabinet finally led to one of the largest and most complex reorganizations the Dutch government had ever seen [5]. The new Police Act of 1993 put emphasis on "decentralizing things, whenever and wherever possible." In hindsight though, the reorganization, in which the current regions were formed, was a clear break with a past which for a large part was composed of 148 municipal forces. Especially in the administrative management sphere, the landscape had changed dramatically. In practice, final responsibility for administrative management was put in the hands of just 26 newly appointed police administrators.

2. The Organization of the Dutch Police System

2.1. A Dominant Logic

If one considers that the whole post World War Two debate on the organization of the Dutch police has been primarily dominated by the question as to what extent the police should be centralized, it is not at all surprising that the current debate closely mirrors the former one.

Traditionally, both in the 30-year discussion leading up to the 1994 reorganization and in the current debate, the question how best to (re)organize the Dutch police has been framed in terms of the need for more or less hierarchical coordination. One could say that the dominant logic underlying the organization of Dutch police has largely been a vertical one, dealing with questions of the structure, the size of police regions and the division of competencies of police regions only. The debate centers around the question on which scale the authority and administrative management over the Dutch police forces should be organized, with viewpoints ranging from either a complete local orientation on the one hand of the imaginary spectrum to a complete national orientation on the other.

In its current form the Dutch police system is neither local nor national. As said before, the current system is a compromise consisting of regions that are bigger than the municipalities. At the same time most of them are considerably smaller than the

Dutch provinces. This results in an awkward fit with the 'backbone' of Dutch administration, which comprises of the municipal, the provincial and the state levels. Internally, the individual regions are organized along territorial lines (in districts) as well as along functional lines (in divisions). The police system as a whole is geographically deconcentrated and individual forces have a high degree of legal autonomy. In the current system the Netherlands has no such thing as a national police force headquarters.

The recent proposal made by the cabinet can be seen as a continuation of the dominant vertical orientation. On the basis of its recent evaluation the cabinet concluded that during the past 12 years, the Dutch police forces have made few successful efforts to collaborate with each other. The proposal builds on arguments stating that an effective and efficient provision of police services can best be guaranteed by more centralized forms of coordination and control in the sphere of administrative management. The cabinet speaks of a need for unity in administrative management [1: 7]. It wants to aim at standardizing work processes and information products, thus hoping to improve intelligence gathering and crime analysis [1: 7]. Furthermore, in the eyes of the cabinet, regional and national interests could be better balanced if only one police organization existed.

2.2. What About the Rise of the Network Society?

One could pose the question whether this dominant vertical orientation is as appropriate now as it might have been in the past. Today, society as a whole can be characterized by an ever-increasing 'horizontalism' triggered by an increased complexity of societal problems. Horizontalism [6, 7] points to a development wherein classical pyramidal, hierarchical views on the relation between societal actors are no longer sufficient for understanding the way public administration and society as a whole work. Nowadays, not just vertical authority and power relationships based in law but also negotiation and the creation of a shared understanding between interdependent actors are of great significance if one wants to act successfully in the public sphere. The increasing complexity of societal problems makes attempts at regulation, rationalization or a disentanglement of relations from an imaginary societal 'cockpit' increasingly futile and less effective [8]. Reorganizing the legal basis of the Dutch police force with the single aim to create better unity in administrative management might therefore not be the panacea sufficiently suited to deal with the complex problems today's society is faced with.

Safety, a police concern par excellence, is a prime example of a multifaceted problem, which cannot be solved from an imaginary cockpit. Like other issues the police have to deal with, it is of an extremely complex character involving a multitude of actors. Even if the final responsibility for administrative management were to reside with one body, the various parts of the police system would still need to cooperate with each other and other societal actors to be successful in addressing such issues. Therefore, horizontal alternatives to hierarchical coordination merit attention. However, before we go into these an understanding of the reasons behind the historic failure of collaboration between the Dutch police forces is necessary.

2.3. Some Historical Impediments for Collaboration

The cabinet's proposal to organize the Dutch police force as a single legal entity –
thereby creating unity in administrative management – springs from the notion that
collaboration between the 26 forces has thus far been the exception to the rule. This
lack of collaboration originates for the most part from the 1993 Police Act itself.

The 1994 reorganization had major consequences for police performance. The
creation of the new police regions consumed a lot of energy. The better part of it was
directed inwards, towards getting the regions up and running. This process had
detrimental effects on police effectiveness in the following years. Not surprisingly,
little attention was given to solving problems that superseded the regional level. When
it came to fighting crime, each region was on its own. Collaboration between the
different forces was the exception to the rule. Where collaboration did occur it was well
intentioned but often noncommittal in character.

More importantly however, until recently the 1993 Police Act itself did not provide
for any (legal) instruments to promote collaboration between the police regions. The
act sharply focused on regional autonomy and lacked legal or other incentives to
encourage collaboration. A good example of this lack of incentives is the fact that
neither the National Council of Police Administrators (*Korpsbeheerdersberaad*) nor the
National Council of Chief Constables (*Raad van Hoofdcommissarissen*) are mentioned
in the 1993 Police Act. They are consultative bodies that do not enjoy any legal status.
In the end it is up to every individual police administrator and chief constable to decide
how to act on decisions that were collectively made by their respective councils.

Besides these and other practical impediments, the lack of a legal basis has
hampered collaboration between the police forces in many ways. Whenever
cooperative efforts were organized on a larger scale than the regions, the implications
for authority, administrative management and allocation of costs over the different
forces became unclear, making chief constables, majors, public prosecutors and police
administrators hesitant to strive for interregional collaboration.

It is precisely this lack of collaboration that the Dutch cabinet wants to circumvent
with its call for unity in the sphere of administrative management. One of the best
examples of the lack of collaboration has long been police informatization. The cabinet
actually refers to this example in its proposal [9]. Yet, surprisingly, it is here that the
seeds for more horizontally oriented governance structures have been sown in the
recent past. But before we deal with this an understanding of the cumbersome history
of police informatization is required.

3. Police Informatization

3.1. The Feudal Roots of Police Informatization

Police informatization has had a long and troublesome history in the Netherlands. The
first attempts at informatization started in the sixties. After a decade of experiments, an
entanglement of different systems had been created within the various municipal police
forces. The 1993 Police Act changed this situation markedly, but did not really improve
it. Instead of municipal 'schools' of police informatization each championing a
different system, it was now police regions that autonomously shaped information
systems [10, 11, 12, 13]. Furthermore, the Departments of Justice and the Interior had

huge differences of opinion about the future roadmap for police informatization. Similar differences also existed between central government on the one hand and the 26 police regions on the other. Every region regarded itself as unique. Often several regions teamed up to form 'schools' of informatization to compete with other regions. After 1993 developments in informatization became intertwined with the reorganization of the police system itself. Understandably enough, internal informatization was given priority over sharing information with other regions and over building information systems that would actually be able to accommodate such a goal.

One could say that fragmentation prevailed over making connections. Referring to Davenport this situation can be described as a form of feudalism in which: "business units (…) control their information environments like lords in so many separate castles" [14: 72]. Even today several information systems for the support of the police's basic processes are in use, which to a high degree perform the same functions (like for example Xpol, BPS and Genesys). The same goes for information systems supporting more specialized activities such as intelligence gathering and record keeping in criminal investigation processes (RBS and Octopus). Even if regions use the same type of system, they have different builds or customized versions at their disposal, which are not easily compatible with similar but different systems in other regions. What is more, data definitions are region specific, seriously hampering the analysis and sharing of information.

3.2. First Steps Away From Feudalism

The fact that police informatization is still considered to be troublesome does not imply that important steps were not taken to improve this situation. From 1999 onwards a concerted effort has been made to put an end to the feudalism that has characterized police informatization for so long.

In 1999 – when the potential of ICTs were becoming obvious to the general public, raising expectations about their usage in the public domain – police informatization still lagged behind in comparison to what was customary in other sectors of society. Unsurprisingly, then, in 1999 the Dutch Minister of the Interior concluded that: "wide circles agree on the view that the police lags behind significantly in the field of ICT. (…) The police's arrears are manifest in four areas: the infrastructure is obsolete, computer applications and information systems lag behind, the coordination of innovation between regions is insufficient and operational management could be more transparent" [15: 1].

Unlike more recent experiences abroad, such as in the United Kingdom with the Bichard enquiry [16], no single reason stood out for political and public indignation over the worrisome state of police informatization. Still, there was a widespread feeling that concerted and decisive action was needed to improve this situation. For this reason it was decided in the autumn of 1999 to bring together all of the relevant stakeholders in a new collaborative effort: the 'Board of Management' (*Regieraad*) for police ICTs. Elsewhere we have described the way in which it came about [17].

The Board of Management for police ICTs is composed of representatives from five stakeholders: two members of each of the consultative bodies of chief public prosecutors, police administrators and police constables, as well as one representative from the Department of the Interior and one from the Ministry of Justice. All representatives were given a mandate by their respective stakeholders. Together they were given the responsibility of formulating a roadmap for police informatization in the years to come and oversee its actual implementation.

This resulted in a governance mechanism which enabled collaboration between police regions and the two police departments; a mechanism that had hitherto never existed, and which put an end to the noncommittal character of previous attempts at collaboration. The Board of Management was able to make decisions which would be binding for all stakeholders [18: 6]. A unique factor was that these parties, who in many respects were on the opposite ends of a hierarchical relationship, were able to collaborate on the basis of equality. The aim of the board was to create a single information infrastructure *(één informatiehuishouding)* for all of the regions which would enable unrestricted sharing of information.

3.3. Creating a Single Information Infrastructure

In the eyes of the board, creating a single information infrastructure implied standardizing data definitions and setting up standards for data collection, recordkeeping and exchange of information under a single information architecture. Second, it implied replacing the legacy of ICT based information systems obstructing such a goal – meaning both the software applications and the underlying technological infrastructure – with new systems. Finally, an important side target was to improve overall cost management and transparency in the costs of police informatization. By 1999, large scale developments of new communication systems intended to be used by the police, fire departments as well as ambulance services which had started in the mid-nineties, were exceeding original budgets by the tens of millions of euros[2]. No clear agreement existed on the way in which the final costs of these developments, and more notably the costs associated with the actual future operational use of these systems, would be allocated over the various emergency response organizations. This made the stakeholders in the effort to create a single homogeneous information infrastructure for the Dutch police hesitant of such a new undertaking. This hesitation was increased by the fact that the police regions themselves could not present systematic and comparable figures of their costs involved in running and maintaining the information systems in use at that time. We shall see that the newly created governance structure could address these issues with some success.

3.4. ICTs and Informatization As Catalysts to Organizational Innovation

While the Board of Management for police ICTs had the difficult task to formulate the roadmap and oversee its realization, the actual realization itself was entrusted to two newly formed organizations (in February 2002).

The first of these, called CIP *(Concern Informatiemanagement Politie)* was to function as a central customer organization that had to articulate and bundle the police forces demand for information management services and the underlying technology. The second, called ISC *(ICT service coöperatie Politie, Justitie en Veiligheid)* was to develop, procure and manage the delivery of IT and communication systems in support of the police and criminal justice organizations. Thus resembling similar organizations

---

[2] Most notably the digital mobile communications network C2000 and joint emergency room information system (GMS).

abroad such as the Police Information Technology Organisation (PITO) in the United Kingdom.

What makes these organizations special in the context of the Dutch police system is not their mission or actual operations, but the governance structure that was created for them. The 1993 Police Act did not provide for any legal instruments to promote or facilitate collaboration between the 26 forces. CIP and ISC could therefore not be founded as public bodies. The solution was to be found in private law. Both organizations were set up as utility cooperatives, the members being all 26 forces. That way each police force – being both member and customer – would be a shareholder with equal say as every other member of the cooperative. This unlike investor-owned utilities where the amount of say is governed by the amount of shares held. To become a member of the two utility cooperatives, which all regions agreed on, each region had to transfer part of their financial resources for the development and management of information systems and all of their information systems and ICT-personnel to the two cooperatives. Although the transfer of resources, systems and ICT-personnel happened reluctantly, it did occur. Traditionally, police informatization had been regional. Now suddenly each police region found itself a 1/26 shareholder in two national utility cooperatives.

The decisions reached in the two cooperatives were no longer noncommittal. The general meetings of both cooperatives decide on the yearly policy plans and budgets for each cooperative. In a formal sense, decision-making is characterized by majority rule and by the fact that it is legally binding. This established a horizontally-oriented regulative structure, based on deliberation and negotiation between 26 forces which suddenly found themselves dependent on the performance of the two cooperatives. The provision of ICT services to a police region was no longer controlled by each force individually. In the end, noncommittal behaviour and a reluctance to cooperate would only damage the forces themselves. It is this type of decision-making mechanism which enables the solution to be found to all sorts of collective action problems that have prevented collaboration in police informatization in the past [19]. It is, what Van Duivenboden describes as, a prime example of 'horizontal intergovernmental cooperation' [20].

What makes the effort of creating a homogeneous information infrastructure truly innovative is the fact that it marks a watershed in the history of the Dutch police system. A watershed that divides a police system that is open to a degree of horizontalism in the coordination of the actions of the different forces, from a past that was dominated solely by a vertical orientation and a lack of incentives to cooperate.

Why did this change occur? Why was the hierarchical, vertically-oriented logic that dominates the Dutch police system as a whole, exchanged for a more deliberative horizontal governance structure in the sphere of police informatization? In this case, why are ICTs and informatization considered catalysts to organizational innovation?

The answer can be found in the characteristics of police work or its 'logic of provision' and the economics of police ICTs. To a large extent, fighting crime depends on intelligence gathering. On the one hand there is no sense in maintaining 26 databases on crime related subjects when there are only limited ways of exchanging or comparing the information stored in them. On the other hand even a single countrywide database would be useless if the 26 forces did not use it and ensure that regional information input is accurate. Therefore, the successful development of a single information infrastructure depends largely on a collective agreement on used standards and data definitions, while its actual operation depends on regional, if not local, input of content and maintenance. Neither a fully centralized, nor a fully decentralized approach to police informatization seems effective. What is more, from an economic perspective it became clear in the late 90s that innovating or even maintaining ICT supported information systems could not be entrusted to individual police regions. Most police regions simply lacked the economic means to do this effectively. The development and maintenance of police ICT systems is an expensive business because a large part of the system has to be especially designed. Forces were required to cooperate together and share their resources because of a 'logic of provision' in police work and of the economics of ICTs and informatization. In 1999, all of the stakeholders realized that the police services, especially the investigation services, would greatly benefit from concerted action in police informatization. Informatization could act as a catalyst to organizational innovation. The creation of a single information infrastructure proved to be such a difficult collective action problem to solve hierarchically that a more horizontal approach was finally introduced into a historically vertically-oriented police system.

4. An Instrumental Assessment

Sadly enough, six years after the establishment of the police ICTs Board of Management , police informatization is still widely criticized. In a 2005, retrospect of its 2003 audit on police ICTs, the Dutch Court of Audit still raised doubts about the likeliness of a homogeneous information infrastructure arising in the near future [21: 146][3]. So what successes can the effort to create a single information-infrastructure boast besides having acted as a catalyst to organizational innovation?

It would be naive to think that changes in the governance structure surrounding police informatization alone, will bring about a single information-infrastructure. Its attainment is dependent on numerous other factors as well. For example, 'a logic of ambitious projects' in which final goals and accompanying timetables are formulated and adjusted 'en route' or the ability of the police forces to absorb the implementation of new ICT systems and the required training of personnel that comes with it. Indeed, looking closely at the achievements in recent years, it becomes clear that the first two formulated goals by the police ICTs Board of Management have yet to be realized. Although steady progress has been made, it has proved difficult to create an information architecture that truly forms a solid basis on which to build new information systems that can replace the legacy of old systems incapable of sharing information between forces. The development and deployment of new ICT systems has proved to be cumbersome. At the end of 2005, the large-scale replacement of legacy systems had yet to be realized. It would seem that police informatization still leaves much to be desired, especially when it comes to technical innovation.

Nevertheless, some modest successes can be mentioned. Cost management and transparency in the costs of police informatization have improved markedly. Since the formation of the Board of Management and the two cooperatives, the police forces have decided collectively to spend a fixed percentage of their yearly budgets on

---

[3] The Court of Audit determines whether public agencies use funds from the public purse correctly and effectively.

informatization; a large part to be allocated by the cooperatives[4]. This has prevented financial unrest to dominate and smother the decision-making process on informatization. Furthermore, with all ICT systems and related personnel 'outsourced' from the individual forces to the ISC cooperative, substantial economies of scale have been made possible. This has led to diminishing projected costs for the day-to-day operations of the legacy systems still in use [22, 23].

On the whole, even with all the police forces supporting the collaborative effort, overall success is by no means guaranteed. From an instrumental point of view the ultimate goal, creating a single information infrastructure for all police regions in the Netherlands, has not yet been realized. However, in this case innovating the ICT systems itself is not the primary effect that informatization has had on the police system. What is important from an organizational innovation perspective is that informatization sparked a horizontal logic in which all concerned parties, police forces in the two utility cooperatives and all stakeholders in the Board of Management, have tried to cooperate on a non-hierarchical basis.

5. An Institutional Assessment

The governance mechanism embodied in the Board of Management and the utility cooperatives challenged the existing vertical logic that has historically characterized the Dutch police system. With its strong horizontal traits, promoting deliberation and negotiation between police forces and other stakeholders in order to bring about concerted interregional action, it contributed to institutional change. On the basis of the experiences with both cooperatives, the 1993 Police Act has recently been changed to allow for the founding of public bodies that accommodate collaborative efforts by the Dutch police forces [24]. In that light, some have called experiences with the police ICTs Board of Management and both cooperatives, resulting in a changed Police Act, "a basis for the concrete, fundamental resolve of wicked problems" in the Dutch police system [25: 200]. The public cooperatives (*samenwerkingsvoorzieningen*) will be the future equivalents of CIP and ISC which still act from a private law framework. The recent changes in the 1993 Police Act are not restricted to the domain of police ICTs and informatization. In the future they can be implemented in other parts of the police system. What is now clear, is that similar arrangements as described here in the case of the Board of Management and both cooperatives, are already starting to arise outside the domain of ICTs. Worth mentioning are the steps taken to create shared services such as the procurement of goods in other domains than ICTs. Or, perhaps more importantly, steps taken in the field of the criminal investigation services. One could point to recent efforts to merge the three Northern Investigation Services into one new organization working for all of the Northern Police Regions[5]. These and other initiatives benefit from the experiences with horizontal cooperation in the field of police ICTs and a newly formed legal basis for collaboration in the changed Police Act.

Nevertheless, the cabinet's proposal to replace the 26 forces by a single legal entity in order to achieve unity in administrative management, balance regional and national

---

[4] Agreement made between police administrators and Minister of the Interior on December 7th 2004, based on the long term policy plans of the two cooperatives.
[5] Noordelijke Recherche Eenheid (NRE) in which the investigation services of the Groningen, Fryslan and Drenthe police regions are merged.

interests and secure cooperation between different parts of the police system is on the table. The vertical logic that it represents is very much alive today. At the same time however, horizontally oriented collaborative efforts are emerging in the Dutch police system today from within the existing legal framework, as was noted by other authors [25: 188]. This would suggest that horizontally oriented alternatives to hierarchical coordination are here to stay.

6. Conclusions and Lessons Learned

In 1999, all parties involved shared high hopes that a single information infrastructure could be a reality within 5 years. From the instrumental assessment we learn that the sole introduction of a new governance mechanism to coordinate combined efforts, however innovative, was not sufficient on its own to achieve this goal. The 'great leap forward' some might have envisioned then, has not yet come about. One could pose the question whether simply introducing a new hierarchical mechanism for coordination, as proposed by the cabinet, would improve the likelihood of the single information infrastructure arising in the near future. What is clear is the fact that both cooperatives have created a solid basis for concerted interregional action in the field of police informatization which is characterized by a feudal past. Therefore, the main contribution to the Dutch police system is not a direct instrumental one, (ICTs have not yet acted as 'enablers' for police forces trying to provide more effective police services). The contribution of the effort to create a single information infrastructure is an indirect institutional one. Through organizational innovation, the introduction of more deliberative horizontal mechanisms for the coordination of interregional concerted action, the vertical institutional logic of the Dutch police system has been challenged and confronted with a viable alternative.

References

[1] Stuurgroep Evaluatie politieorganisatie, *Lokaal verankerd, nationaal versterkt*, Utrecht, 2005.
[2] K. de Ridder, De externe besturing van de politie. Over belemmeringen voor een integrale besturing van de regiokorpsen, *Beleidswetenschap* **13**(3) (1999), 232-259.
[3] J. Koopman, *De democratische inbedding van de regionale politie*, Kluwer, Deventer, 1998.
[4] J.L.M. Boek, *Organisatie, functie en bevoegdheden van politie in Nederland. Juridische beschouwingen over het politiebestel en het politiebedrijf in historisch perspectief*, Gouda Quint, Arnhem, 1995.
[5] C.E. Peters and L.W.J.C. Huberts, Stroperigheid doorbroken. De herziening van het politiebestel in 1989, in: *Schikken en plooien: de stroperige staat bij nader inzien*, F. Hendriks and Th. Toonen (eds.), Van Gorcum, Assen, 1998, 183-197.
[6] J. Naisbitt, *Megatrends*, Warner Books, 1982.
[7] P.H.A. Frissen, *De virtuele staat*, Academic Service, Schoonhoven, 1996.
[8] H.R. van Gunsteren and E. van Ruyven, De ongekende samenleving (DOS). Een verkenning, *Beleid en Maatschappij* **3** (1993), 114-125.
[9] *Kabinetsstandpunt Evaluatie politieorganisatie*, Den Haag, 2005.
[10] W. Ph. Stol, *Politieoptreden en informatietechnologie: over sociale controle van politiemensen*, Vermande, Lelystad, 1996.
[11] W. Ph. Stol, Veranderend politiewerk en ontwikkelingen in techniek, in: *De blijvende betekenis van Politie in verandering*, A. Cachet, E.J. van der Torre and W. van Natijne (eds.), Elsevier Bedrijfsinformatie, The Hague, 1998, 149-163.
[12] J. Rademaker, *De digitale strafrechtspleging: strafrechtelijke informatisering in meervoudig perspectief*, W.E.J. Tjeenk Willink, Zwolle, 1996.

[13] A.R. van Dingstee, *ICT ken(t) zijn grenzen*. Een onderzoek naar de besluitvorming over basisproces informatiesystemen bij de Nederlandse politie, waarbij het uitblijven van regio-overschrijdende of landelijke uitwisseling van gegevens centraal staat, Unpublished master-thesis, Vrije Universiteit Amsterdam, Amsterdam, 2000.

[14] T. H. Davenport, *Information Ecology. Mastering the Information and Knowledge Environment*, Oxford University Press, New York, 1997.

[15] Tweede Kamer (1999-2000), TK 26 345, nr. 41.

[16] see http//www.Bichardinquiry.org.uk.

[17] F.P. Wagenaar and S. Soeparman, The Permanence of Paradigms. The Integration of the Dutch Police's Information Domains and its (Non)Effects, *Information Polity* **8** (2003), 103-116.

[18] Tweede Kamer (1998-1999) TK 26 345, nr. 19.

[19] F.P. Wagenaar and S. Soeparman, Coping with the Dilemma of Common Pool Information Resourcing: integrating information domains in the Dutch Police, *Information Polity* **9**(3/4) (2004), 181-192.

[20] H.P.M. van Duivenboden, *Diffuse Domeinen, over ICT, beleid, uitvoering en interbestuurlijke samenwerking*, Lemma, Utrecht, 2004.

[21] Algemene Rekenkamer, *Terugblik 2005, ICT bij de politie*, 2005, 135-154.

[22] ISC, ICT Service cooperatie Politie, Justitie en Veiligheid (2004), Begroting 2005 .

[23] ISC, ICT Service coöperatie Politie, Justitie en Veiligheid (2005), Begroting 2006 .

[24] Tweede Kamer (2003-2004) TK 29 703, nr. 1.

[25] Politie en Wetenschap, *Uit balans: Politie en bestel in de knel*, Apeldoorn, 2005.

Part 5

Conceptual and Institutional Innovation

Information and Communication Technology and Public Innovation
V.J.J.M. Bekkers et al. (Eds.)
IOS Press, 2006

Empowering Communities for Environmental Decision-Making: Innovative Partnerships in Cleveland (USA)

Arthur EDWARDS[1]
Erasmus University Rotterdam, Faculty of Social Sciences, the Netherlands

Abstract: This chapter investigates environmental partnerships in the city of Cleveland (USA), focusing on how they affect the problem-solving capacity of local communities, in terms of access to environmental information. The case study shows how the innovation agenda of the regulatory agencies, the empowerment agenda of the environmental advocacy community and the aspirations of community-based organizations became linked two each other. Key factor in the success of the partnerships has been the broker roles played by non-governmental organizations. At the national level, NGOs have an important role as 'information-intermediaries' in the nationwide infrastructure for environmental information. In Cleveland, they fulfilled initiating and facilitating roles as 'interaction intermediaries' in the emergent partnerships.

Keywords: partnerships, community empowerment, environmental decision-making, non-governmental organizations, NGOs and environmental information

1. Introduction

In this chapter, we discuss the relation between public innovation and the empowerment of local communities. Specifically, we explore the significance of cooperative public innovation efforts for the capability of local communities to participate in environmental decision-making, focusing on the role of environmental information, and information and communication technologies (ICTs). Our case-study is the city of Cleveland (Ohio) in the United States of America where several citizen-government partnerships have emerged on environmental sustainability and in which the access to information is a major element. A case-study on environmental governance practices in the USA in order to study the role of ICTs in public innovation and community empowerment is very interesting for several reasons. First, in comparison with Europe, the USA is more advanced in public access to environmental information systems. There is a nation-wide information infrastructure in the USA

---

[1] Corresponding Author: Erasmus University Rotterdam, Faculty of Social Sciences, Public Administration Group, P.O. Box 1738, 3000 DR Rotterdam, the Netherlands, E-mail: Edwards@fsw.eur.nl.

encompassing regulatory agencies, businesses and civil society organizations. Second, civil society organizations fulfil key intermediary roles in this infrastructure. They also play an important empowerment role by assisting local communities in acquiring the capabilities to use this information in environmental problem-solving. Third, the innovation practices of the federal Environmental Protection Agency (EPA) and various state and local environmental health agencies provide us with interesting insights about how public agencies try to adapt to new challenges, and how they use ICTs in this. According to the chairman of EPA's Innovation Action Council, "EPA has had innovation as a mandate for over a decade" [1].

We look at public innovations as processes of co-production between public agencies, nongovernmental organizations and community-based organizations. In Cleveland, several models of partnerships have emerged in which the innovation agendas of public agencies, the empowerment agendas of civil society organizations and the aspirations of community-based organizations have been linked to each other. The case-study will reveal how these partnerships have helped to empower local communities, thereby facilitating new forms of environmental decision-making. We provide an assessment of these partnerships from an instrumental and institutional point of view and establish the major factors that may account for their success.

We also present a historical perspective on public innovation. The evolution of public administration is marked by a continuous succession of innovations. Current innovation programs that aim at a 'modernization' of the public sector cannot be viewed in isolation from this evolution. Furthermore, national factors have to be taken into account. In the recent history of environmental governance in the USA, innovations have been interwoven with various political agendas. In the 1980s, the Community Right-to-Know movement gave the impetus to several statutes in which the provision of significant amounts of data on environmental matters was established. In the 1990s, during the Clinton administration, the Environmental Justice debate resulted in policy initiatives that were intended to address the disproportionate public health burdens suffered by minority and low-income populations. Currently, the notion of 'voluntary compliance' has come to the fore. Despite their different political origins, two constant factors are present in all of these agendas: public access to environmental information and community participation.

We present the conceptual framework in the next section. In section 3, we discuss the innovation agenda of the Environmental Protection Agency in a historical perspective. We provide a preliminary characterization in terms of the 'innovation catalogue', which is the focus of this book: process innovation, product innovation, organizational innovation, conceptual innovation and institutional innovation. In section 4, we present a broad overview of the environmental information infrastructure in the USA. In sections 5 and 6, we turn to the case-study. In section 5, we look at the Sustainable Cleveland Partnership and the Cleveland Clean Air Century Campaign, partnerships between regulatory agencies at the federal, state and city level, civil society organizations and community-based organizations. In Section 6 we turn to the neighbourhood level where we describe the recent history of environmental problem-solving in one of the neighbourhoods in Cleveland in more detail. In section 7, we return to the conceptual framework and give an assessment of the innovations that have taken place. We present our conclusions in section 8.

2. The Conceptual Framework

We take an empowerment perspective on public innovation, focussing on how public innovation efforts affect the problem-solving capacities of local communities. Figure 1 depicts the basic conceptual framework.

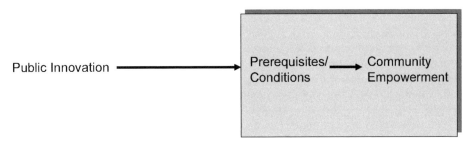

Figure 1. The Relation Between Public Innovation and Community Empowerment

As a starting-point, we adopt the World Banks' definition of empowerment: "the expansion of assets and capabilities of poor people to participate in, negotiate with, influence, control, and hold accountable institutions that affect their lives" [2]. Four key elements of empowerment can be distinguished:
  - Access to information.
  - Local organizational capacity
  - Inclusion and participation
  - Accountability

'Access to information' is broadly understood in this chapter, as including the use of information, the generation of new information, and the adoption of ICTs. Local organizational capacity refers "to the ability of people to work together, organize themselves, and mobilize resources to solve problems of common interest" [2: 17]. Together, access to information and local organizational capacity affect the quality of public participation and the inclusion of communities in (environmental) decision-making. Access to information is also a key factor for insuring accountability.

Access to information (broadly understood) is dependent on various factors. Kellogg [3] distinguishes technical, organizational and personal prerequisites. The presence or absence of these conditions will affect the degree to which community-based organizations will adopt ICTs in their usage of environmental information. Technical prerequisites are associated with (the availability of) hardware and software, capacity for data retrieval and data processing and related factors. Organizational prerequisites include various cultural, structural and functional factors of the organization, ranging from leadership support for ICT usage to presence of staff. Personal skills refer to human skills, knowledge and attitudes. In their discussion of the digital divide literature, Van Dijk and Hacker [4] emphasize the importance of strategic skills in addition to instrumental and informational skills. Instrumental skills include the ability to operate hardware and software. Informational skills enable people to search information using digital hardware and software. Strategic skills enable people to determine their information needs and to use information for one's own purposes, as, for instance, for collective goals in political participation.

The term public innovation refers to efforts to innovate the institutions, forms of governance, organizational forms, processes or products within the public sector (this volume). In this chapter, we explore how public innovations affect the institutional relations and distribution of resources and skills that are related to community empowerment. Generally, in the modernization programs of public administration that have been drafted in the last decade in Western countries, goals have been formulated in terms of a shift toward a more citizen-centred mode of governance [5]. Generally, however, these programs tend to *assume* that citizens are empowered, without addressing the question of whether this is really the case. Against this background, the notion of public innovation as co-production is important. In particular, we assume that nongovernmental organizations can play a key role in linking government-initiated public innovation efforts with community empowerment, especially by helping to provide and enhance the various conditions and prerequisites for empowerment: "Intermediate civil society organizations have critical roles to play in supporting and enhancing communities' capabilities, translating and interpreting information to them, and helping link them to the state and the private sector" [2]. Coproduction can evolve more or less spontaneously, but in Cleveland co-production was achieved in various partnerships, in which the concerted efforts of the partners contributed to the emergence of new practices of environmental decision-making. With this addition, we closely align with the notion of 'conceptual innovation', which refers to "the introduction of new forms of governance, like interactive policy making, or the horizontalization of public control by empowered citizens". Figure 2 indicates the involvement of public agencies, civil society organizations and community-based organizations in relation to the components of the conceptual framework, and it relates these innovation efforts to environmental decision-making. Furthermore, it adds the success factors of public innovation efforts into the framework.

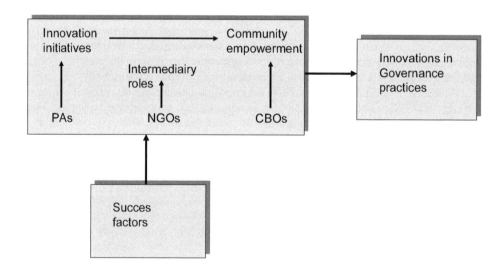

Figure 2. Public Innovation and Community Empowerment as Coproduction

We assume that the intermediary roles of non-governmental organizations are focused on two sorts of functions. As 'information intermediaries' they fulfil functions of selecting, integrating, interpreting and digesting information. As 'interaction intermediaries' they facilitate cooperation between citizens, public and private actors. Innovations, in particular the innovative capacity of partnerships, depend on various success factors, of which we can only highlight a few:

- External pressure to improve results;
- An organizational culture that is conducive to innovation and learning;
- The development of trust.
- Participation of people with the willingness and skills to engage in innovative partnerships;
- The availability of knowledge and expertise.

3. Innovations in the United States Environmental Protection Agency

According to Thomas Gibson, Chairman of EPA's Innovation Action Council, the EPA has a legacy of progress in innovation, but that legacy "is challenged by a growing and increasingly complex set of problems", such as global climate change, the loss of biodiversity, by the influence of large and vital economic sectors, like agriculture, energy and transportation on environmental quality and by various societal trends, such as informatization and globalization. In the EPA strategy 'to guide the next generation of innovation' [6], a broader definition of environmental protection is advocated than just controlling pollution: "Environmental programs should address a broader range of issues than they typically do today. The goal should be greater environmental responsibility and natural resource stewardship across all of society, along with successful integration of environmental, economic and social objectives". In EPA environmental management, results should be emphasized more than the means to achieve them, using regulatory and non-regulatory tools. Specifically, more market-based financial incentives should be created. Furthermore, partnership and stakeholder collaboration are emphasized: "Businesses, government agencies, community groups and other interested stakeholders should become more involved in development of environmental solutions". The innovation strategy focuses on four elements:

- Strengthen the innovation partnership with states and tribes. EPA considers its partnerships with states and tribes as the most important ones. In 1998, EPA and the states signed an Innovations Agreement. This agreement addresses the development, testing and implementation of regulatory innovations. In this agreement, one of the principles is Stakeholder Involvement
- Focus innovation efforts on priority environmental problems: reduce greenhouse gases, reduce smog, restore and maintain water quality and improve the water infrastructure.
- Diversify the agency's environmental protection tools and approaches. One of the priorities is to improve the use and deployment of information resources and technology. Specific goals include (1) providing better information to the public (as a tool for supporting public participation), (2) handling information exchanges with states and regulated communities more efficiently, and (3) linking information more directly with state and EPA decision-making processes.

- Foster a more innovative culture and organizational systems: "…innovation must become an attitude, and an integral part of EPA's daily work, management systems and culture".

In terms of the innovation catalogue developed in this book, we can conclude that EPA' s innovation strategy is a complex mixture of innovations, the core of which are *conceptual* innovations. They include the philosophy of performance enhancement, partnerships, stakeholder collaboration, and public participation. Other sorts of innovations can be regarded as supporting the conceptual innovations, namely *organizational* innovations, such as the development of better outcome-based performance measures, *product* innovations, such as market-based policy instruments, and *process* innovations, in which information resources and technology are prominent elements.[2] With its focus on stakeholder collaboration, performance and results, its orientation on a holistic systems approach of environmental management, its preference for market-based incentives and outcome-based performance measures, this innovation agenda can be clearly designated as a 'modernization agenda' (see also [7]).

Innovation agendas of public agencies are partly shaped by normative discourses in society and policy programs of national administrations. In the 1980s and 1990s, two normative discourses have been prominent in the domain of environmental governance in the USA, the Right-to-Know movement and the Environmental Justice debate. Current policy practices still bear the legacy of these two discourses. The Right-to-Know movement urged for the right of employees and local communities to have access to information about the health hazards of industrial production processes. In 1986, the movement reached a 'limited' victory with the adoption of the federal Emergency Planning and Community Right-to-Know Act [8: 189-190]. An underlying premise of legislation based on Right-to-Know principles is that expanding and improving upon the information provided to the public will improve the quality of public input into regulatory processes. Geographic Information Systems might have a great potential to strengthen the role of the public and their community organizations in environmental decision-making [9]. Another aspect is that public information can be used as a tool to encourage voluntary improvements in environmental performance by the regulated facilities. This agenda was taken up during the Bush Sr. administration. In the Pollution Prevention Act (1990) the use of voluntary programs was made a national priority.

The Environmental Justice debate also began as a grass-roots movement in the USA. The term has been associated most commonly with concerns about distributional inequalities, in particular the disproportionate burden of environmental contaminants faced by many poor or minority residents [10]. In 1994, President Clinton issued an Executive Order to establish environmental justice as a priority for the administration's environmental policy. Each Federal agency was ordered to develop an agency-wide environmental justice strategy to (1) promote enforcement of all health and environmental statuses in areas with minority and low-income populations, (2) ensure greater public participation, (3) improve research and data collection relating to the health of and environment of minority populations and low-income populations and (4) identify differential patterns of consumption of natural resources among these populations.

---

[2] We do not identify any institutional innovations. However, the delegation of responsibilities in environmental governance from the federal level to the state and local level in the 1990s might be regarded as institutional changes facilitating the above-mentioned conceptual innovations.

Public participation and information are key elements in this strategy. Seven years later, a study conducted by the National Academy of Public Administration [11] concluded that the EPA had not adequately integrated environmental justice and community participation into its permit process and that despite the EPA's efforts to disseminate environmental information, "disproportionately impacted community members want better access to technical information that will enable them to participate more effectively in negotiations about permit terms and conditions" [11: 4]. In a memorandum signed in August 2004, EPA's Administrator Christine Todd Whitman confirmed the EPA's 'firm commitment' to the issue of environmental justice and its integration into the EPA's programs, policies and activities.

What we want to argue is that the innovation agendas that have emerged in the history of environmental governance in the USA are a legacy that still informs current practices of the EPA, including the implementation of its most recent innovation agenda. Put in theoretical terms, innovation efforts of public agencies are path dependent endeavours shaped by the succession of organizational choices made in the past. This idea of successive 'generations of innovations' is depicted in figure 3.

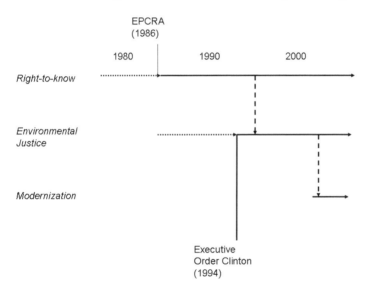

Figure 3. EPA's Innovation Agendas and Their Interconnections.

We return to these time lines in section 5 when we show how the two partnerships in Cleveland can be related to the history of EPA's innovations.

4. The Environmental Information Infrastructure in the USA

Since the 1980s, a nation-wide infrastructure for the flow by electronic environmental information has emerged between regulated facilities, regulatory agencies and the public. Under the Emergency Planning and Community Right-to-Know Act (EPCRA) of 1986, the Toxic Release Inventory (TRI) was established. Manufacturing facilities must report their releases, transfers, and waste management activities to the federal EPA. This database is made available to the general public. The TRI can be seen as the 'first generation' of agencies' databases on the basis of right-to-know principles. TRI data have several limitations: (1) they are made available to the public two years after it is reported to the EPA, (2) the reports only provide raw data about emissions, (3) they do not reach to the neighbourhood level. Some large national NGO's have undertaken to digest and interpret the data for use by local communities. Furthermore, the EPA has developed 'second' and 'third generation' online resources.

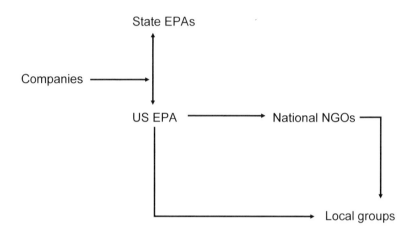

Figure 4. The Infrastructure of Environmental Information Flows in the USA

Two major resources provided by NGO's are the Right-to-Know Network and Scorecard.

The *Right-to-Know Network* (RTK NET) was started in 1989 in support of the EPCRA. It is operated by OMB Watch, a non-profit 'government watchdog organization' dedicated to "open government, accountability and citizen participation" (www.rtknet.org). *Scorecard* integrates various scientific and governmental databases in order to generate customized profiles of local environmental quality and toxic chemicals. Environmental Defense, one of the major national non-profit organizations on the environment, provides the Scorecard (www.scorecard.org).

New generation online resources provided by the EPA are Envirofacts and Window to my Environment. *Envirofacts* provides access to several EPA databases about environmental activities that may affect air, water and land. By entering his zip code, the user gets an overview of the relevant facilities and their emissions (www.epa.gov/enviro).

W*indow to My Environment* (WME) is a new website sponsored by the EPA in partnership with federal, state, and local partner organizations. WME represents an effort to develop a 'geographic portal' for integrating data and information that is shared among EPA, States, Tribes, localities and other data partners. Particular features of WME include state-of-the-art interactive mapping tools, data on 'ambient' environmental conditions, access to analytical and reporting tools and local governmental services and contacts (www.epa.gov/enviro/wme).

The EPA has also began working with the states on a new electronic exchange network: http://exchangenetwork.net. The main purpose of the Exchange Network is to overcome system incompatibility, allowing the partners (EPA, state agencies, tribes, territories and regulated facilities) to securely and automatically exchange environmental data.

5. Environmental Partnerships in the City of Cleveland

5.1. The Context

Cleveland is situated on the southern shore of Lake Erie, northeastern Ohio. The city has about 500,000 inhabitants. Greater Cleveland sprawls along the lake for about 145 km and runs 40 km inland, encompassing more than 70 suburban communities. The total population of the area, including the suburbs, is about 2.9 million, making it the 14th largest metropolitan area in the United States. Heavy industry is basic to the city's economy. Similar to many metropolitan areas, Cleveland experienced since the 1960s a decline in heavy manufacturing and population. Suburban living became more popular for those who could afford the lifestyle. With money leaving the city, the downtown neighbourhoods deteriorated. There were cutbacks in public services, and crime rates increased. However, today, Cleveland is gaining much recognition as a city experiencing a turnaround. Because of its environmental problems and the presence of an active civil society sector, Cleveland is often chosen as a model city for several new initiatives in environmental governance, in particular for partnerships between the federal, state, local and neighbourhood level. The environmental justice agenda, in particular, is highly relevant for Ohio and the city of Cleveland. Ohio ranks 3rd in the nation with the highest number of commercial hazardous waste handling facilities located in communities with above the national average percent of colour.

In this section, we discuss two environmental partnerships in Cleveland, (1) the Sustainable Cleveland Partnership that started in 1997 and (2) the Cleveland Clean Air Century Campaign that started in 2001.[3] The following actors participated in these partnerships:

- The United States Environmental Protection Agency (Region 5 Office in Chicago/EPA Cleveland Office). The Cleveland Office of Region 5 focuses on a 'Community-Based Environmental Protection' approach.
- The Ohio Environmental Protection Agency (Northeast District Officer). The State of Ohio has laws and regulations that are at least as stringent as most of the federal laws and regulations enforced by the U.S. EPA. For most federal laws and regulations, U.S. EPA delegates to the state EPAs the responsibility for issuing permits and for monitoring and enforcing compliance.
- Agencies at the county and city level: Cuyahoga County Planning Commission and several departments of the City of Cleveland. A further devolution of tasks has taken place toward the local level. Ohio EPA has delegated several monitoring tasks to the city.
- Non-governmental organizations: The Sustainable Cleveland Partnership is administered by the Earth Day Coalition (EDC), a non-profit environmental education and advocacy organization. The American Lung Association of

---

[3] For a discussion of sustainable cities programs: [12, 13].

Ohio administers the Cleveland Clean Air Century Campaign. Other civil society organizations involved in these partnerships include Environmental Health Watch and Cleveland Green Building Association.

- Community-based organizations (CBOs): CBOs are non-profit organizations that operate in urban neighbourhoods to benefit residents and address their concerns. CBOs have a long history in the US, beginning in the later 19th century. They are characterized foremost by their close working relationships with neighbourhood residents and their block-based associations [3: 447]). Participants in both partnerships are the St. Clair Superior Neighborhood Development Association and the Lee-Seville-Miles Citizens Council.

- Other societal actors, including the Center for Families and Children, the Neighborhood Centers Association and educational institutions (the Levin College of Urban Affairs at Cleveland State University and Cleveland Municipal School District). One element in the mission of Cleveland State University (CSU) is helping efforts to strengthen the empowerment of local communities in the city.

- Businesses: businesses that participate in the Cleveland Clean Air Century Campaign include Alcoa, BP Products North America Inc., Greater Cleveland Regional Transit Authority, RPM, Northeast Ohio Regional Sewer District, and Goodrich Landing Gear.

5.2. The Sustainable Cleveland Partnership

The Sustainable Cleveland Partnership (SCP) grew out of a common recognition of similar interests and emphases on community-based information access and environmental justice issues. It became clear that residents had rarely participated in the decision-making processes that had shaped environmental problems, and that inadequate access to environmental information resources and tools was a root cause of this [14]. Earth Day Coalition started the partnership, which began meeting in early 1997.

The partners adopted four programmatic goals [14: 579]: (1) enhance the availability and relevance of environmental information provided by government agencies and non-profit organizations to urban neighbourhoods; (2) improve the capacity of community leaders to use the Internet as an information access tool; (3) improve their capacity to use the information from the Internet (and other sources) effectively to address environmental problems these leaders identified as priorities; and (4) facilitate new and enhanced working relationships among neighbourhood-based organizations, regulatory agencies and the environmental advocacy community.

The first goal was addressed primarily through the development of an Environmental Health Action Guide (1997-1998). The issues covered in the Guide were based on solicited information about the environmental health issues that concerned neighbourhood leaders and residents. The second and third goals were accomplished through a series of workshops held in various neighbourhoods in the city of Cleveland (1999-2000) and the Neighbourhood Audit Profile project (1999). The workshops addressed instrumental skills, informational and strategic skills. Apart from a basic Internet training, the workshops' topics included a review of the major environmental laws and the framework of regulatory agencies, urban sustainability and environmental justice issues, problem-solving and information management needs, and action strategies. In this way, a cadre of environmental leaders was created who could assist other organizations and residents in the community. The Neighbourhood Audit Profile project was designed to orient participants to the identification and collection of data specific to their neighbourhood. Community leaders, fellow residents and student assistants developed a profile of environmental attributes, collected data using the Internet, and created a GIS map to illustrate the location of these attributes. The maps generated considerable discussion among the participants, which shortly led to the discovery of a problem that had to be investigated by the neighbourhood leaders [14]. Furthermore, training modules were developed and delivered to neighbourhood groups about risk assessment and management (2001). The various projects have fostered networking and collaboration among divergent groups in Cleveland, thereby accomplishing the fourth goal of the SCP to facilitate new and enhanced working relations among Cleveland's neighbourhood-based organizations, regulatory agencies and environmental advocacy groups. At the outset of the project, the initiators found a deep mistrust of the agencies among the residents.

The SCP has gained regional and national recognition, a testament to its innovative approach and unique mix of partners. It has proven a replicable model in other cities. Residents and community leaders learned to access information about their own neighbourhood from environmental databases, such as Envirofacts and Scorecard. Most importantly, Kellogg and Mathur [14: 581] conclude "the leadership team graduates have demonstrated an improved capacity for using information to address problems, both because of their enhanced understanding of environmental issues and of how information is generated and used in decision making". Among the first graduates were residents and leaders in the St. Clair-Superior neighbourhood to which we turn in section 6.

5.3. The Cleveland Clean Air Century Campaign and EMPACT

The Cleveland Clean Air Century Campaign is a voluntary, community-based initiative to reduce health and environmental risks from air toxics in Northeast Ohio. The CCACC began in 2001 with the establishment of a Working Group of community volunteers representing Cleveland's neighbourhoods, businesses and environmental, educational, and governmental organizations. The projects are all targeting reductions in both indoor and outdoor air toxins through voluntary community efforts, ranging from the upgrade of school buses with new particulate filters to the reduction of exposure to harmful toxins emitted from mercury-containing devices in households. With its emphasis on concrete results (measurable emission reductions for specific pollutants), non-regulatory voluntary approaches and collaboration with stakeholders, the CCACC fits well with the recent modernization agenda of the EPA. The EPA has made an initial investment in the campaign and is mainly fulfilling an expert function in providing technical assistance. Some projects have been funded by money from local Ohio EPA enforcement settlements with businesses in the city. Instead of the traditional civil penalties for violations of hazardous waste laws, Ohio EPA negotiated innovated agreements in 2004 with two businesses to spend about three-quarter of the money to a CCACC project, allowing redirecting the rest of the penalty to investments that would reduce the amount of hazardous waste.

Before the start of CCACC, the EPA had initiated its EMPACT Project (Environmental Monitoring for Public Access and Community Tracking).[4] EMPACT

---

[4] http://www.epa.gov/empact/index.htm

funded proposals submitted by EPAs and local government applicants. Proposals were required to have three critical components: environmental monitoring, information management and communication. This project covered 39 states, under which Northeast Ohio (NEO EMPACT) was one of the successful projects[5]. The goal of the NEO EMPACT project was to build an improved air monitoring network and an ecological computer-modelling tool to bring people up-to-date (real-time) local information about air pollution and its effects on health via the Internet. Again, this project was implemented in a partnership with the Northeast Ohio community, including Earth Day Coalition, Eco City Cleveland, the Northeast Ohio Area-wide Coordinating Agency, Kent Sate University, University of Akron, and others.

6. Environmental Decision-Making: St. Clair Superior Neighbourhood

St. Clair Superior has about 40, 000 residents. Originally, St. Clair Superior was mainly populated by people from East-European origins who worked in the factories in the neighbourhood. In the 1960s and 1970s, many businesses disappeared. East-Europeans moved to the suburbs; black people (from the southern states) came in and found jobs in service industries outside the neighbourhood. As a result of these developments, social trust in the neighbourhood disappeared. In 1976, the St. Clair Superior Coalition (SCSC) was formed. In 1999 the SCSC merged with the St. Clair Business Association to form the St. Clair Superior Neighborhood Development Association (SCSNDA).

The two major environmental concerns within the neighbourhood are air quality and hazardous waste. In 1996, the Environmental Committee was formed in response to resident concerns and to help residents organize around environment issues. Initially, the committee was educational in nature. In these years, the committee members participated in the projects of the Sustainable Cleveland Partnership. The committee became more action oriented with the pending review of the Title V (major source) air permits for the CEI Lakeshore Plant (1999) and Day Glo. With regards to CEI, the company sought to retain the ability to start up some old generation boilers that had been grandfathered under the Clean Air Act. These units, however, are several times more polluting than those with new source-pollution controls. With regards to Day Glo, the neighbourhood was concerned about odour and particulate emissions. The committee advocated for knowledge and experts sitting around the table, and made an environmental justice petition to the Ohio EPA. With the assistance of local NGO's, among which the Earth Day Coalition and the Sierra Club, a collaborative meeting process developed between the Environmental Committee and representatives from the Ohio EPA. The Environmental Committee chaired the Working Group, and Ohio EPA acted as facilitator and secretary. The U.S. EPA and the Cleveland Department of Air Quality were requested to participate in monthly meetings designed to address neighbourhood concerns. This may have been the first initiative in the United States to bring the state, federal and city environmental agencies into a monthly neighbourhood working group setting to address environmental justice concerns. Through the collaboration in this Working Group, the opportunity for more community input was secured, including an informal review and comment period. CEI was prevented from bringing the old boilers online without a full new source review.

---

[5] http://empact.nhlink.net

The Environmental Committee also composed a list of 'companies of concern', based on community concerns, toxic release inventory data, visual behaviour indicators and type of business. Again, a collaborative process followed, in which the regulatory agencies provided information on permits and inspections. The committee received, when possible, copies of permits and the most recent inspection reports. Moreover, the state and city agencies used the community input to conduct several unannounced inspections in addition to the standard inspections within the neighbourhood. Initially, the list of 'companies of concern' caused negative reactions from the businesses. It certainly contributed to the power position of the Environmental Committee. However, this in turn seems to have contributed to the emergence of more collaborative relations later on.

In 2003, the Committee and the Working Group were consolidated. The merger of the two groups marked a new phase in environmental problem solving in St. Clair Superior, a transition from a confrontational style to a more collaborative style toward the companies in the neighbourhood. A turning point was the Phillips Electric case. This company was found to be in violation of hazardous waste regulations. When a fine was imposed that would absorb its complete annual profit, the company approached the committee for consultation. The two parties found a solution that would not put the business in financial peril but still address the desired health and safety concerns of the community. The committee decided to support Phillips Electric in its dealings with the Ohio EPA. Because of the relationship that developed between the committee and the Ohio EPA, the agency clearly considered the committee's recommendation in its penalty decision. The company's director even joined the environmental committee. Another 'company of concern' that received a Notice of Violation from EPA Hazardous Waste inspectors agreed to pay $30,000 to a 'Supplemental Environmental Project' (SEP) to have neighbourhood school buses retrofitted with particulate filters, a project of the Cleveland Clean Air Century Campaign. The neighbourhood's new policy line was the outcome of intense discussions between SCNDA board members and the committee. Community leaders in the former residents-based committee only reluctantly agreed with the agreement with Phillips Electric. The committee embarked on an ongoing dialogue with Day-Glo Color Corporation to create an informal "Good Neighbour" relationship. The committee hopes that it can be used as a template for similar relationships with other companies in the neighbourhood. This new line is in congruence with the federal policy of 'voluntary compliance'. We may conclude that community leaders within the SCNDA are shifting their policies toward voluntary approaches, which aligns with the U.S. EPA's current modernization agenda.

The combined Committee now focuses on five areas: 1) regulatory and enforcement action; 2) voluntary pollution reduction and good neighbour relationships; 3) monitoring and information gathering; 4) advocacy and education and 5) replication of the model in other neighbourhoods. The goal of the SCNDA is to build a community for all stakeholders. Efforts have to be directed at "mending fences, building connections, and producing positive energy" (interview). It is acknowledged that sustainability requires a broader approach than regulatory measures. It is a step-by-step process, in which 'economy' and 'ecology' have to go together. Education efforts have to be directed to residents and small businesses that do not have the resources to acquire the necessary environmental knowledge themselves. Ohio EPA looks at SCSNDA as a model to conduct small business assistance on a local neighbourhood level. Moreover, through the collaborative meetings, U.S. EPA and Ohio EPA have further strengthened the partnerships between themselves, local agencies and with the neighbourhoods they serve. Ohio EPA is replicating the same process in some other neighbourhoods in Cleveland. For the regulatory agencies, collaboration with active citizens may yield efficiency benefits.

7. Analysis

In the two partnerships we looked at in this chapter, three sorts of agendas are linked with each other:
- The innovation agenda of the EPAs.
- The empowerment agenda of the environmental advocacy community.
- The aspirations of community-based organizations with regard to environmental decision-making.

In the Sustainable Cleveland Partnership (SCP), the agenda of the EPAs and the environmental advocacy community were marked by a combination of right-to-know and environmental justice concerns. Linchpins in both are public access to environmental information and community-based public participation. However, (online) information provision and public participation are also key elements in the U.S. EPA's (as well as Ohio EPA's) current modernization agenda with its emphasis on performance, results and voluntary approaches. This is highlighted in the Cleveland Clean Air Century Campaign (CCACC). The partnerships had a clear impact on the history of environmental decision-making in the St. Clair Superior neighbourhood, which was marked by a gradual transition from a confrontational to a more collaborative style of action.

Against this background, we first present an instrumental assessment of the innovation projects, in terms of its goal achievement, and then proceed to an institutional assessment focused on the project's impact on practices, positions and relations in environmental decision-making. For the U.S. EPA and the Ohio EPA, the SCP, the SCSNDA Environmental Committee, and CCACC accomplished the following:
- A model for addressing environmental justice issues.
- A model for voluntary approaches of environmental problems at the community level.
- (A model for) improved partnerships between regulatory agencies at the federal, state and city level, and with the stakeholders.

For the non-governmental organizations, such as Earth Day Coalition, the partnerships enhanced their knowledge and experience with regard to their empowerment agenda. For the involved communities the projects resulted in improved access to information as well as enhanced community control over environmental problem-solving. This brings us to an institutional assessment of the innovation projects. First, the projects fostered networking and new working relations among neighbourhood-based organizations, regulatory agencies and environmental advocacy groups. Second, improved access to information contributed to the leverage of local communities in environmental decision-making. Third, this helped to set the stage for the emergence of voluntary and collaborative approaches. Public access to information has in itself a potential to encourage voluntary improvements in environmental performance by companies, away from traditional enforcement practices. This also means that enhanced community empowerment that has been the outcome of innovation efforts that started on the basis of right-to-know and environmental justice concerns may contribute to the success of the EPA's modernization agenda in the future.

If we look at the success factors specified in the conceptual model, we conclude the following. The first instrumental success factor is the already existing nationwide infrastructure for environmental information, build up by regulatory agencies and civil society organizations. A second factor is the availability of knowledge and expertise from universities, regulatory agencies and non-governmental organizations. Another important success factor is the availability of staff and activists ('leaders'), both within the agencies and the communities. However, within the U.S. EPA's local offices and state EPAs, 'reaching out' may be dependent on a few people with the attitude, skills and willingness to do this work. Self-sustaining communities that are fully dependent on volunteers may face a serious succession problem when the former activists retire. From an institutional point of view, the following factors come to the fore. A commonly felt urgency to combat the environmental problems in the city of Cleveland formed the basis of the partnerships. It must be noted that this urgency was previously less felt at the municipal level. The city administration had given priority to economic concerns above the environmental burdens felt in poor neighbourhoods. For the federal EPA, the Sustainable Cleveland Partnership was an opportunity to implement the national guidelines on community involvement. However, the regulatory agencies had to develop a culture of innovation in partnerships. As one interviewee put it, "They had to learn to think in terms of how neighbourhoods feel and perceive problems. They had to 're-invent' their way of communication" (see also [15: 168]). Trust has been a major success factor of the partnerships. According to all the interviewees there was, initially, a great mistrust and a lot of tension between the regulatory agencies and the communities. Furthermore, residents had to get acquainted with regulatory culture and language. They had to understand what agencies can do and what they cannot do. Building individual relationships with community leaders and creating room for communication in informal settings have been essential. A major success factor from both an instrumental and institutional perspective is the prominent role of non-governmental organizations as experienced 'intermediaries' in the public domain. At the national level, non-governmental organizations have a key role as 'information intermediaries' in the national information infrastructure; in Cleveland, non-governmental organizations fulfilled initiating and facilitating roles as 'interaction intermediaries' in the emergent partnerships. In sum, non-governmental organizations were crucial for accomplishing the empowerment goals for local communities in Cleveland.

8. Conclusions

In this chapter, we took an empowerment perspective on public innovation, focused on how public innovation efforts affect the problem-solving capacity of local communities. We looked at these public innovations as processes of co-production between public agencies, non-governmental organizations and community-based organizations. Two environmental partnerships in Cleveland were studied, the Cleveland Sustainable Partnership that started in 1997 and the Cleveland Clean Air Century Campaign that started in 2001. By taking a historical perspective on public innovations, we were able to relate these two partnerships to the history of successive innovations in environmental governance in the USA. Community empowerment by improved access to information was the focus of the SCP; stakeholder collaboration and voluntary approaches were in the forefront of the CCACC. Clearly, the latter program closely aligns with EPA's current modernization agenda. The basis for the leverage of empowered communities in this program was laid down in the SCP with its framework of Right-to-Know and Environmental Justice concerns.

A key factor in the success of both partnerships has been the broker roles played by non-governmental organizations. Apart from the role of national NGO's in the environmental information infrastructure, NGO's had a major initiating and facilitating role in Cleveland's partnerships. This underlines that public innovations that have the pretension to modernize public administration, in terms of a shift toward a more citizen-centred mode of governance, are dependent on the empowerment efforts of NGO's.

Acknowledgements

The author wishes to thank Wendy Kellogg, Chris Kious, Lyn Luttner, Anjali Mathur, Bill Skowronski, Diane Swander, Chris Trepal and Elvin Vauss for their time and attention.

References

[1]   Th. Gibson, The Innovation Imperative, *The Environmental Forum* (2002), March-April, 23-32.
[2]   World Bank, *Empowerment Sourcebook*, Washington DC, 2002.
[3]   W.A. Kellogg, Community-based Organizations and Neighbourhood Environmental Problem-Solving: A Framework for Adoption of Information Technologies, *Journal of Environmental Planning and Management* **42**(4) (1999), 445-469.
[4]   J. van Dijk and K. Hacker, The Digital Divide as a Complex and Dynamic Phenomenon, *The Information Society* **19** (2003), 315-326.
[5]   V.J.J.M. Bekkers, H.J.M. Fenger and E.H. Korteland, *Governance, Democracy and the Modernizing Agenda*, Paper presented at the EGPA conference, Bern, September 2005.
[6]   Environmental Protection Agency, *Innovating for Better Environmental Results: A Strategy To Guide The Next Generation of Innovation at EPA*, 2002.
[7]   P. Leroy and J. van Tatenhove, Political Modernization Theory and Environmental Politics, in: *Environment and Global Modernity*, G. Spaargaren, A.P.J. Mol and F.H. Buttel (eds.), Sage, London, 2000, 187-208.
[8]   B.A. Williams and A.R. Matheny, *Democracy, Dialogue, and Environmental Disputes*, Yale University Press, New Haven and London, 1995.
[9]   S. Carver, A. Evans, R. Kingston and I. Turton, Accessing Geographical Information Systems over the World Wide Web: Improving Public Participation in Environmental Decision-Making, *Information Infrastructure and Policy* **6**(3) (2000), 157-170.
[10] B.M. Illsley, Good Neighbour Agreements: The First Step to Environmental Justice?, *Local Environment* **7**(1) (2002), 69-79.
[11] National Academy of Public Administration, *Environmental Justice in EPA Permitting: Reducing Pollution in High-Risk Communities is Integral to the Agency's Mission*, NAPA, Washington DC, 2001.
[12] K. Warner, Linking Local Sustainability Initiatives with Environmental Justice, *Local Environment* **7**(1) (2002), 35-47.

[13] K. Portney, Civic Engagement and Sustainable Cities in the United States, *Public Administration Review* **65**(5) (2005), 579-591.

[14] W.A. Kellogg and A. Mathur, Environmental Justice and Information Technologies: Overcoming the Information-Access Paradox in Urban Communities, *Public Administration Review* **63**(5) (2003), 573-585.

[15] H.C. Boyte, *Everyday Politics. Reconnecting Citizens and Public Life*, University of Pennsylvania Press, Philadelphia, 2004.

Information and Communication Technology and Public Innovation
V.J.J.M. Bekkers et al. (Eds.)
IOS Press, 2006

The UK's Electronic Mixed Economy of Public Service Delivery: A Preliminary Evaluation

Eleanor BURT [a,1] and John TAYLOR [b]

[a] School of Management, University of St Andrews, United Kingdom
[b] Caledonian Business School and University of Oxford, United Kingdom

Abstract. This chapter sets out the UK Government's proposal for an electronic mixed economy that will engage public, private, and voluntary organizations as "intermediaries" in the delivery of public services. Using a case study of the Citizens Advice service, a leading UK voluntary organization, the conceptual foundations, institutional and technological arrangements underpinning the electronic mixed economy are evaluated. The chapter concludes by bringing forward recommendations designed to ease and bring about more effective implementation.

Keywords. E-Government, Electronic Mixed Economy, Intermediaries, Voluntary Organizations, Innovation

1. Introduction

The UK government is seeking to bring about the modernization of public services delivery, in part through the creation of an "electronic mixed economy" that is expected to deliver innovative services that are highly responsive to citizen needs, both in relation to substantive service needs and the need for new forms of access to those services. Sitting at the heart of the electronic mixed economy are public, private, and voluntary sector "intermediary" organizations that will deliver public services to citizens from within their own portfolio of service provision. So as to illustrate key emergent issues arising from this initiative this chapter examines the case of the Citizens Advice Bureau (CAB), a UK nation-wide voluntary organization which has been engaged closely from the outset of the intermediaries initiative with the Government's Department of Work and Pensions (DWP) and other public sector bodies. Drawing upon this case study we bring forward recommendations for government policy-makers and senior administrators leading the development of the electronic mixed economy. The lessons that we draw from the case study have relevance too for public and private sector intermediaries.

---

[1] Corresponding Author: School of Management, University of St Andrews, The Scores, St Andrews, KY16 9AL, United Kingdom; E-mail: eb19@st-andrews.ac.uk.

While our focus is upon the evolving relationship between the UK voluntary sector and UK Government, the issues surrounding this relationship also have wider international significance. Governments elsewhere are also seeking new relationships with this sector, including electronically intermediated relationships [1, 2, 3, 4]. The emerging issues and insights from this present study concern generic governance issues such as trust, investment and public accountability, making them broadly comparable and transferable within these other national contexts.

The chapter begins by positioning the electronic mixed economy against the broader backcloth of the UK e-government programme and the desire to bring about the fundamental transformation of the way that Government does business and connects with citizens (section 2). Then, in setting out the Citizens Advice case study, emergent challenges in the conceptualisation and implementation of the electronic mixed economy are illustratively drawn out for the reader (section 3). Building upon this case study analysis, the authors offer an evaluation of the main challenges besetting the intermediaries initiative from the perspective of both Government and voluntary sector intermediaries (section 4). The chapter ends with the drawing out of key lessons and recommendations designed to have utility for Government and other key stakeholders engaged in the implementation and shaping of the electronic mixed economy (section 5).

2. The Modernization Project: Aims, Orientation, and Characterization

The UK e-government programme was born of ambitious aims for the fundamental transformation and modernization of public services delivery and the way that government does business [5, 6]. The intermediaries initiative that now sits within this broader programme of e-government is rooted specifically in the Government's aims to generate scale economies in the delivery of public services as well as enhancing their effectiveness, and to re-build public trust and confidence in Government and its institutions, including through the delivery of more "citizen-centric" services. More ambitious still is the increasingly and strongly stated commitment by Government not simply to the broad aim of being citizen-centric in service provision, but more profoundly to the provision of "personalised" public services [7, 8 ,9, 10, 33].

It is anticipated that opening up government to new relationships with intermediaries from the private and voluntary sectors will shock and disrupt embedded and deep rooted institutional arrangements [11], thereby enabling sought for innovations and new relationships with citizens. Thus, the intermediaries initiative involves changed and new relationships between Government and organizations from the voluntary sectors, with these new relationships founded upon access to, and exchanges of, management information between the parties involved; a matter that is giving rise to concerns both from within and from outside Government [12, 13]. Moreover it is these attempts on the part of Government to challenge and transform deeply embedded arrangements and relationships that leads us to conceptualise this particular innovation as primarily "institutionalist" in orientation, though it clearly cuts across those other forms of innovation that Bekkers, Van Duivenboden and Thaens designate "conceptual", "product", "process", and "organizational". Thus, the process of innovation that is being played out within the intermediaries initiative can be conceived of as multi-layered (Table 1). The conceptual dimension lies in the idea and vision of the electronic mixed economy as a mechanism for the delivery of intermediated public services, underpinned by high commitment on the part of intermediaries to market and provide these services effectively and to high quality standards. The ambition to serve the "whole citizen" is also a fundamental and crucial innovation at the conceptual level. Evidence of product innovation is twofold. It lies firstly in the opportunities that the initiative presents for more highly personalised services to be delivered through intermediaries that are intimately knowledgeable about their customers. Secondly it lies in enhanced access to services for citizens through the increased "channels" that intermediaries provide on behalf of Government. There is process innovation in the complex new arrangements for the flow and sharing of information between Government and public, private, and voluntary sector actors in the electronic mixed economy, and in the opportunities this brings forward for the design of service delivery around the whole citizen. Finally, organizational innovation is evident in the new back office practices, protocols, and other arrangements that enable new forms of information sharing to emerge, new access channels to be made available, and new and more personalised services to be offered.

Conceptual innovation	i.e., the envisioning of intermediated delivery of public services to "whole citizens"
Product innovation	i.e., enhanced product quality through personalisation; increased access channels through intermediaries
Process innovation	i.e., new arrangements for the flow and sharing of information emerge and are embedded
Organizational innovation	i.e., the emergence and embedding of new practices, protocols and other arrangements between actors in the electronic mixed economy
Institutional innovation	i.e., historically embedded organizational arrangements are broken down at the deepest levels, enabling deep shifts and transformations to occur

Table 1. Multi-level Innovation in e-Government

The arguments from managerial and political perspectives set out above are infused by other technologically-inspired arguments about the capacity of Internet-based service delivery channels to deliver both customised and personalised outcomes. The success of some well known virtual firms and internet-intensive companies [14], is seen as deriving from the customer focussed strategy of such businesses to accumulate data about individual purchasing and browsing records and habits and, thereby, consumer tastes and preferences. From this perspective, information and communications technologies (ICTs), including the Internet, are viewed as lifting the business/consumption nexus away from the production of mass product development, delivery and consumption and towards a future, based in customisation and, more ambitiously, personalisation. Moreover, and from a government perspective, the application of these principles to public services, in part through the access channels of the emergent electronic mixed economy, signals the end of the policy norm of universalism, as public service outcomes become highly individuated and personalised at the point of consumption.

Currently, 520 public services are targeted for potential delivery through intermediary organizations [15, 16, 17]. Intermediaries will "own" these services together with the customer-relationship itself. In so-doing they will carry responsibility for service successful delivery and for subsequent innovation including the personalisation of hitherto mass-produced and undifferentiated public services. This "ownership" raises issues concerned with the legitimacy of delivering public services in this way and the management of public accountability and trust in this relationship.

We turn now to set out how the intermediaries initiative is playing out in practice, drawing upon a case study of the Citizens Advice service in order to do so.

3. Citizens Advice

The Organisation

The Citizens Advice (CA) service is a large, well-known, highly trusted organization within the UK's voluntary sector. It is heavily dependent upon central Government and wider public sector funding, with these institutions accounting for 90.7% of its £43m income in 2003/4 the latest year for which figures are available, at the time of writing.

The core values that have underpinned the Citizens Advice service throughout its 65 year history remain firmly embedded and it is one of the UK's most highly trusted voluntary organizations. The core values of CA are to act impartially and independently on behalf of citizens; to provide a confidential service to citizens; and to provide a service that is free and available to all. It is its deep commitment to these cherished values that is shaping its engagement within the intermediaries initiative, seeking as it is to ensure that its ability to act independently and in the interests of its clients remains foremost. Thus, *"Our definition of an 'intermediary' in the context of electronic services is embedded in our concept of independent and impartial advice. We are clear that advisers will continue to act in the best interests of clients"* [18: 11].

The CA is organised for universal provision of service, operating from 3,200 locations through its network of 496 Citizens Advice Bureaux situated throughout England, Wales, and Northern Ireland. The CA service is provided by 5,617 paid staff and 20,973 volunteers, delivering services on a face-to-face basis, by telephone, and on-line [19].

In 2003/4 its bureaux dealt with 5,605,000 enquiries ranging from benefits enquiries, to housing, employment, and asylum issues: all areas with high resonance for government, including e-government. Moreover, the identifiable "decline" in enquiries made to bureaux from 6.43 million in 1997 to just over 5.5 million in 2003/4 is undoubtedly in large measure attributable to citizens now actively favouring engagement with Citizens Advice's web-based advice service over other "off-line" channels. This latter also makes Citizens Advice and the Citizens Advice Bureaux highly attractive to Government as the intermediaries initiative is taken forward. That clients are selecting its web-based services over other channels, suggests that Citizens Advice is offering the high quality web-based delivery essential for the successful delivery of e-government. 1.6 million visits were made in 2003/4 to the Citizens Advice website www.adviceguide.org.uk [19].

The Citizens Connect Project

Citizens Connect is the electronic 'backbone' through which the Citizens Advice service is delivering web-based services to citizens and clients, in partnership with Government. Underpinned by the new "CASE" system that "captures" client information within a secure "e-filing system" in which client records can be generated, accessed, and exchanged rapidly and easily, Citizens Connect is said to be saving client and administrative time and effort. Thus, client information need only be entered once under the CASE system, advice given to clients can be more easily monitored, and automated reminders to bureaux advisers mean that impending deadlines are more visible. The capability to retrieve client information instantly from throughout the bureaux network also means that clients should have the flexibility of consultation through whichever bureau or outreach facility is most convenient at a particular time. Moreover, by capturing and drawing in client CASE information from across the virtual private network (VPN) that connects the bureaux and administrative office, Citizens Connect is also generating new statistics through which the effect of public policies upon citizens can be identified, monitored, analysed, and understood, conveying the potential to make new evidence available to Government and to strengthen the Citizens Advice "voice" within the public policy arena.

Citizens Connect also provides the means through which e-Government services are made accessible to clients of the Citizens Advice service, many of whom will not have alternative access to online services or the confidence or capability to engage independently on-line. Thus, to take the example of the town of Woking in southern England, the local CA bureau has, as an authenticated and authorised "trusted intermediary" [20], automatic and unprecedented new levels of access to aspects of Woking Borough Council's back-office IT systems, including customer records. This access enables the bureau to generate a detailed profile of a client's situation, including their benefits situation or their position on the housing list [21, 20]. Citizens Advice has also been working with the Inland Revenue and Department of Work and Pensions (DWP) to pilot an initiative that will provide citizens advice bureaux advisers with similarly unprecedented forms of access to clients' benefits and tax records. Potentially, such access circumvents the need for telephone calls and written communications. Citizens Advice has also engaged closely with Government in the shaping and delivery of the major National e-Benefits Project that is to enable benefits entitlements to be calculated and claims made on-line [22, 23]. Here too, the concept and application of "trusted intermediary" status is core. Clearly, with the majority of the six million or so enquiries received by Citizens Advice requiring liaison with Government departments and other public sector bodies, there are significant opportunities to shape and take forward e-government through the intermediaries initiative and the prospect of gains to be had for citizens, Government, and intermediaries alike.

The Problems for Citizens Advice

Despite these signs that e-government and the intermediaries initiative are moving forward, progress remains slow within UK central Government. The piloting of the

National e-Benefits Project has been scaled down, a pilot to test the "trace and track" function of the Inland Revenue's new Tax Credits system has not progressed, and several e-enabled DWP systems that run to 2006 and beyond do not currently support third party access [23]. The signs are that it will be some time before e-government has the capability both to implement the electronic mixed economy fully and to engage effectively with intermediaries such as Citizens Advice, whose "*modus operandi is to deal with the whole person*" [24]. At local government level the indications are more positive, however, and a number of bureaux, in similar form to Woking, are developing processes for the tracing and tracking of housing benefit claims and their electronic submission, with benefits to clients in the form of reduced rent arrears and evictions. Here, the trust and confidence that is generated through closer personal relationships between local government councillors and officers and bureaux personnel has been highly significant in enabling agreements to be reached on protocols for access, data sharing, and verification of client identity [13].

Our analysis of the intermediaries initiative through the case of Citizens Advice shows a number of inter-related factors to be problematic and inhibitory from the perspective of that organization. These broadly cohere around two thematic areas that include the failure of Government to re-position around the information systems involved; and the failure to develop a consistent set of understandings of intermediary status within Government. These outcomes are shaped by and derive from embedded institutional arrangements, legacy ICT systems, and social and political constructions of legal and regulatory requirements, and their dynamics are well rehearsed and understood by social scientists [25]. It is the outward manifestations of these factors and the issues they raise for voluntary sector intermediaries that is our interest in this article. We set these out below.

The Failure to Re-position Around Information Systems

Even at the most basic technical levels within Government Departments, e-Government is some way from enabling integrated, on-line, customer-responsive services. For example, the DWP's "Winter Fuel Payment" application form is available in PDF format. However, claimants, and intermediaries such as the Citizens Advice Bureaux, are advised that they should print the form, complete it in writing, and post it to the DWP, together with the claimant's birth certificate. A second example, the "Housing Benefit and Council Tax Benefit" form, is also available in PDF format. It is 39 pages long, is designed so that it cannot be completed electronically and must be either hand-written or completed on a traditional type-writer and, like the Winter Fuel Payment form, there is no facility for on-line submission. Here, too, various additional items confirming the claimant's identity and status must accompany the form and various signatures are required, including that of the claimant's landlord. A third example, the "Disability Living Allowance" claim form, is also available in PDF format and, whilst it can be saved to the claimant's computer, this cannot be done once the form is opened in an internet browser. As with the other forms, this form too has no facility for on-line submission or electronic receipt, and follow-up communications are by letter. As these examples demonstrate, both the customer-facing and back-office services remain predominantly paper-based arrangements, shaped around historically embedded, compartmentalised, departmental arrangements together with similarly institutionalised regulatory 'norms' and practices.

Moreover, and at the more overarching infrastructural level, it is probable that significant numbers of claimants will have entitlements to all of these allowances and, though each allowance falls within the remit of the DWP, there is no integrated on-line application process, and neither the instructions to claimants and intermediaries nor the electronic interface operate to common standards. The DWP's historic envisioning of the (e-enabled) citizen is demonstrably "one-dimensional" and episodic, far removed from the holistic, highly personalised understanding conveyed by Citizens Advice. In theory, the types of underlying technical problem described here can be overcome as legacy systems are phased out and new customised systems are brought into place, including on-line. However, as CA has counselled, the conceptual and practical foundations for next generation customer-centric e-services need to be laid forthwith, with the intermediaries relationship embedded from the outset. Other aspects, such as re-conceptualising the citizen in holistic form and bringing forward new means of validating the status of clients that are compatible with an e-enabled service environment, are considerably more difficult barriers to overcome, not least because they threaten established patterns of power and influence and require strong leadership and incentives to drive them through.

Lack of Consistency in Defining and Understanding Intermediary Status

Deep challenges are generated around the nature and status of "intermediaries", as how this concept is understood impacts upon issues of accountability, legitimacy, confidentiality, and trust and how these are managed within the electronic mixed economy. In its documents outlining the proposal for the electronic mixed economy the Office of the e-Envoy (OeE) is clear that intermediaries "do not offer services on behalf of the public sector, and shall not represent themselves as so doing" [17: 18]. The OeE also states that intermediaries will act on behalf of, and, indeed, "own" the customer-relationship; so far, so clear. However, elsewhere in these same documents, the OeE also suggests that under some circumstances intermediaries may additionally deliver services on behalf of Government, as "government-commissioned intermediaries" [17]. Further down the same page is the statement that "The intermediations that this policy seeks to encourage are those which result in the customer viewing a government service the intermediary delivers as wholly owned by the intermediary". Later in this document the OcE indicates that "adapted public sector content is no longer 'public sector' and cannot be branded as such without the endorsement of the original service owner" [17: 28]. We are also told that "The Government service may have such a strong or established brand that the intermediary would prefer to be visibly associated with it, or the intermediary may wish to present its service as wholly its own" [17: 26]. These statements convey a fundamental lack of clarity around the definition of intermediaries and the nature and status of their relationship with Government and citizen. If intermediaries do not "own" Government services how can they legitimately and lawfully "re-invent" them? How can they "brand" and "represent" a service as their own if it is a Government owned service? Will citizens have confidence that intermediaries are acting in their interests if the same intermediaries are also delivering government-commissioned services to citizens?

These are profoundly important questions for organizations such as CA, as their clients must be assured and confident of the impartiality and independence of the CA service from Government. It is also in the interests of CA and indeed voluntary sector intermediaries generally that in the event of problems occurring with an intermediated public service, clients understand that the service is Government owned, and thereby hold Government to account, so safeguarding the intermediary's reputation and relationship with its customers [12]. The problem described here is magnified throughout Government departments, where there is little or no common understanding of intermediary status and no consistent policy for their engagement and nothing to suggest that this will alter in the foreseeable future.

4. Assessing the Intermediaries Initiative

The electronic mixed economy is in the early stages of implementation and it will be some time before the extent to which its contribution to the Government's ambitious aims of "modernizing government" around the delivery of highly citizen-centric public services can be fully evaluated. What is already evident though, is that there are significant instrumental and institutional challenges to be met as the initiative is taken forward.

4.1. Instrumental Assessment

An instrumental evaluation of the intermediaries initiative brings forward three sets of issues.

First, while the intermediaries initiative clearly has the potential to generate cost-savings it is also conceivable that costs will rise for both Government and intermediaries. The delivery of high volume, personalised services, through a wide range of channels should increase take-up of e-government, on the one hand, while delivering significant cost-savings to Government, on the other. For VSOs the potential benefits of intermediary status lie almost entirely in enhancements to service quality through new access to and integration with Government information systems, thereby enabling VSOs to support their consumers of service more effectively. It is possible, too, that this more integrated service will generate cost-efficiencies for VSOs as their service users are enabled to engage directly with Government through public services that have been appropriately customised by VSOs on their behalf. It is also conceivable that the capability to enter Government information systems on behalf of their service users will lead to reduced transaction times and errors, thereby also generating potential cost-efficiencies for VSOs of the sort identified by CA. At this early stage in the delivery of the electronic mixed economy these benefits remain unproven. What is already clear, however, is that there are significant challenges to be resolved in its conceptualisation, shaping, and implementation, including the potential for costs to government and intermediaries to rise rather than reduce as demand for services expands or, indeed, as customisation and personalisation generate higher costs.

Second, the "ownership" of public services by intermediaries brings considerable opportunities for government and voluntary sector, as well as significant risks in particular to public trust [26, 12]. For government, opportunities include off-loading responsibility for services that are under-performing, whilst risk attaches mainly to the capabilities of VSOs to take on these service provisions as well as in establishing clarity over the locus and process of public accountability. The opportunities for VSOs lie in providing an expanded portfolio of services that they provide and which they are also able to re-package and deliver in ways that are highly attractive and accessible to consumers of their services. Together, these bring opportunities for voluntary intermediaries to grow their service users and their membership. Additionally, cost-savings garnered through performance enhancing relationships of the type achieved by Woking CAB and opportunities to provide some services on a "for-profit" basis enable "surplus" to be ploughed back into further service enhancing and charitable activities. The risks for these organizations are most in evidence over threats to organizational independence and public trust should services fail to meet contractual obligations or consumer expectations, for it is from their autonomy and public trust that VSOs draw considerable strength and unique "voice" [27].

Third, there will need to be substantial strategic investment in developing and sustaining ICT capacity and capability throughout the voluntary sector if VSOs are to be significant actors, alongside public sector institutions and private sector enterprises. Yet, the costs of generating ICT infrastructural development throughout the voluntary sector on a scale that will enable VSOs' engagement within the electronic mixed economy are prohibitive. To take the case that forms the empirical core of this chapter, the Citizens Advice service's Citizens Connect IT programme, that extends throughout its English and Welsh bureaux, is underpinned by a £20 million grant from the Government's Capital Modernisation Fund [28, 20]. Without such subvention investment on this scale would not have been possible. However, levels of funding such as this are not possible across the voluntary sector as a whole and nor is it within the scope of most VSOs to generate such investment funding from other sources.

4.2. Institutional Evaluation

Two fundamental insights on the institutionalist challenges of the intermediaries initiative derive from the case study of CA.

First, for there to be effective and meaningful engagement with citizens there needs to be a profound shift in the way that the business of national Government is organised, including in its relationships with intermediaries. That e-enabled services continue to be provided in ways that are both partial and fragmented is not only attributable to lack of interoperability across Government ICT systems, it is symptomatic too of the deeply institutionalised arrangements and autonomies and other 'legacy arrangements' that still reside within the organizational architecture of UK national Government.

Second, there needs to be sensitivity to the core values and underlying principles that shape the relationships – particularly the trust relationships – that are so fundamentally important between VSO and client. New arrangements for the management, including the sharing, of information can be highly disruptive to those values and principles. The capability to deliver service enhancements attuned to customer requirements means that consumers of these services need to surrender personal information to the voluntary sector intermediary, so enabling the voluntary organization "to get to know the customer better". In this way, the voluntary organization becomes more and more a repository of vital information on its client group of citizens if it is to discharge its new obligations to provide public services effectively. While some personal information will be used to construct profiles of "customer segments" and will not be garnered or utilised by intermediaries or Government in ways that are revealing of the individual customer's identity, by their very nature many public services do require variable levels of inherently personal and private information for their effective delivery. While this personal information has always been a feature of the public service landscape, it is the intensification of its collection and the new transparencies between Government and intermediaries that online personalisation demands that give rise to concerns metaphorically encapsulated by the concept of the "glass citizen" [29], the citizen whose privacy is threatened under the "electronic gaze". While the "glass citizen" is an improbable outcome of relationships between Government and intermediaries in which legislative and institutional arrangements and value and trust-based concerns combine to ensure that information will never be fully, openly shared, nonetheless the electronic mixed economy raises not insignificant questions about the stewardship of information. If the electronic mixed economy is to operate effectively, and the Government's vision of delivering personalised services is to be achieved, the sharing of information that was previously "off-limits" will become the norm. In the complex organizational milieu that the electronic mixed economy will generate it will be difficult to know the destinations of information, once released. Thus, the electronic mixed economy generates crucial questions regarding the stewardship of information. Who "owns" it? How will the sharing of information be managed? Who is accountable for the ways that it is used? And to whom is that accountability owed? Who will be empowered and disempowered in the emergent relationships? What safeguards will ensure that information is not wrongly attributed, with the implications and consequences that this conveys? How will information be managed so voluntary sector intermediaries are able to retain their deeply valued and crucial high levels of public trust?

5. Conclusions, Key Lessons, and Recommendations

The electronic mixed economy of public service provision has the potential both to generate significant economies of scale and to deliver highly customer-responsive services, as government owned services are channelled through intermediaries drawn from the voluntary and private sectors. Their status as relatively high trust organizations and their reputation for delivering personalised services responsive to the needs of individual clients makes voluntary organizations such as CA particularly attractive partners within this environment. However, as this analysis of e-Government through the case of CA demonstrates, there is a number of significant challenges to be overcome and lessons to be learned if the electronic mixed economy is to be delivered effectively.

The first profound challenge for Government and the voluntary sector is how to manage risk and public accountability within the intermediary relationship and most particularly those risks and accountabilities associated with the stewardship of information (as we identify in the section on instrumental assessment), for these are the foundations upon which effective collaborative arrangements and public trust rest.

The second challenge that our evaluation identifies is to develop a consistent and shared understanding of the nature and status of intermediary organizations. Crucially, this understanding must take account of the value that voluntary organizations place upon independence and impartiality and upon the provision of universal services freely available, as it is in these and other deeply cherished values that high public trust in this sector is generated and sustained. It is a crucial part of this shared understanding too that Government accepts that, implicit in the intermediaries concept, is the necessity for access to be granted to secure Government systems and for new protocols and authentication processes to be implemented that will allow organizations such as

Citizens Advice new levels of access to confidential and hitherto private client information as they seek to serve the whole citizen.

The third clear challenge is to develop, deliver and sustain a vision of (e-) Government that both embeds, and is shaped around, deep commitments to both the "whole citizen" and "the intermediated delivery of public services". Organizations such as CA have a wealth of experience and expertise to bring through this process and there are gains to be had in engaging VSOs in dialogue around how best to shape and deliver e-Government, including, importantly, how to do so in ways that do not place at risk the independence of VSOs from Government or their high-trust relationships with vulnerable clients.

The fourth challenge that our assessment points to is how to generate and sustain the very significant funding that is required if the voluntary sector is to engage effectively within the electronic mixed economy. Several major studies have shown that the sector has consistently failed to invest in ICTs and to re-position strategically around e-enabled services [30, 31, 32] and large-scale financial investment is required if the situation is to be adequately redressed.

Fifthly, our analysis has shown that the Government's sought-for innovation in the form of the intermediaries initiative does not straightforwardly encompass a single dimension of innovation. Instead, innovation within this context is a multi-layered phenomenon wherein some layers are more deeply embedded and concretised than others: the institutional layer being the most deep-set and yet the one upon which fundamental and sustained change at the other levels is dependent.

In conclusion we set out briefly a number of recommendations for Government and the Voluntary Sector as they move forward with the intermediaries initiative. Either singly or jointly they should:

- Consider carefully how public accountability is to be managed in respect of the intermediaries initiative;
- Consider carefully how the stewardship of information is to be managed, perhaps developing a mutually arrived at protocol to aid judgements about the parameters for information sharing in settings such as these;
- Consider carefully what is meant by the "whole citizen" and ensure that this sits at the centre of strategic development of public services at UK, regional, and local levels of government;
- Consider how the independence and autonomy of VSOs can be safeguarded within this environment;
- Work together and with other stakeholders to develop a clear and coherent and inclusive strategy for generating and sustaining ICT capacity and capability in the voluntary sector;
- Be aware that innovation of the magnitude of the electronic mixed economy is a complex, multi-level process in which each level must be attended to if transformation is to be effective and sustained.

References

[1]   A. Evers and J-L. Laville, *The Third Sector in Europe*, Edward Elgar, Cheltenham, 2004.
[2]   S.P. Osborne (ed.), *The Voluntary and Non-profit Sector in Japan: The Challenge of Change*, RoutledgeCurzon, New York, 2003.

[3]   U. Josefesson and A. Ranerup, Consumerism Revisited: The Emergent Roles of New Electronic Intermediaries Between Citizen and the Public Sector, *Information Polity* **8**(3/4) (2003), 167-180.

[4]   W. Cukier and C.A. Middleton, Evaluating the Web Presence of Voluntary Sector Organizations: An Assessment of Canadian Websites, *IT and Society* **1**(3) (2003), 102-130.

[5]   Cabinet Office, *Modernising Government*, London, CM 4310, 1999.

[6]   Performance and Innovation Unit, e.gov., *Electronic Government Services for the 21st Century*, London, 2000.

[7]   Strategy Project Team, *Transformational Government: Enabled by Technology*. Report to the CIO Council and the Service Transformation Board (Internal, working document), London, 2005.

[8]   T. Blair, *The Labour Party Manifesto*, London, 2005.

[9]   G. Brown, Speech by the Chancellor of the Exchequer to the Social Market Foundation, 18 May, London, available at: www.hm-treasury.gov.uk/newsroom_ and_speeches/press/2004/press_49_04.cfm, 2004.

[10] C. Leadbetter, *Personalisation through Participation: A New Script for Public Services*, DEMOS, London, 2004.

[11] F.R. Baumgartner and B.D. Jones, *Policy Dynamics*, University of Chicago Press, Chicago, 2002.

[12] I. Kearns, *Intermediaries and the Electronic Delivery of Public Services: a Mixed Economy in e-Government*. A Public Response to the Government Consultation Paper, IPPR, London, 2004.

[13] J. Wheatley, Citizens Advice On Course To Be Intermediaries?, PublicTechnology.net, 9 February, available at: http://www.publictechnology.net/print.php?sid=564, 2004.

[14] A.M.B. Lips, S. van der Hof, J.E.J. Prins and A.A.P. Schudelaro, *Issues of On-line Personalisation in Commercial and Public Service Delivery*, University of Tilburg, 2004.

[15] Office of the e-Envoy, *Policy framework for a mixed economy in the supply of e-government services: a consultation document*, London, 2003.

[16] Office of the e-Envoy, *Policy framework for a mixed economy in the supply of e-government services. Official response to public consultation*, London, 2003.

[17] Office of the e-Envoy, *Policy framework for a mixed economy in the supply of e-government services. Implementation guidelines*, **1**, London, 2003.

[18] Citizens Advice, *Electronic Government Services: Key Priorities for the Citizens Advice service*, London, (n.d.).

[19] Citizens Advice, *Citizens Advice Strategic Plan 2004-2008*, London, 2004.

[20] Citizens Advice, Citizens Connect, available at: www.ciitizensadvice.org.uk/print/index/aboutus/citizensconnect.htm?x=9&y=9, 2005.

[21] RSeconsulting & Evolve Business Consultancy, *e-Pay National Project*, 2004.

[22] e-Benefits, About the Project, available at: www.ebenefits.org.uk/, 2005.

[23] J. Wheatley, Citizens Advice Bureaux are Not Yet Acting as Intermediaries for e-Services, 20 March, e-Gov Monitor, 20: 26, available at: http://www.egovmonitor.com/node/56 , 2005.

[24] D. Harker, eGovernment in the Spotlight: Citizens Advice CEO Speaks Out at PITCOM Meeting, 25 November, PublicTechnology.net, available at: http://www.publictechnology.net/print.php?sid=258 , 2003.

[25] C.A. Bellamy and J.A. Taylor, *Governing in the Information Age*, Open University Press, Milton Keynes, 1998.

[26] J.A. Taylor and E. Burt, Managing Trust, Generating Risk – Incorporating the Voluntary Sector in UK e-Government, *Information Polity*, Special edition on 'Risk and Trust in the Internet Era', 2005.

[27] R.E. Goodin, *Reflective Democracy*, Oxford University Press, Oxford, 2002.

[28] Citizens Advice, *The Charity for Your Community. Citizens Advice Annual Report 2003/2004*, London. 2004.

[29] E. Mayo, *The Age of Identity*, Speech, The Foundation of Science and Technology, February, 2005.

[30] E. Burt and J.A. Taylor, *Information and Communication Technologies: Re-shaping the Voluntary Sector in the Information Age?*, Centre for the Study of Telematics and Governance, Caledonian Business School, Glasgow Caledonian University, Glasgow, 1998.

[31] Hall Aitken, *E-enabling the Voluntary and Community Sectors*, Final report, London, 2001.

[32] J. Saxton and S. Game, *Virtual Promise*, The Future Foundation, London, 2003.

[33] G. Brown, *Politics as a Moral Duty*, Labour Party Conference, 26 September, Brighton, 2005.

Information and Communication Technology and Public Innovation
V.J.J.M. Bekkers et al. (Eds.)
IOS Press, 2006

Identity Management as Public Innovation: Looking Beyond ID Cards and Authentication Systems[1]

Miriam LIPS [a,2], John TAYLOR [b] and Joe ORGAN [c]

[a] *Tilburg University and University of Oxford, United Kingdom*
[b] *Caledonian Business School and University of Oxford, United Kingdom*
[c] *University of Oxford, Oxford Internet Institute, United Kingdom*

Abstract. Governments are introducing, managing and using digitized personal identification and authentication systems in their service relationships with citizens in addition to, and increasingly in replacement of, traditional forms of personal identification and authentication. An important question is to what extent these developments are causing innovation in the sense of a renewal of traditional institutions in the government domain. By presenting public debate with regard to the recently proposed UK National Identity Cards initiative we will show that a public administration perspective is needed to be able to detect more fundamental forms of innovation in government.

Keywords. Identity Management, Personal Identification, Authentication, e-Government, ID card, Citizenship, Passport

1. Introduction

Governments around the world are introducing, managing and using digitized personal identification and authentication systems in addition to, and increasingly in replacement of, traditional forms of personal identification and authentication. Digitized personal identification systems can offer customer convenience; citizen mobility and empowerment; efficiency and/or effectiveness of public service provision, including joined-up government; and the enhancement of public safety and security, including general law enforcement. These systems therefore not only appear to enable the modernization of government; they also enable government to fulfil its service providing functions, through its ability to authenticate personal identifiers provided by citizens in e-government relationships. Authentication, or the assurance that a person is who (s)he says (s)he is, is generally acknowledged as an essential requirement for the

---

[1] This chapter has been based on ongoing research sponsored by the ESRC; Personal Identification and Identity Management in New Modes of E-Government. Ref: 'RES-341-25-0028', A.M.B. Lips, J.A.Taylor and J. Organ.
[2] Corresponding Author: Oxford Internet Institute, University of Oxford, United Kingdom and Tilburg Institute for Law, Technology and Society, Tilburg University, Tilburg, The Netherlands. E-Mail: miriam.lips@oii.ox.ac.uk.

provision of many government services to citizens. Digitized personal identification and authentication systems thereby become the *sine qua non* of successful e-government. The innovative potential of these systems seems to be substantial, therefore; but is innovation in government actually happening as a result of the implementation and use of these systems, in what form and to what extent?

It is clear that e-ID, e-authentication and the broader field of Identity Management (IDM) can be observed as important topics emerging on national and international policy agendas, in e-government and other policy domains (e.g. the EU Ministerial e-Government Declaration of 2005 [1]). These concepts however are relatively new terms, whose meanings remain unsettled, at least from a social science perspective [2]. In many countries the clarification and implementation of these concepts and their related personal identification and authentication systems has started only recently, leaving us without a clear perspective on what ultimately they will change or offer to governments. We observe in some countries that the introduction of these topics is surrounded by considerable public debate, indicating popular anticipation of a profound impact of new forms of personal identification and IDM on the machinery of government and its relationships with citizens. In the United Kingdom (UK) for instance the introduction of Identity Cards, *inter alia* an important component of the UK antiterrorist legislation, is causing heated public discussions about their pros and cons. In other countries, although with much less public attention or concern, comparable developments in the field of IDM are taking place in society. For instance, perceived as an eID best practice and copied by governments (e.g. Portugal) and even commercial organizations (e.g. Microsoft) the Belgian eID Card is being used in an increasing number of public and commercial services and has an uptake of at least 1.5 million, virtually without public debate.

Unquestionably these developments in the field of IDM will have some impact on the future management and organization of electronic public service provision to citizens. The question is then if, and if so in what respect and to what extent, these developments are causing innovation in the sense of a renewal of traditional institutions. Are new forms of personal identification and IDM actually bringing about what Schumpeter [3] has called a process of 'creative destruction', in this case of the traditional relationships including the information practices between government and citizens? Or are these developments merely conceptual innovations, 'old wine in new bottles', with limited change implications for existing practices? Our main argument in this chapter will be that we need to make use of a public administration perspective, i.e. an *institutional* assessment of modernization efforts in government, to be able to detect more fundamental forms of innovation in government as a result of the introduction of these digitized personal identification and authentication systems. At present, the two dominant perspectives regarding e-ID, e-authentication and IDM in general in the policy making arena are a technical design perspective based on the application of technical logic to complex public problem solving and a 'privacy-advocacy' point of view based on normative assumptions about the importance of privacy to human freedoms. Both perspectives can be acknowledged as *instrumental* assessments of the modernization efforts related to the introduction of new digitized personal identification and authentication systems in public administration. We will further illustrate these perspectives on the basis of the recently proposed UK national identity cards initiative. But before we do so we will introduce the innovative potential related to emerging digital forms of identification, authentication and IDM.

2. New Forms of Identification, Authentication and Personal Identity

Traditionally, personal identification of the citizen resides at the heart of many forms of government service delivery, from health services to policing, social services, housing and taxation, to cite some general examples. Historically and archetypically, such identification has been undertaken through manual form filling, coupled to the verification of personal identity through paper-based authentication processes. Through time authentication processes related to the use of paper-based authentication systems, such as the passport, have been largely constant. The passport holder shows his or her passport to the person officially recognised to check and verify that the document carrier is the person shown referred to through the information, including photograph, included in the document. Set within a traditional environment of trust, these authentication processes often have been supplemented by informal assessment of the citizen by the official, based upon their appearance of honesty or upon the official's knowledge of the citizen within the local community.

Within this archetype of personal identification of the citizen, public organizations delivering services to the public became vast repositories of stored paper records, gathered together as the proof of entitlement that was required before access to the service could be authorised. Moreover, the entitlement to service was realised through a form of administrative equity that saw citizens being 'handled' *seriatim*: the citizen claimant for service, for example, was included onto a waiting list, in line, and was provided service and thereby taken off that waiting list in the strict order in which the waiting list was entered. Furthermore, the service accessed by citizens was 'universal', deriving from the administrative equity principle of 'equality under the law' i.e. within any particular governmental jurisdiction (national, regional, local, functional), rights to the same service level were afforded to all citizens [4].

Now, in the rapidly developing on-line activities of government new forms of personal identification are being used in which the identity of the citizen increasingly is being established through the gathering of personal or person-related information in electronic relationships rather than in face-to-face relationships between the citizen and government. Emerging within the digital era are three main ways of identifying a person operating within an electronic environment; accepting a self-declared statement of identity that draws upon details known by that person about who they are (e.g. a username, registration number, address details, password, PIN); accepting an item of identity the person physically possesses (e.g. a smartcard, electronic tag, mobile phone); scrutinising aspects of the physiological identity of the person (e.g. fingerprint, iris, face, DNA). Moreover these means of identification can be used in combination, as an affirmation of identity and as a step towards authentication of that identity (e.g. showing a credit card and supporting it with a PIN).

With the increasing use of these new forms of personal identification and authentication we can observe new types of 'personal data' being involved in citizen-government service relationships. In the abstract, these new types of personal data can be perceived in concentric circles at varying distances from the individual's core identity [5]. The outermost circle is that of individual information which includes any data which can be linked to a person, for instance a license plate, email-address or click behaviour on the Internet; the most inner circle represents the individual's core identity based on biological ancestry and family relations. In between are concentric circles of private, intimate and sensitive information, followed by unique identification.

Combinations of different types of personal data are at the basis of new forms of e-government service provision. Examples of these new forms are personalised public service provision and Customer Relationship Management (CRM). Within these new forms of public service provision we may observe new and more complex ways of categorising, segmenting and grouping citizens that enable different modes, levels and paces of service provision to be implemented. With that, these developments offer possibilities to set aside the historically arrived at administrative logic of 'service by waiting list' derived from the policy norm of universalism and the legal principle of equality under the law [4].

Moreover in the emerging electronic public service environment we recognise the multiple relationships that the citizen has with government agencies, each supported by an assembled form of a citizen's personal data [6]. For example, the citizen has an Inland Revenue taxpayer's identity, a Health Service patient identity, a Social Security identity as a contributor and claimant within the system, a driver's identity, and a resident identity within a public housing scheme. Traditionally, a separate citizen's identity profile was constructed, managed and used for each of these relationships. In the current digital environment it has become much easier in principle to create and manage an integrated identity profile on the citizen, for instance through the use of a unique number (e.g. social security number), or for the citizen to make use of a singular personal identification and authentication system to access a variety of government services. Potential IDM solutions such as these are being looked into by many governments around the world and, more specifically, practices in this last respect can already be found in for instance New Zealand, the Netherlands (DigiD-initiative), and the UK (Government Gateway Project).

3. Informational Trends Resulting From New Identification Technologies

These new modes, levels and paces of e-government service provision are developing on the basis of several general informational trends we may empirically observe [5]. We describe these trends below, without making any judgements about their nature or direction:

- an increasing use of digital forms of identification and authentication of personal data instead of physical forms;
- an increase of the ability to discover and track personal information in real time across physical barriers, locations and over time;
- an increasing integration of life activities with the generation of personal information (e.g. the use of credit cards or mobile phones);
- an increased blurring of lines between public and private places makes personal information more publicly available;
- an increased merging of previously compartmentalised personal data; and
- an expansion of ways of measuring and classifying citizens, with greater precision compared to traditional measures, such as paper-based methods.

These informational trends lead to different outcomes in society, which happen simultaneously and may be mutually contradictory. For instance, as a result of these informational trends an individual's ability to remain unnoticed and, after being noticed, to remain unidentified in society has declined significantly. In many cases we can observe a development towards the construction of (more) complete identity profiles on individuals [7]. This expanded ease of identity construction also has led to increased requirements of some form of identity validation in public and commercial activities. We can observe for instance a major expansion of laws, policies and procedures mandating that individuals provide personal information. Another related development is to more and more require personal identification with the heaviest possible means of identification, i.e. biometrics (Ibid). Arguments for using this far-reaching form of identification are often related to convenience (e.g. efficiency and increased speed of service delivery), combat of fraud or crime.

At the same time we may observe an increased freedom of choice for individuals to present their identity. Especially as a result of the expansion of impersonal, digital interaction, for instance supported by the Internet, an individual's personal identity is becoming relatively less unitary, homogeneous, fixed or enduring. Moreover in presenting the self, as indicated earlier, an individual is able to make use of new functional alternatives to his or her core identity. Different types of pseudonyms (e.g. email-address, phone number, credit card details, unique number) for instance can be used to present the self for various purposes in interactions with others. In doing so, but also through other available methods nowadays, an individual has increased possibilities to protect personal data that is more closely related to his or her core identity. As people play different roles in social processes (e.g., as employee, citizen, customer, or family member), each individual is in fact owner of many different identities, and is known to his environment under many different pseudonyms such as an e-mail address and GSM phone number. As Goffman has extensively shown, we cannot avoid conveying information about ourselves every moment that we are in the presence of others, but we may be able to affect the way in which those impressions are given to others [8]. Moreover, parallel to the observed expansion of lawful personal information requests, we can observe a significant expansion of laws, policies and management approaches that restrict and regulate the collection of personal information and its subsequent treatment.

4. Identity Cards as a Technical Domain of Understanding

At present governments clearly have discovered these informational trends resulting from the availability of new technologies for detecting and validating personal information. Governments seem to have acknowledged these new identification and authentication technologies as contributors to information security and to increased confidence in the identity of individuals in electronic relationships therefore [9]. The implementation and use of these technologies in government service provision have become strongly recognised in the digital era, both for more optimal security provision and to support the spread and successful uptake of e-Government [10, 11: 27, 12]. Generally, the introduction of a more robust form of IDM in citizen-government relationships is perceived as an essential solution for a variety of policy problems.

At present a prime example of the introduction of a new means of personal identification in government is the proposed UK national identity card legislation. The aims of the UK central government are to introduce a national identity card containing three biometric identifiers together with a national identity register acting as a central database in which a range of details about individuals will be stored. In the short term ID cards will be voluntary, though anyone renewing a passport or drivers' licence will automatically receive an ID card, and foreign visitors will have to obtain a biometric residence permit; in the longer term the ID card will become compulsory [13: 1].

The UK government has defended its proposals for a variety of reasons, including prevention of benefit fraud, prevention of terrorism, prevention of identity theft and authentication in e-government services. Although the core policy objective is difficult to ascertain the location of the ID card legislation within the Home Office is believed to especially support the policy need to uphold security, law and international migration protocols [11: 34]. Research findings show that UK citizens are generally supportive of an ID card [14: 114, 15, 16), or even consider their introduction as inevitable [13: 6]. This is in accordance with situations in other European countries where the implementation of ID cards did not cause strong public debate (e.g. Belgium, Austria, Finland).

In the UK context, however, critics have pointed to the overemphasis in the public debate on the visible, technical means of identification proposed by the UK government, the ID card itself, and, with that, the lack of public attention for the more invisible aspect of how citizens' data will be handled by the UK government [e.g. 11: 38, 17]. Other critical voices point at seemingly unrealistic technical expectations of the ID card scheme, using arguments such as the fact that neither the major contractors nor the government have shown themselves capable of organizing and implementing an outsourced IT scheme on this scale: no country has attempted to use biometrics technologies to register a population the size of the UK [18]; the proposed requirement for 100 per cent accuracy: has there ever been an identification system which is 100 per cent accurate? [19]; trials of the card scheme have demonstrated that a substantial number of specific groups of the UK general population (e.g. disabled people) may not be able to enrol on biometrics based verification schemes [20]; from industry, 'a national ID card for the UK is overly ambitious, extremely expensive and will not be a panacea against terrorism or fraud, although it will make a company like mine very happy' (as stated by biometrics specialist Tavano[3]); and, from a collective group of LSE academics, that the government proposals for a secure national identity system are too complex, technically unsafe, overly prescriptive, massively more costly than government is itself estimating and lack a foundation of public trust and confidence [18: 3].

This ID card debate illustrates the traditional way in which IDM issues have been tackled by governments so far. Optimal security, technical reliability, ID "theft[4]" and accuracy repeatedly have been important topics in public decision making about available personal identification and authentication systems at many occasions in the past. This debate therefore is not a new debate emerging in the current era, but can be observed for instance for the paper-based passport system on a regular basis in many national public decision making arenas. Interestingly, if we look at personal identification and authentication systems in practice, such as the use of the passport in authentication procedures, there have not been notable changes in this authentication system through time. Moreover this similarity in restricted, technically focused IDM topics may explain the current ease with which governments are trying to copy ID card systems or authentication systems from 'best practices' available in other countries. From a technical perspective new forms of personal identification, authentication and

---

[3] Tavano works for Unisys, one of the companies considering bidding for contracts. Quoted in The Guardian, 21 October 2005.

[4] ID theft as a concept has only emerged recently. The theft or fraudulent use of ID documents however exists for a long time.

IDM can be perceived as improved technical means to be used in similar identification and authentication practices compared to the past. In terms of innovation these new means may bring about process innovation for governments, but their actual use in practice would need to demonstrate that type of innovation before it can be confirmed.

5. Identity Cards as a Legal-Normative Domain of Understanding

Where a non-technical perspective is being used actively to approach the informational trends that we have noted here the perspective that is most common is 'legal-normative', one that derives especially from data protection legislation. The potential uses of identification and authentication technologies and their implications for individual citizens' privacy are often couched by privacy advocates in Orwellian big brother scenarios. They usually claim that a contradictory societal outcome of leaving more control to the individual over his or her personal information would be in accordance with legally defined civil rights and therefore a more appropriate scenario for which to strive. Privacy in this sense may be understood as the right to informational self-determination, i.e. individuals must be able to determine for themselves when, how, to what extent and for what purpose information about them is communicated to others.

We can observe the presence of this legal-normative perspective in the UK national identity card debate. A general conviction is that, with the introduction of an ID card, UK citizens are required to trade an element of their privacy for increased security [11: 26]. Proposals are for instance that personal details to be stored on the register will include three biometric identifiers, residence, former residences, and details of change of residence; moreover it will contain information about numbers allocated to the individual and official personal documents. For reasons of 'public interest' the Home Secretary would be able to pass on to other parties information kept on the national register, without the individual's consent and without the individual being entitled to know how his/her data is being used [11: 35].

These proposals have convinced the LSE to comment that this legislation would conflict with data protection legislation, on the basis that the function of the register is too ill-defined [18]. Also several other critics, including the UK Information Commissioner, expressed concerns about the lack of clarification in the UK legislation proposals about the nature and extent of personal information which will be collected and retained, plus the reasons why such a large amount of information needs to be recorded as part of establishing an individual's identity [17]. In addition, the centralization of this information has been questioned, as alternative models for data storage could be chosen, such as for instance more data storage on the ID card and less data in the national register.

Proponents of this legal-normative perspective generally also try to explain that the dominant information principle in these government proposals is in keeping with the social norm attaching to identification of the citizen, rather than an alternative norm such as the acceptance or encouragement of anonymity. With anonymity as the guiding principle, the minimal collection of personal information by government would be the norm. However, with the current ease of collecting, managing and using of various types of personal information, the dominant information principle of individuals' identification seems to become widespread in the information society. A guiding principle of anonymity in the emerging information society appears to be far removed therefore, both empirically and normatively [21].

Nonetheless, the developing IDM expert community in which information security specialists, (former) data protection commissioners, and privacy advocates can be recognised, has adopted more or less a set of laws for digital IDM, in which the principle of anonymity guides thinking. One illustration of this attention to anonymity is to be found in the Seven Laws of Identity[5], which have been embraced by many IDM experts as IDM *principles* (see for instance a paper of the former Australian Federal Privacy Commissioner Malcolm Crompton [9]):

1. *User Control and Consent*: Digital identity systems must only reveal information identifying a user with the user's consent;
2. *Limited Disclosure for Limited Use*: The solution which discloses the least identifying information and best limits its use is the most stable, long-term solution.
3. *The Law of Fewest Parties*: Digital identity systems must limit disclosure of identifying information to parties having a necessary and justifiable place in a given identity relationship.
4. *Directed Identity*: A universal identity metasystem must support both "omnidirectional" identifiers for use by public entities and "unidirectional" identifiers for private entities, thus facilitating discovery while preventing unnecessary release of correlation handles.
5. *Pluralism of Operators and Technologies*: A universal identity metasystem must channel and enable the interworking of multiple identity technologies run by multiple identity providers.
6. *Human Integration*: A unifying identity metasystem must define the human user as a component integrated through protected and unambiguous human-machine communications.
7. *Consistent Experience Across Contexts:* A unifying identity metasystem must provide a simple consistent experience while enabling separation of contexts through multiple operators and technologies.

Interestingly, several of these 'laws' on identity can be recognised as similarly looking to the OECD's basic principles for the protection of personal data[6]. These laws therefore seem to propose to integrate the protection of civil rights in digital identity systems and to create what may be called 'privacy enhanced' IDM systems.

Through time we can observe that privacy and security values often have been balanced by governments with regard to the use of identification systems. The history of the use of the passport shows us that personal identification procedures mainly changed during moments of societal crisis, such as the French Revolution, the First World War and the Second World War [22, 23]. Although the authentication system itself, the paper-based passport, more or less stayed the same through time, the frequency and intensity of its use, as well as the officials executing the authentication process usually changed during these periods of war. A similar effect can be observed in more recent times after the events of 9/11 and the London bombings.

---

[5] Cameron, 2005, see http://www.identityblog.com.
[6] See for instance the OECD Guidelines on the Protection of Privacy and Transborder Flows of Personal Data.

Another general observation is that the introduction of new technologies in society, such as in the case of ID cards in the UK[7], inevitably raises public concerns, however muted they might actually be in public discourse, regarding individuals' privacy (see for instance [24]). The introduction of new identification technologies in itself cannot logically imply however that the monitoring and disciplining capabilities of these technologies will be used in practice and that privacy will be diminished *per se*. Our own research findings confirm this point of view by showing that new identification technologies can be introduced and used with few if any implications for individual privacy [2]. From a legal-normative point of view new forms of personal identification, authentication and IDM can be perceived as new vehicles to re-open a continuous, more profound battle for improving civil rights. In terms of innovation the introduction of these new technologies can be perceived as conceptual innovation, as it moves the focus in governance away from more restricted concerns regarding individuals' privacy to a more comprehensive personal identity point of view which for instance simultaneously takes into account privacy and security values.

6. Identity Cards as a Public Administration Domain of Understanding

"One of the properties of effective digital innovation is that it is often rendered invisible to the public, while remaining a transformative social presence" [11: 1]. What Davies seeks to indicate with this remark is the importance of looking beyond a new technology and its introduction and public use to be able to observe its innovative impact. We would like to add to this the importance of broadening the perspective and in so-doing looking behind the face value impressions of the technology. As ID cards in the UK have not been implemented thus far we would like to illustrate our point by focusing again on the history of the passport as an important predecessor of the ID card; two identification technologies with many characteristics in common.

If we look at the history of the passport we can observe what could be called a *révolution identificatoire* in the public domain of nation states [22]. Whereas the power to regulate citizen movements used to belong to private institutions like the church, or market institutions like serfdom, national governments succeeded in increasingly gaining authority over activities in which a person's status of national citizenship needed to be confirmed. By issuing official national identification papers like the passport, nation states have established the exclusive right to authorise and regulate the movement of people. As identification papers evolved into an administrative expression of national citizenship, citizens have become dependent on nation states for the possession of an official "identity" which may significantly shape their access to various spaces and activities.

Interestingly the first passports and passport controls for that matter were not so much used to regulate citizens' access to spaces beyond their home country as we are used to today, but to *prevent* people from leaving their home territory. Consequently those citizens leaving their Kingdom (for instance under the old regime in France) were required to be in possession of a passport authorising them to do so. The main purpose of these documentary requirements was to forestall any undesired migration to the cities, especially Paris [22: 21].

---

[7] Interestingly the generally acknowledged successful eID in Belgium did not raise any public concerns at its introduction but had a socially accepted paper-based ID card predecessor since the 2nd World War.

When geographically based citizen registrations were created and used for providing the personal details in passports, social distinctions started to be made between true 'citizens' and 'non-citizens', also to look for traitors who would obviously belong to the alien, non-citizen category. At that time the French government for instance decreed the establishment of civil status (*l'état civil*), which determined that an individual could only exist as a citizen once his or her identity had been registered by the municipal authorities, according to regulations that were the same throughout the national territory. Consequently passport controls to *enter* countries or districts became more extensive.

In the 19th century in Prussia, the practice could be found whereby incoming travellers were provided with a passport from the receiving state rather than by the state of the traveller's origin. These passports were no longer issued by local authorities but by higher-level officials. The foreigners and unknown persons circulating in the country were to be subjected to heightened scrutiny by the Prussian security forces, with the assistance of specific, legally defined[8] intermediaries like landowners, innkeepers and cart-drivers [22: 60]. In the late 19th century a generally liberal attitude of governments toward freedom of movement could be observed; a development which was stopped in the 20th century by national government's desires to regulate immigration, also targeted to restrict immigration of specific national groups (e.g. USA) and to stimulate economic opportunities for their own citizens abroad (e.g. Italy), to be able to better protect their country for suspicious people in times of war (e.g. Germany, UK, France), or to have the possibility to track their own nationals for conscription into their armies (e.g. Germany). Generally in the 19th and 20th century we may observe a development towards two models for citizenship attribution and the related issuing of passports to citizens, namely on the basis of *ius soli* ("law of the soil") and *ius sanguinis* ("law of the blood") (see for instance [25]). The latter model had to do with the development of enhanced mobility of citizens beyond the state's territorial boundaries, especially for economic reasons, and the possibility for nation states therefore to continuously keep a relationship with citizens living abroad.

It is very interesting to see the changing meanings, uses, and values attached to a similar technical means and process for personal identification through time, the passport. Besides values which seem to be obviously related to a citizen's personal identity, e.g. security and privacy, we can observe ownership, public safety, service, economic, and international migration values being applied by those institutions issuing passports. This historical analysis also makes us aware of the importance to perceive the use of IDM systems in non-evolutionary ways. For instance to look for 'punctuated equilibria' [26] in the evolution of identification systems, e.g. the periods of crisis during the history of the passport, as important moments where radical shifts happen in the use of these identity systems.

Moreover it provides us with several insights in shifts within and between public and private sector involvement in official identification and authentication processes, 'trusted third parties', such as city officials, higher level public officials, but also landowners, innkeepers and cart-drivers. Together with the passport issuing institutions these 'trusted third parties' have played an important role in the attribution of citizen's rights.

Insights like these may be of further importance when looking at current developments in IDM in e-government service provision. For instance, e-authentication

---

[8] The 1813 passport law in Prussia.

systems for electronic public service relationships between government and citizens are being developed which introduce new 'trusted third parties' or intermediaries outside government, so-called 'authentication solution providers', to check citizens' identity for electronic services that require stronger authentication levels. Examples of these intermediaries are banks, telecommunication providers, software companies and credit reference agencies.

From a public administration perspective we can observe that the introduction and use of the passport has fundamentally changed the relationship between governments and citizens, and has led to alternative developments and designs in citizenship attribution. We can conclude therefore that at least this particular identification technology has caused a *révolution identificatoire* and, through that, institutional innovation in the public domain between governments and citizens. From an innovation point of view the question remains over what new forms of personal identification, authentication and IDM will occur.

7. Further Analysis: Implications for Institutional Innovation

Looking through these different perspectives shows us that beyond the technical designs of newly available forms of personal identification and authentication for e-government service provision, which appear to have remarkable similarities, a whole variety of nuances resulting from differently chosen or confronted governmental, managerial, and democratic design aspects come to the surface. Where *technical* or even *legal-normative* standardization of these new identification and authentication systems for e-government service provision may appear to be an obvious development, other *public administration* factors of importance to the application and deployment of these systems seem to point in an opposite direction. In many countries we may acknowledge the presence of similar *instrumental* assessments of modernization efforts through the introduction of IDM, namely technical or legal e-ID and e-authentication policy designs, but with different *institutional* implications for further development of the e-government service domain in terms of governance, citizen-government relationships and citizenship.

What the public administration perspective reveals to us is the profound influence these new forms of personal identification and authentication may have on the governance of citizen-government relationships. Institutional innovation, the renewal of traditional citizen-government relationships as a result of the creation and development of new information practices, appears to be happening as a result of the introduction of IDM in e-government. As a result of these identification and authentication measures the nature of citizenship, which can be considered as a function of citizen-government relationships, is changing. Similarly to the analysis of the passport's history we may observe that borders between customers and non-customers of government organizations; identified or non-identified subjects of the state; authenticated citizens or non-authenticated citizens, are being reset as a result of these newly available forms of authentication and identity management in e-government relationships. Not only does the same authentication allow the possibility for government to provide people with access its virtual territories; it also allows governments to keep people out of them. Analogously to the Prussian era where intermediaries like landowners, innkeepers and cart-drivers supported the government in the checking and validation of a person's identity, new trusted third parties are emerging in the e-government domains in these countries to help government to check people upon their trustworthiness.

With these new digital forms of personal identification, authentication and identity management we seem to have arrived into a new *révolution identificatoire* in the public domain, where a law of informational identity, a so-called *ius informationis*, may soon replace the existing models of citizenship attribution in the analogue world, *ius soli* and *ius sanguinis*. We are now seeing the reworking of information on and about the citizen-as-consumer so as to classify, to "sort", the citizen in ways that enable the segmentation of the service being provided [27]. Citizen sorting opens the possibility that these forms of remote checking and validation will shape access to service in a variety of ways largely hidden to the end consumer, breaking down the historic eligibility of the citizen to service consumption, based on a universal access conception of citizenship.

What will happen in eras of crises with the application of this newly developing model of citizenship attribution remains to be seen. Whilst there is this chief concern with enhancing e-government service provision to entitled, trusted citizens, there is, nonetheless, recognition that the security agenda of modern government is adding to a climate wherein the identification of the citizen is seen as of paramount importance. If services to the citizen are to be provided effectively, then identity issues come to the fore. If enhanced personal and State security is paramount then, once more, the means of identifying individual citizens becomes of crucial importance.

References

[1] *EU Ministerial Declaration on e-Government*, 24 November 2005, Manchester, Ministerial eGovernment Conference 2005, Transforming Public Services, 2005, available at: http://www.egov2005conference.gov.uk/documents/proceedings/pdf/051124declaration.pdf.
[2] A.M.B. Lips, J.A. Taylor and J. Organ (2005), *Electronic Government: Towards New Forms of Authentication*, Citizenship and Governance, paper contribution to the Oxford Internet Institute's Cybersecurity Conference, 8-10 September 2005.
[3] J.A. Schumpeter, *Capitalism, Socialism and Democracy*, Harper, New York, 1942
[4] J.A. Taylor, A.M.B. Lips, and J. Organ, Freedom with Information: Electronic Government, Information Intensity and Challenges to Citizenship, in: *Freedom of Information: Perspectives on Open Government in a Theoretical and Practical Context*, R. Chapman and M. Hunt (eds.), Ashgate: Aldershot, 2006 (forthcoming).
[5] G.T. Marx, *Varieties of Personal Information as Influences on Attitudes Toward Surveillance*, Paper prepared for a Conference on 'The New Politics of Surveillance and Visibility', available at: http://web.mit.edu/gtmarx/www/vancouver.html, 2003.
[6] J. Fishenden, *eID: Identity Management in an Online World*, paper presented at the 5th European Conference on e-Government, Antwerpen, 2005.
[7] J.E.J. Prins and M. de Vries, *ID or not to be? Naar een doordacht stelsel voor digitale identificatie*, Rathenau Institute, Den Haag, 2003.
[8] E. Goffman, *Relations in Public; Microstudies of the Public Order*, Free Press, New York, 1971.
[9] M. Crompton, *Trust, Identity and Connected Government*, paper presented for The Evolution of e-Government: from Policy to Practice, a forum for the Research, Development and Evaluation Commission, Taipei, 24 June 2005.
[10] S. Hof, Arguments for a Holistic and Open Approach to Secure e-Government, in: R. Traunmüller and K. Lenk (eds.), *EGOV 2002*, LNCS 2456, Berlin/Heidelberg: Springer-Verlag, 2002, 464-467.
[11] W. Davies (2005), *Modernizing with Purpose: a Manifesto for a Digital Britain*, London: Institute for Public Policy Research, 2005.
[12] European Commission, *eEurope Action Plan 2005*, available at: http://europa.eu.int/information_society/eeurope/2005/all_about/action_plan/index_en.htm, 2005.
[13] Cragg Ross Dawson, *Public Perceptions of ID Cards,* Qualitative Research Report, COI Ref: 262 151, 2004.

[14] W.H. Dutton, C. di Gennaro & A. Millwood Hargrave, *The Internet in Britain: The Oxford Internet Survey* (OxIS), Oxford Internet Institute, University of Oxford, Oxford, 2005.

[15] Home Office (2003), *Identity Cards – A Summary of Findings from the Consultation Exercise on Entitlement Cards and Identity Fraud*, Cm 6019, London, 2003.

[16] Detica, *National Identity Cards: The View of the British Public*, 2004

[17] UK Information Commissioner press release, *'Information Commissioner Publishes Concern on IdentityCcards'*, 30 July 2004.

[18] The LSE, *The Identity Project. An Assessment of the UK Identity Cards Bill & its Implications*, The LSE Identity Project Interim Report, March 2005.

[19] Neville-Jones, Dame P Former Chair of QinetiQ. Reported on 18/10/05 by silicon.com, Lack of "balls" in 'Whitehall will hinder ID cards' Will Sturgeon, available at: http://www.silicon.com/publicsector/0,3800010403,39153447,00.htm.

[20] UK Passport Service Biometrics Enrolment Trial Report', available at: http://www.passport.gov.uk/downloads/UKPSBiometrics_Enrolment_Trial_Report.pdf, 2005.

[21] D. Bailey, *The Open Society Paradox: Why the 21st Century Calls for More Openness – not less*, Potomac Books, Virginia, 2004.

[22] J. Torpey, *The Invention of the Passport: Surveillance, Citizenship and the State*, Cambridge: Cambridge University Press, 2000

[23] J. Agar, *The Government Machine: a Revolutionary History of the Computer*, The MIT Press, 2003.

[24] A.F. Westin, Social and Political Dimensions of Privacy, *Journal of Social Issues*, **59**(2) (2003), 431-453.

[25] R. Brubaker, *Citizenship and Nationhood in France and Germany*, Harvard University Press, Cambridge, 1992.

[26] F. Baumgartner and B. Jones (eds.), *Policy Dynamics*, University of Chicago Press, Chicago, 2002.

[27] D. Lyon (ed.), *Surveillance & Social Sorting: Privacy, Risk and Digital Discrimination*, Routledge, London/New York, 2003.

Part 6

Instrumental and Institutional Assessment

Information and Communication Technology and Public Innovation
V.J.J.M. Bekkers et al. (Eds.)
IOS Press, 2006

E-Government is an Institutional Innovation

Albert MEIJER [a,1] and Stavros ZOURIDIS [b]

[a] *Utrecht School of Governance, the Netherlands*
[b] *Tilburg School for Politics and Public Administration, the Netherlands*

Abstract. The development of e-government stagnates in many countries. In this chapter we explore three different explanations for the difficulties of this type of innovation in the public sector. The first explanation concerns technological barriers and we conclude that these barriers are present but fast technological developments can be expected do deal with it. The second explanation concerns organizational barriers but these barriers cannot explain the overall stagnation of e-government innovations. The third explanation relates to institutional barriers and we conclude that these barriers may be difficult to overcome. We conclude that e-government should be seen as an institutional innovation. Following this conclusion we stress that institutional innovation may have undesired effects: technology may change the meaning of government and hollow out fundamental values. Therefore, we call for a public debate on the institutional innovation of government.

Keywords. E-government, Technological Barriers, Organizational Barriers, Institutional Change

1. Introduction

E-government has been presented as a key innovation in government. Throughout the world, e-government has become a key element of modernization and government reform programs. E-government has put a spell on public administration from Singapore to Uruguay and from the United States to Hong Kong. This worldwide movement is interesting from the perspective of information science and public administration science. For example, an interesting aspect of the worldwide e-government movement is the remarkable similarity between the e-government programs. On the surface, e-government initiatives appear to be somewhat similar throughout the world. Governments have redesigned their social security organizations, tax departments and education agencies to be able to put informational and transactional services on the world-wide web. Of course, different nations work at a different pace towards this goal and some countries are far ahead (like Singapore, Hong Kong and Korea) while others lag behind. But still the similarity between the programs

---

[1] Corresponding Author: Utrecht School of Governance, Bijlhouwerstraat 6, 3511 ZC Utrecht, the Netherlands; E-mail: a.meijer@usg.uu.nl.

and the direction in which e-government evolves is striking. E-government consultants and specialists tell us that it is only a matter of time before every government has made the transition to e-government.

All countries are developing e-government initiatives because e-government seems to offer a better future for government. The OECD highlights the 'case for e-government' which provides a good overview of arguments for e-government [1]. The OECD indicates that e-government improves efficiency and services and can help to build trust between governments and citizens. E-government helps to achieve specific policy outcomes and can contribute to economic policy objectives. And, finally, e-government can be a major contributor to reform in government. In view of all these desirable effects, the broad range of e-government initiatives around the world is hardly surprising.

How inspiring these digital dreams may be, the practice of e-government is much more a question of 'muddling through' [2]. This side of e-government is not very prominent at international conferences. We are dazzled by the success stories and case studies, sometimes told by the project champions (consultants and civil servants). Their principle message is: "in our country we used to have paper government in this policy sector (education, tax, social security), but now as you can see (via a direct Internet connection) we now have e-government." However, as impressive these case studies may sound, their resemblance sometimes becomes boring. This resemblance may also point to another phenomenon. Perhaps only the easy part of e-government has been achieved in most 'premier league' countries. After some basic transaction and information services have been put on the web, we tend to hear less about these e-government programs. And, in fact, in some countries we even observe a stagnation. A recent investigation, for example, shows that the development of e-government in Switzerland is stagnating [3]: "This stagnation is revealed by the freezing of the e-ID card project, the slow digitisation of public administration processes, the current failure of the e-government portal to become a true one-stop shop for public e-services, and the uncoordinated development of individual e-government applications by local authorities, due partly to insufficient exchange of best practices among public bodies."

What causes the stagnation of e-government after the primary public services have been put on the World Wide Web? Why are the promises of e-government not realized? Are technological problems to complicated to overcome? Is it because of the economic recession that innovative programs are being postponed? Do obscurantists and Luddites dominate public administration outside the basic services and prevent further development of e-government? Do we observe the usual implementation problems which are well known in public administration science? Ever since Pressman & Wildavsky's pioneering work on implementation we know that policy programs are seldom carried out according to plan. Is it just a matter of having more patience? [4]

In this paper we explore three possible groups of explanations. First, we assess whether the stagnation has to do with the *technology*. Does the technology not work adequately or are the beautiful simulations and prototypes difficult to implement in real organizations? Does the complex reality of public administration require solutions that present technology can not yet deliver? Second, we look at *organizational* barriers. Do bureaucratic politics hinder the exchange of information across organizations? Is it the power of professionals with an old-fashioned idea that implementing law should be a matter for humans instead of machines? Finally, we deal with the possibility of fundamental *institutional hindrances*. Does e-government clash with fundamental values that underlie public administration? Are democratic arrangements threatened by technological developments?

We conclude that the three groups of explanations for the slow development are relevant but observe that the institutional perspective receives little attention in debates on e-government. E-government is too often only regarded as a product, process and organizational innovation and substantial attention for e-government as an institutional innovation is lacking.. The discussion has moved from a debate on technological issues to a debate on organizational aspects. The institutional dimensions of technological developments in government have been recognized by scientists but still play a limited role in debates about e-government [5, 6, 7]. Patterns of signification, domination, and legitimation are neglected. We argue that ICT-students should learn to reflect on institutional transformations in government and, that a public debate about the institutional transformation of government is needed to make sure that we conclude with the kind of government we want. Substantial attention for institutional innovation is called for.

2. Immature Technology?

Governments all around the world have discovered the Internet and are using it to inform their citizens. Most governments have a central portal which offers access to a great variety of information about the government [8]. In that respect one could argue that the openness of government has increased and citizens are better informed about the dealings of their governments. However, the promises of e-government go much further than that. ICTs will not only improve the dissemination of government information but hold the potential for interaction, transaction and, finally, transformation. So far, however, not many governments have come much further than information and interaction [9, 10, 11, 12].

Janssen en Rotthier have conducted a comparative study on e-government implementation in eight countries [8]. Most government initiatives do not pass the point of the dissemination of information and interaction with citizens and few initiatives can be classified as transactions between government and citizens. Janssen en Rotthier show that the countries main aim is to realize e-service delivery but fail to realize their aspirations because they are still faced with deficient possibilities for a unique online authentication of citizens (cf. chapter 12 on Identity Management). Other technological requirements include the identification of citizens in the back office, security issues and a service delivery architecture. These identified barriers, however, are not of a permanent and structural nature.

In several countries, the technologies required for the further development of e-government are being developed at a high pace. Interesting projects in the Netherlands include the development of electronic authentication, a structure for trusted third parties and a Public Key Infrastructure (ww.minbzk.nl, www.digid.nl). The Belgium government has already developed an identity card for all citizens which enables digital identification and may speed up electronic service delivery (www.registrenational. fgov.be). The necessary technology for online transactions has already been implemented in the private sector and several governments have already developed successful applications for online transactions. Technological development is extremely fast and, although security will remain an issue that demands attention, the general opinion seems to be that the required technologies for e-government development will be developed in the next couple of years.

Another technological barrier may be the limited number of citizens who have access to the Internet. Governments can developed interesting applications for government transaction but if a majority of the citizens cannot access these websites, the use of the technology and thus the impact of e-government will be limited. The capacity of a country to profit from e-government is sometimes referred to as 'e-readiness': "the degree to which a community is prepared to participate in Networked World" [13]. Especially in Western Europe, the United States and Southeast Asia this can no longer be a valid argument for arguing against e-government since the Internet coverage and use has become high (although the digital divide does still merit attention). Finally, the bandwidth has enormously increased during the last decade. Nowadays even more sophisticated services can cheaply be distributed via the Internet.

At this point, proponents of e-government will emphasize that governments will need to tackle these technological issues. Technology may still be immature but it is maturing rapidly. Interesting approaches stress the relevance of information architectures that tackle the fragmented nature of technological solutions [14]. Solutions to technological problems and architectural designs will open the way for further development of e-government and create the opportunity to move on to the transaction and transformation phases.

A focus on technological barriers is usually found when e-government is regarded as a form of process and product innovation. One may wonder, however, whether these technological issues are the only barrier for the further development of e-government. Research has convincingly shown that the successful use of ICTs requires more than adequate technologies. Organizational factors influence the success of technological development (see [15] for a vivid illustration). A more sophisticated perspective on e-government also focuses on the organizational innovations in the public sector.

3. The Organization: Resistance and Leadership

It is generally acknowledged that adequate use of technologies requires an adequate organization. Organizational innovation is needed to realize the full benefits of information and communication technology. A classical adage of the IT business perfectly expresses this need: "If you automate a mess, you get an automated mess." Stories of organizational resistance to technological change are abundant (see [16] for some good examples). The importance of organizational change has been most clearly expressed by the Business Process Re-engineering (BPR) School [17, 18, 19, 20]. Proponents of BPR emphasize that we should deliberately put aside the existing system and redesign the process on the basis of the original meaning and its mission. Taylor et al.: "BPR's appeal lies in the simplistic rationalistic approach to the reconfiguring of the organization." [16: 15] One could argue that the rationalistic approach appeals to information managers working on the development of e-government.

The importance of overcoming organizational barriers for a transformation from government to e-government is clear and has been highlighted by various researchers [19, 21]. It is often stressed that back offices of government need to be reorganized for good front office service delivery. These changes especially concern standard processes for the production and distribution of public services (benefits and allowances, permits and grants). The processes in government organizations have to be rationalized and standardized to be able to profit from technological innovations. Also, the organization structures have to be adapted to the redesigned processes and this can be rather complicated (for example, the dissemination of government information via one portal). Organizational change can be hard to achieve. Within organizations, professionals often resist the implementation of information systems because they feel that their autonomy is threatened [16, 22]. On the interorganizational level, organizations are also hesitant to cooperate [23]. In public administration, cooperation across policy sectors is often considered to be difficult.

Change management is a key concept in theories on business process redesign. Management has to find ways to guide the organization through a process of change. This change seems to be hard to achieve, harder than in the private sector. Because of the lack of market pressures and incentives in public administration, change and innovation have to be explicitly enforced. In addition, public administration as an institution functions rather conservatively (see for example [24]). Caldow suggests that the role of leadership in promoting this change is crucial [25]. Strong leaders in public administration should have a firm view on e-government and convince employees and public organizations to proceed on the route to e-government. Furthermore, they need to be patient in order to implement the necessary transformation of persistent standard operating procedures.

The OECD has also emphasized the importance of leadership in e-government and has described key areas where leadership is particularly necessary for successful e-government implementation [1]. These areas are vision and political will, common frameworks and collaboration, customer focus and international cooperation. According to the OECD leadership can speed the process of government implementation, promote coordination within and among agencies and help reinforce good governance objectives: "Leaders drive e-government planning by setting a broad vision. At the same time, specific objectives can motivate action" [1: 2]. The OECD stresses that leaders play an important role in overcoming barriers to the development of e-government.

The question is not whether strong leadership and adequate change management are needed, we certainly agree on the need for leadership and change management, but whether they are sufficient. Is public administration lagging behind the private sector because there is a lack of strong leaders and inadequate change management? Or are there other factors to be considered? We suggest that the change from government to e-government is not only slow because of a lack of technological solutions and strong leaders but also because meaning, power and norms underlie present forms of government. E-government is a form of institutional innovation and, as is generally acknowledged, institutional change is a slow process. To understand the change from government to e-government we need to look at these institutional factors. Of course, 'organization' and 'institution' are two concepts that are connected to one another. While 'organization' refers to the level of processes, structures, strategies and systems, the concept of 'institution' encompasses the fundamental values, norms and belief systems that are deeply embedded in the organization's patterns of signification, domination and legitimation.

4. Government's Core Institutions: Obscurantist or Misunderstood?

Although the alleged inherent institutional meaning of information and communication technology has been disputed ever since its existence, there is hardly anybody who still holds the naive belief that information technology is a neutral instrument. An early interesting institutional approach of the interaction between information technology and its (organizational, cultural, and political) context can be found in the work of Shoshana Zuboff [26]. She argues that information technology always has two dimensions: an intrinsic dimension and a situational dimension. The intrinsic dimension refers to the potential of change that is connected with technology. At the same time, the changes that occur cannot be attributed solely to the technology. She argues: "Between the turning of the rim and the emergence of a new pattern, there is another force that infuses the final configuration with meaning: the human activity of choice" [26: 388].

In her widely acclaimed article Orlikowski has used Giddens' structuration theory to understand the relation between information technology and organizations [27]. She stresses the duality of technology: institutional properties influence humans in their interaction with technology and at the same time interaction with technology influences the institutional properties of an organization. Following Giddens' work, Orlikowski indicates that there are three fundamental elements of social interaction: meaning, power and norms. Interpretative schemes play a key role in constituting and communicating meaning and result in structures of signification. Power is understood as 'transformative capacity' and results in structures of domination. Norms are expressed in normative sanctions and result in structures of legitimation. These three structures structure social interaction but are also reinforced and challenged through social interaction.

Institutional theory has always played a key role in the science of public administration and this theory is helpful for understanding processes of institutional innovation. This paper is too confined to deal with all the relevant institutions. Some of the most important institutions – structures of signification, domination and legitimation – are discussed to indicate how these institutions work and why they are so important to understand the transition from government to e-government. The stagnation of e-government may be due to the following institutions:

Division of powers. The division of executive, legislative and legal powers is a core institution in public administration. This division is regarded to be crucial in preventing the abuse of public authority. In e-government, the division of powers may be challenged since, from an ICT-perspective, it may be rational to integrate information systems of executive, legislative and legal powers. This seems more efficient but it leads to questions concerning safeguards against the abuse of public authority.

Rule of law. The rule of law provides safeguards against the power of state organs in western societies. Governments do not only function in democratic contexts but also have to abide by general rules. Governments cannot decide freely on their actions and decisions, but they are disciplined by legal principles, such as legal security and legal equality. In the context of e-government, these rules can form obstacles to effective and efficient information systems and from an ICT-perspective these rules often seem irrational.

Government by the people. In essence democracy is based on government by the people and for the people. This implies that government decisions concerning the design of information systems can be altered when the people, for example through elections, have indicated that they do not agree with these decisions. From an ICT-perspective government can then seem to be lacking stability and this can hamper the development of large information systems.

Bureaucracy. The term 'bureaucracy' is often used in a derogatory manner but also embodies important values like neutrality, equal treatment, and democratic control. Hierarchy is an essential element of bureaucracy but communication technologies can challenge this hierarchy. Bureaucracies have been criticized for their failure to deal with dynamic environments and network organizations seem more rational from an ICT-perspective. The uncertainty is, however, whether neutrality, equal treatment, and democratic control can be preserved in network organizations.

These institutional barriers are sometimes regarded as legal obstacles: law and regulations should be changed to enable e-government (see e.g. www.egovbarriers.org). Although this argument may have some validity – e.g. certain legal regulations do not allow for digital signatures while these present a functional equivalent to paper signatures – institutions also point to a the values that underlie laws and regulations. Laws may be changed and allow for new practices when there is broad consensus about the need for these changes. Law making is then a technical exercise that requires much expertise and should be carried out well. The Dutch law concerning the digital signature is an example of overcoming legal barriers to e-government [28]. When key institutions of government are at stake such as the division of powers and government by the people, law making is not a technical expertise but is directly related to structures of signification, domination and legitimation.

These institutions can help us understand why good technology and strong leadership may sometimes not be sufficient for a transformation to e-government since this transformation takes place within these institutional structures. The structuration theory and Orlikowski's interpretation of it also stress that structures are not only reinforced but also challenged in social interactions. This means that the transformation from government to e-government results in institutional innovation. We call for a better understanding of this process of institutional innovation.

5. Government as an Information Machine and a Seamless Web

Since we are now in the middle of a process of institutional innovation in government, it is difficult to grasp the essence of the changes. Snellen & van de Donk have tried to catch the essence of the present institutional changes in ten 'statements' [6]. These statements refer to themes such as the territorial foundations of the state, the balance between the public and the private sphere, discretionary power of bureaucrats, the foundations of bureaucracy and the structure of policymaking processes. These statements are meant to form the 'embyonic' building blocks of a theory on public administration in an information age. They admit, however, that their answers are still somewhat ambiguous.

Snellen & Van de Donk's approach is based on a careful analysis of empirical research into the use of ICTs in government. Is there another way to comprehend the institutional innovation in government? Marshall McLuhan's 'the medium is the message' can help us to understand the present institutional transformation in government [29]. Following Marshall McLuhan, Neil Postman argues that a specific ideology is hidden behind every technology. Every seemingly neutral technical instrument is tied up with (hidden) ideological bias. Although one is able to use a hammer in numerous ways, to a man with a hammer everything looks like a nail. Postman proceeds: 'To a man with a pencil everything looks like a list. To a man with a camera, everything looks like an image. To a man with a computer, everything looks like data. And to a man with a grade sheet, everything looks like a number' [30]. Crucial to Postman's argument is the idea that the use of technology leads to a change in the meaning of concepts. He indicates that the introduction of writing changed what is meant by 'wisdom' from 'knowing much about life' to 'having read many texts'. The question we are facing now is what is going to happen with the concept of 'government'. How is technology changing the meaning of 'government'?

Technology has changed the meaning of 'government' before. Before the introduction of bureaucracy, personal preferences and a personal treatment were seen as crucial elements of government. Postman describes how the introduction of bureaucracy has led us to think of government as an impersonal machine as described most explicitly in Kafka's novels [30: 83–87]. Bureaucracy has also changed our ideas of what domains government should work in and government now claims sovereignty over all of society's affairs. Bureaucracy also changed our view of the work of civil servants: government work is no longer requires moral judgments but consists of loyal execution of tasks. In that sense, as Postman provocatively indicates, Adolf Eichman is the basic model and metaphor for a bureaucrat.

Now let us try to develop a perspective on present changes in the meaning of the concept 'government'. According to the ideology of information technology, everything is essentially a matter of information collection, information processing and information dissemination. When we believe the e-government ideology, government essentially becomes a matter of information. Whether this is done manually or by computers, it will be the same process. Citizens are better served when the computers process the information, because they are more efficient and more reliable. An interesting example concerns discussion on the exchange of information concerning criminal justice [31]. In the United Kingdom the complex separation of powers and of functions is challenged by the introduction of by an information system meant to coordinate information exchanges between the various actors. This system makes government more efficient but does it provide adequate guarantees against abuse of power? Government is not only about efficient policy execution and efficient service delivery but also about competing values. In criminal justice the values of efficiency and protection against the abuse of power are competing. Will there still be room for fundamental debates on competing values in e-government or will all debates be framed in terms of efficient information processing?

The ideology behind communication technologies seems to be "making connections" [32]. In their rich description of changes in organizations that occur when electronic communications are introduced, they highlight that people start communicating that were previously divided by organizational barriers. Boundaries disappear when communication technologies are introduced since time and place become less important. Building on Sproull and Kiesler's argument, Bekkers indicates that the boundaries between public organizations are fading away [33]. And, following Castells, these boundaries concern boundaries between countries, boundaries between the different powers within a state and boundaries in organizations [34]. Translating this argument, one could state that government may turn into a seamless web. This seamless web will not be limited to the public sector: communication technologies will also increase the connections with citizens and the private sector. This development seems desirable: exclusion of people on other sides of boundaries may be a thing of the past. Yet, as Castells describes, not everybody will be included in this web. You are either in the web or outside of it. The excluded may turn to crime, fundamentalism, and even terrorism. Will e-government – in spite of all the efforts aimed at diminishing the digital divide – be government for all people or government for those tuned in to the network?

6. Debating the Future of Government

In line with McLuhan's 'the medium is the message' we have indicated a probable outcome of the institutional innovation of government. In the future 'government' may refer to a network for efficient information processing. Efficiency may develop into the core value of government and it may work for those that are tuned into the network. In line with Giddens' structuration theory we want to emphasize that these outcomes are not deterministic. Orlikowski also indicates that technologies are interpretively flexible [27]. Shaping of e-government takes place through the actions of a wide variety of actors ranging from ICT-specialists to public managers and lawyers. Postman adds that technologies have advantages and disadvantages and every society needs to deal with this: "A bargain is struck in which technology giveth and technology taketh away" [30: 5].

This leads us to the following questions that direct our attention away from technological and organizational innovation and towards institutional innovation. How we can use the interpretative flexibility of information and communication technologies to reshape public institutions? Can we avoid the transformation of government to a single-minded information machine? Can we avoid large groups of people being excluded from government? What can we learn from the history of current institutions and how can these lessons be used in the formation of the institutions of e-government? Underlying these questions is the fundamental question: what kind of government do we want?

These questions concerning the future of government cannot be answered by experts and civil servants. Baptista warns us that "the transnational e-government agenda provides a number of pre-made choices deemed to be applicable to all situations regardless of political preferences and often presented as the inevitable result of technological progress" [35: 493]. He argues for politicizing e-government and emphasizes that e-government should be debated in the *political system*. In regard of the impact of these institutional changes, we argue for not only a debate in the political system but think that a *public debate* on the transition from government to e-government is required. Institutional innovation will catch us by surprise as long as the debate about e-government is only seen in technological and organizational terms. E-government is not only a government that is more effective and efficient, e-government is about new structures for signification, domination and legitimation. Because e-government is a political and institutional movement, it needs to be politically and institutionally debated (see for example [36]).

Shaping a public debate about the future of government is not easy. It is extremely difficult to get a grasp of the changes that are taking place around us. But the alternative seems even less preferable. Up to now, the institutional innovation of our governments takes place implicitly. Currently, scholars, consultants, and public managers concentrate on the instrumental and technical levels. We think that a debate should take place in a formal setting such as in Parliament and in universities but also in informal settings like on the Internet. Furthermore, we should not only focus on a rational debate but should stimulate artists and science fiction writers to join in the debate. This debate will not result in collective decision-making but will enhance the level of collective reflection and therefore, hopefully, improve decisions on e-government.

References

[1] OECD, *Checklist for e-Government Leaders*, Policy Brief, available at: http://www.oecd.org/dataoecd/62/58/11923037.pdf (accessed 7 June 2005), 2003.
[2] C.E. Lindblom, The Science of Muddling Through, *Public Administration Review* **19**(2) (1959), 79-88.
[3] European Communities, 'Swiss e-Government Still Below Expectations, Survey Reveals', eGovernment News, March 2005, available at: http://europa.eu.int/idabc/en/document/4025/5791 (accessed 7 June 2005), 2005.
[4] J.L. Pressman and A.B. Wildawsky, *Implementation*, University of California Press, Berkeley, CA., 1973.
[5] C.A. Bellamy and J.A. Taylor, *Governing in the Information Age*, Open University Press, Milton Keynes, 1998.
[6] I.Th.M. Snellen and W.H.B.J. van de Donk, Towards A Theory Of Public Administration In An Information Age, in: *Public Administration in an Information Age. A Handbook*, I.Th.M. Snellen and W.H.B.J. van de Donk (eds.), IOS Press, Amsterdam, 1998, 3-19.
[7] J.E. Fountain, *Building the Virtual State. Information Technology and Institutional Change*, Brookings Institution, Washington, DC., 2001.
[8] D. Janssen and S. Rotthier, *How Are They Doing Elsewhere? Trends and Consolidations in e-Government Implementation*, Paper presented at the annual EGPA Conference, Oeiras, 2003. (In their research they have compared the following countries: Belgium, Canada, Finland, France, Germany, Ireland, the Netherlands and the United Kingdom).
[9] Accenture, *eGovernment Leadership - Realizing the Vision*, available at: www.accenture.com, 2002.
[10] Cap Gemini Ernst & Young, *Online availability of Public Services: How does Europe Progress?*, Web Based Survey on Electronic Public Services, available at: www.capgemini.com, 2003.
[11] Gartner Group, *Western Europe Government Sector: IT Solution Opportunities*, available at: www.gartner.com, 2000.
[12] UN-ASPA, *Benchmarking E-government: A Global Perspective. Assessing the Progress of the UN Member States*, New York, 2002.
[13] Center for International Development at Harvard University, Readiness for the Networked World, *A Guide for Developing Countries*, available at: http://cyber.law.harvard.edu/readinessguide/guide.pdf, (accessed 7 June 2005), 2003.
[14] M. Janssen and R. Wagenaar, Developing Generic Shared Services for e-Government, *Electronic Journal of e-Government* **2**(1) (2004), available at: www.ejeg.com (accessed 7 June 2005).
[15] S. Clarke, B. Lehaney and H. Evans, A Study of a U.K. Police Call Centre, in: *Information Technology and Organizations: Trends, Issues, Challenges and Solutions*, M. Khosrow-Pour (ed.), Idea Group, Hershey PA, 2003, 216 – 219.
[16] J.R. Taylor, C. Groleau, L. Heaton and E. van Every, *The Computerization of Work. A Communication Perspective*, Sage Publications, Thousand Oaks, 2001.
[17] M. Hammer and J. Champy, *Reengineering the Corporation. A Manifesto for Business Revolution*, Harper Collins, New York, 1993.
[18] T.H. Davenport, *Process Innovation: Reengineering Work Through Information Technology*, Harvard Business School Press, Boston, 1993.
[19] C. Bellamy and J.A. Taylor, Reinventing Government in the Information Age, *Public Money and Management* **14**(3) (1994), 59-62.
[20] J.A. Taylor, I.Th.M. Snellen and A. Zuurmond, *Beyond BPR in Public Administration*, IOS Press, Amsterdam, 1997.
[21] O. O'Donell, R. Boyle and V. Timonen, Transformational Aspects of E-Government in Ireland: Issues to Be Addressed, *Electronic Journal of e-Government* **1**(1) (2003), available at: www.ejeg.com (accessed 7 June 2005).
[22] A. Zuurmond, *De infocratie: een theoretische en empirische heroriëntatie op Weber's ideaaltype in het informatietijdperk*, Phaedrus, Den Haag, 1994.

[23] V.M.F. Homburg, *The Political Economy of Information Management. A Theoretical and Empirical Analysis of Decision Making regarding Interorganizational Information Systems*, Labyrint Publication, Capelle aan de Ijssel, 1999.

[24] J. Jacobs, *Systems of survival. A Dialogue on the Moral Foundations of Commerce and Politics*, New York, 1994.

[25] J. Caldow, *Seven E-Government Leadership Milestones*, available at: http://www.ieg.ibm.com/thought_leadership/Seven_E-Gov_Milestones.pdf , (accessed 9 September 2003), 2001.

[26] S. Zuboff, *In the Age of the Smart Machine. The Future of Work and Power*, Basic Book, New York, 1988.

[27] W.J. Orlikowski, The Duality of Technology: Rethinking the Concept of Technology in Organizations, *Organization Science* **39**(3) (1992), 398-427.

[28] M.M. Groothuis, *Beschikken en digitaliseren. Over normering van de elektronische overheid*, Sdu Uitgevers, Den Haag, 2004.

[29] M. McLuhan, *Understanding Media: The Extensions of Man*, McGraw-Hill, New York, 1964.

[30] N. Postman, *Technopoly. The Surrender of Culture to Technology*, New York, 1993.

[31] C. Bellamy, ICTs and Governance: Beyond Policy Networks? The Case of the Crminal Justice System, in: *Public Administration in an Information Age. A Handbook*, I.Th.M. Snellen and W.H.B.J. van de Donk (eds.), IOS Press, Amsterdam, 1998, 293-306.

[32] L. Sproull and S. Kiesler, *Connections. New Ways of Working in the Networked Organization*, The MIT Press, Cambridge (Massachusetts), 1991.

[33] V.J.J.M. Bekkers, Wiring Public Organizations and Changing Organizational Jurisdictions, in: *Public Administration in an Information Age. A Handbook*, I.Th.M. Snellen and W.H.B.J. van de Donk (eds.), IOS Press, Amsterdam, 1998, 57-78.

[34] M. Castells, *The Rise of the Network Society*, Blackwell Publishers, Cambridge MA., 1996.

[35] M. Baptista, The Transnational e-Government Agenda: Key Policy Issues for the European Union and its Member States, in: *Proceedings of the 5th European Conference on E-Government*, D. Remenyi (ed.), Academic Conferences, Reading, 2005, 493-501.

[36] S. Zouridis and M. Thaens, E-government: towards a public administration approach, *The Asian Journal of Public Administration* **25**(2),159-184.

[37] H. Mullen, Ethical Problems for e-Government: An Evaluative Framework, *Electronic Journal of e-Government* **2**(3) (2004), available at: www.ejeg.com (accessed 7 June 2005).

Information and Communication Technology and Public Innovation
V.J.J.M. Bekkers et al. (Eds.)
IOS Press, 2006

Creative Destruction of Public Administration Practices: An Assessment of ICT-Driven Public Innovations

Hein van DUIVENBODEN [a,1], Victor BEKKERS [b] and Marcel THAENS [c]

[a] *Capgemini & Tilburg University, Tias Business School, the Netherlands*
[b] *Erasmus University Rotterdam, Faculty of Social Sciences, the Netherlands*
[c] *Ordina & Erasmus University Rotterdam, Faculty of Social Sciences, the Netherlands*

Abstract. What conclusions can be drawn from a comparison of the previous chapters regarding the nature of ICT-driven public innovation? After a brief description of the main findings, we conclude that enhancing efficiency is the most important goal or value which lay behind many public innovation projects. We conclude that the public innovation agenda has a rather mechanistic character, which also influences the use and appreciation of ICT. A managerial , and thus internal, perspective prevails. This one-sidedness can be diminished, if ICT-driven public innovations focus on the concrete manifestations of societal problems. An alternative public innovation strategy is elaborated.

Keywords. Public Innovation Assessment, Efficiency, Ecology, Evolution, Social Embedding, Trust, Multi-rationality, Societal Agenda

1. Introduction

As stated in our introductory chapter, the aim of this book has been to asses the innovation potential of ICT for different kinds of public innovations, the conditions under which these innovations take place and the innovative effects that actually have occurred due to the use of ICT. In this chapter, we will shortly summarize the answers to these questions, based on the contributions in this book. First, we will present a birds-eye view of the findings of previous chapters (section two). Secondly, we will go deeper into these findings and will present a number of striking observations. One of these observations is that many ICT-driven public innovations have a rather internal oriented driver, which is efficiency. The use of ICT to create a more responsive government, which tries to place the potential of ICT in the centre of societal problems, like the social quality of neighbourhoods, the regeneration of regions or the effects of the aging of the population, is rather scarce. Therefore, we conclude that the modernization agenda of public administration is rather one-dimensional. A rather

---

[1] Corresponding Author: Capgemini and Tias Business School, Public and Non-Profit Department, Tilburg University, P.O. Box 90153, 5000 LE Tilburg, The Netherlands; E-mail: h.vanduivenboden@tias.edu.

mechanistic view prevails (section three). In order to overcome this one-sidedness we will present an alternative ICT-driven public innovation strategy (section four).

2. A Birds-eye View on ICT-driven Public Innovations

We have started our *tour d'horizon* with a comparison of a number of modernization policy statements of different European countries. When comparing and analyzing the official Danish, Dutch, British and German modernization programs, it seems that changing societal conditions and a lack of problem-solving capability call for a transformation of public administration into a new, more responsive and citizen-oriented government, but that a profound analysis of these conditions in relation to the role and position of government has not been made. This also influences the way in which the use of ICT is being assessed. Bekkers and Korteland notice that the main emphasis lies in the improvement of the quality of public service delivery: 'demand-orientation, public participation and improving openness and responsiveness are all relevant aspects which return in the documents studied.' In practice, however, it looks like improving internal efficiency is a by far the most important goal of the innovation projects, which also lies beyond the most dominant shift of governance, which has been detected in the policy documents studied. Self-regulation and self-government are being viewed as necessary shifts in governance to contribute to the internal efficiency of public administration. These shifts have been further operationalized in terms of decentralization to local, regional and functional bodies of government, a larger role of the private sector and the civil society in providing services and a greater responsibility of the citizen, primarily as an active consumer who participates in the design of service delivery processes. ICT is viewed as instrument to achieve these goals and to facilitate this shift of governance. As a result, Bekkers and Korteland see the rise of a new public administration. They observe the emergence of a consumer democracy, blended with ideas about New Public Management, complementary to the existing democratic order. Modernization primarily takes place through a shift of governance towards the citizen as a consumer, which a) should be empowered so that he is able, more than before, to act as a 'homo economicus' who actually has a choice (Denmark), b) can obtain more client-friendlier and more cost efficient services (Denmark, UK, Netherlands, Germany), c) can participate as co-producer in the way services should be provided (Denmark, UK) in order to strengthen the responsiveness and need-orientation of the public service delivery process (Denmark, Germany, UK). The second implication is that government can only meet the challenges of a more integrated, more responsive way of delivering public services, if it functions as an efficient machine, which can be achieved by a) deregulation, b) reducing 'red tape' and c) monitoring the outcomes produced by the machinery of government in terms of value for money, focussing on quality and efficiency, d) improving the collaboration between the 'cogwheels in the machinery of government' (collaboration between layers of government and agencies), e) through the introduction of more 'management techniques' which come from the private sector and f) strengthening the central control of the functioning of machinery of government by on the one hand giving more autonomy but on the other hand focussing on specific parameters. From this point of view ICT is primarily seen as an instrument to improve the functioning of the cogwheels in the machinery of government, because service delivery processes can be redesigned in a more efficient and effective way, while at the same time it offers new possibilities for designing an administrative system which functions as an cybernetic system in which more and better information – for instance about the outcomes of the service delivery process and the needs of citizens – enables government to govern more effective. From this point of view government is seen as an 'information processor' in which the use of ICT is primarily defined as information management. This observation has been confirmed by the many contributions in this book. Therefore, we will address this issue more in detail in the next sections.

Process Innovation

In the category of process innovation, which focuses on the improvement of the quality and efficiency of the internal and external business processes, like processes of rule application and service delivery, Snijkers has presented two Belgian case studies: the Crossroads Bank for Social Security (CBSS) and the Crossroads Bank for Companies (CBC). In both cases ICT played an important role in redesigning processes of several parties involved. In the case of the CBSS, a distinction was made between the official goals of more efficiency, customer orientation and better policy support versus an unofficial but perhaps just as serious goal of better fraud detection and prevention. For political reasons, the formal focus was on 'positive goals', which would facilitate an increase of customer satisfaction, instead of on increasing law enforcement activities that could irritate one of the major stakeholders in the project – the trade unions. In practice, however, fraud detection and prevention has become an important feature of CBSS-related activities. On the issue of institutional innovation, because the Crossroads Banks function as clearing houses no large reorganization of structures has become visible, but some adjustments in task allocation between the different administrations have been made. Interesting is the role of private parties in the case of CBC: they have joined the modernization project as they could see that the new Company Counters would present new possibilities for them in offering services to companies in the near future, such as insurances or HR-services. For these private intermediaries in the public sphere, new forms of collaboration with government agencies seem to be worthwhile if there's a prospect of increasing commercial activities.

On the basis of an international research project of best practices of ICT in European public administration, Driessen has given a description of four cases in which different ICT-innovations were implemented to improve public service delivery: the Danish State Education Fund (SU-Agency), the Estonian Tax and Customs Board (e-Maksuamet), the Finnish Ministry of Environment (VAHTI) and the German Bremen Online Services (BOS). These cases behold of various types of process innovation, such as the introduction of pro-active services, automation of risk assessment processes and online transaction processes on the basis of a public private partnership. All of these practices show that the use of ICT alone is not sufficient to create new, innovative forms of public administration practices; organizational changes in the back office of all parties involved were needed to actually improve service delivery and internal efficiency (see also chapters 8 and 11). Driessen also states that ICT-projects tend to fail if the take-up by citizens or business is insufficient because then the goals of modernization will simply not be attained (see also chapter 7). In terms of institutional change one can observe that these changes often follow changes in the division of power, which, in turn, are often founded on alterations in the control over data and information. The motto 'knowledge is power' still seems to be true, but in slightly different sense; it used be important to possess knowledge itself, but now it becomes much more important to have power over the (ways of) distribution or data, information and knowledge. The cases Driessen describes show that whoever plays a dominant role in controlling the ICT-system, also has a power advantage over other parties involved. At the same time, technology often can be seen as a driver for (public of public-private) collaboration, which may offer smaller parties or even citizens or individual businesses advantages that fit a new, more responsive government (e.g. SU-Agency or Maksuamet).

Thaens, Bekkers and Van Duivenboden focus on combinations of political, technological, economic and legal agreements (as aspects of an information architecture) which organizations develop to exchange information in a flexible way within a policy chain or network. Two types of information architectures in the Dutch social security (RINIS and Suwinet) are presented in order to answer the question, whether organizations collaborating in a policy chain or network, will be able to adapt to changing circumstances once many information-processing processes have been computerized. Flexibility is seen as an important condition for process innovation. In both cases information politics has played an important role in the development of information architectures that will facilitate further improvement of efficiency and effectivity. Depending on the outcomes of political 'negotiation processes' in different organizational settings sets of multi-party agreements have been made which vary in form and flexibility. In this process of architecture development, the politico-administrative setting and judicial context prove to be of more influence than information management or technological aspects. Therefore, one of the conclusions is that technology itself is not a bottleneck for flexibility of information architectures; the structure of the policy chain and the quality of the collaboration process are much more important when it comes to building robust partnerships that strengthen the adaptive capacity of cooperatives.

Product and Technological Innovation

Cases of product and technological innovation, in which the emphasis is on the creation of new public services and products through the creation of new technologies, are described and assessed by Bekkers and Moody (Geographic Information Systems – GIS – and mobile government) and Smith and Webster (Interactive Digital Television, iDTV). The GIS cases demonstrate the innovative potential of a special technology (GIS) to enhance the rationality of policy design process in public administration. Two advantages can be put forward. First, GIS makes it possible to enhance the transparency of rather 'wicked policy problems' through the combination of different data and data models with location-based information. The second advantage is that GIS can help to visualize the 'state of the art' of specific problems as well as visualize the effects of specific developments or policy measures. However, is this potential being realized? From an instrumental point of view it is reported that GIS has contributed to the rationality of the policy formulation process, but that the possible advantages of GIS were not fully used because of: a) the lack of nation wide geographical infrastructure, b) the lack of a systematic information strategy in which basic geographical needs were explicitly addressed and c) the fact that geo-information and GIS are important powerful resources in negotiation processes. From an institutional point of view Bekkers and Moody have observed some contradictionary results. First, they witness that GIS provokes resistance and may frustrate innovation, because it touches upon the existing working practices and routines of the involved professionals. GIS presupposes standardization, which is perceived as a threat to the discretion of these planning professionals. Secondly, GIS has been strategically used to generate information that is used to legitimize the decisions that have been made afterwards. Thirdly, and perhaps this is the most interesting observation, GIS could contribute to a policy formulation mode that can be described as 'reversed mixed planning'.

In the case of iDTV, a number of initiatives have been reviewed which aimed at testing the feasibility of interactive technology to deliver services directly to citizens. In doing so, Smith and Webster have looked into the possibility of this new form of service delivery being responsible for changes in the citizens-state relationship. Parallel to the cases of Driessen (chapter 4) the iDTV cases show us that it is important for the success of modernization initiatives to mobilize the actual use of the new services that have been introduced. In doing just that, it helps if one makes use of pilots to let users get accustomed to rather far-reaching technological changes and to learn from these pilots by trial and error. Furthermore, it is essential for the success or failure of innovation projects to base its form and contents on the actual wants and needs of the citizens instead of letting the possibilities of new technologies lead the format of the new services. This so-called citizen-oriented approach can be further improved if innovations are closely connected to the existing manners and technologies that people already feel comfortable with; innovations should not be introduced and presented as a completely new form of service delivery without any relation to current ways of interacting between citizens and government. Finally, as also observed in other chapters (e.g. 3, 4 and 13), one can only observe a modest number of institutional changes as a result of modernization projects – in terms of shifts in positions or governance structures.

Organizational Innovation

Organizational innovations focus on the creation of new organizational forms, the introduction of new management methods and techniques, and new working methods. In this book, Wagenaar et al. deal with the dilemmas and trade-offs that can play an important role when deciding on the implementation of Shared Service Centres (SSC's). An interorganizational HRM-SSC project in the Netherlands (P-direct) shows us many of the risks involved and dilemma's one faces in design and implementation of this popular form of organizational innovation. In the chapter of Wagenaar et al. the importance of the implementation phase is further highlighted by pointing at the key role standardization of technology and procedures (cf. chapter 6) can play together with the idea that there's no successful ICT-innovation without the necessary adjustments of organizational structure or routines such as operating procedures (see also chapters 2, 4 and 12).

Soeparman and Wagenaar look into the efforts to create a national information infrastructure in the Dutch police sector, where ICT seems to have been functioning as a catalyst for organizational innovation. Interestingly, they show us some indirect effects of ICT by illustrating that the introduction of a joint ICT-infrastructure can lead or at least contribute to the development of more horizontal forms of coordination and collaboration. They also state that in some cases financial resources are indeed crucial for ICT-innovation – especially if the allocation of budget on a central (or joint) level is necessary in order to create sufficient 'economies of scale' (see also chapters 4 and 11).

Conceptual and Institutional Innovation

If innovations occur in relation to the introduction of new concepts, frames, references or even new paradigms (of governing or steering policy or implementation processes), *conceptual innovations* could be in place. In line with this, *institutional* innovations are focused at the renewal of traditional institutions and institutional structures (including existing practices, positions and relationships within public administration). Edwards discusses the relationship between public innovation and the empowerment of local communities in terms of their capacity to participate in decision-making processes. He presents the case of the city of Cleveland (Ohio, USA) that shows us several citizen-government partnerships in the area of environmental sustainability. This case learns us that the success of innovation often depends on a variety of factors such as the availability of a (national) infrastructure that serves as a platform for further development (see also chapters 5 and 9) or certain minimum of relevant knowledge and experience of the people or organizations that develop or have to work with new systems or services. Furthermore, in Cleveland's innovation project (mis)trust shows to be of substantial importance for the success or failure – trust between partners in the modernization initiative but also trust between e.g. regulatory agencies and citizens (cf. chapter 3).

Burt and Taylor evaluate the UK government's proposal for an 'electronic mixed economy of public service delivery' that should engage public, private, and voluntary organizations as intermediaries in the delivery of public services. They make use of the case of the Citizens Advice Service to assess the conceptual, institutional and technological arrangements that underpin this form of public innovation. Parallel to the observations made by Driessen and by Soeparman and Wagenaar (chapters 4 and 9), the allocation of costs and benefits is of substantial importance in the implementation phase of innovation projects. Not seldom there is a chance of an unequal distribution of costs and benefits amongst all the parties involved in which case the availability of a central fund could offer a way out – as has been the case in the initiative of the Citizens Advice Service and in the case of Bremen Online Services. Furthermore, like many other authors, Burt and Taylor show us that the development or availability of a joint (standardized) infrastructure that is used by a large number of organizations is one of the key success factors for innovation. Another critical factor for the success of the electronic mixed economy is the development of good collaboration practices between public and private organizations (cf. chapter 3 and 4).

Lips, Taylor and Organ look into the phenomenon of identity management (IDM). More specifically, they deal with the question if, and if so in what respect and to what extent, forms of electronic identification and authentication (e.g. using identity cards) are actually causing a renewal of traditional institutions within the sphere of public administration. As drivers for IDM they point at customer convenience, citizen mobility and empowerment, efficiency and/or effectiveness and the enhancement of public safety and security. Interestingly, they connect the issue of public safety and security to the issue of general law enforcement, which in turn seems to be primarily aimed at increasing efficiency and effectivity (as is the case in many public innovation initiatives). Like other authors, they place some question marks on the feasibility of the plans when it comes to the actual implementation of the promising initiatives. For example, on the introduction of ID-cards they state that '(…) critical voices point at seemingly unrealistic technical expectations of the ID card scheme, using arguments such as the fact that neither the major contractors nor the government have shown themselves capable of organizing and implementing an outsourced IT scheme on this scale: no country has attempted to use biometrics technologies to register a population the size of the UK.' And: '(…) has there ever been an identification system which is 100 per cent accurate?' These kinds of questions express the general feeling of more authors who seem to be concerned about underestimating the complexity of the implementation phase (e.g. chapter 8). The introduction of many ICT-driven public innovations is dominated by a one-sided focus on technology. As a result, there is too little attention for the innovative potential of the modernization initiatives themselves and for the possibilities to challenge existing practices and positions. In other words, in most cases the 'creative destruction' is often limited to destructing the currently used technologies and does not include reinventing the existing politico-administrative or democratic processes. However, Lips et al. do see some possible indirect effects of IDM-related innovations that could have a deeper impact on the way government interacts with citizens and businesses than many direct (and formally stated) goals and their effects: 'What the public administration perspective reveals to us is the profound influence (…) new forms of personal identification and authentication may have on the governance of citizen-government relationships. Institutional innovation, the renewal of traditional citizen-government relationships as a result of the creation and development of new information practices, appears to be happening as a result of the introduction of IDM in e-government. As a result of these identification and authentication measures the nature of citizenship, which can be considered as a function of citizen-government relationships, is changing.'

3. Beyond A Mechanistic Oriented Public Innovation Agenda?

In chapter 13, Meijer and Zouridis have given several explanations (concerning technological, organizational and institutional barriers) for what they call the stagnation of eGovernment in many countries and conclude that the concept of eGovernment itself should be seen as an institutional innovation in order to be able to discuss the future of public administration properly. Like Lips et al., they show us that public innovations can have important indirect effects, but not only in a positive way. If (electronic!) government will become 'a matter of information collection, information processing and information dissemination', this might lead to a one-sided focus on efficient policy execution and service delivery with less room for fundamental debates on competing values such as efficiency versus the protection against the abuse of power. Groups of people that are excluded from the 'seamless web' of government 'may turn to crime, fundamentalism, and even terrorism.'

The idea that efficiency 'may develop into the core value of government' is closely related to our observation that government is on the way to been seen as an information processor in which the use of ICT is primarily defined as information management. In the previous chapters a substantial number of ICT driven innovations in public administration have been described and analysed, in which the emphasis has been on efficiency and technology. Although the selection of the cases does not match normal statistical requirements, it is interesting to look, in a more reflective way, what the nature is of the modernization process in public administration is. What do these case studies tell us about the essence of public innovation? What are remarkable issues that have to be discussed when talking about modernizing government?

Efficiency as a Legitimizing Driver

In the general overview of modernization programs in four countries (chapter 2) as well as in the majority of the presented cases (see especially chapters 3, 4, 5, 8, 9, 11, 13), we see that efficiency has indeed been one of the most important goals c.q. political values used to legitimize the modernization of public administration and the use of ICT, although it has sometimes been hidden behind more political goals, like the improving the quality of public services, the openness of government etcetera. In order to do so public administration should be reshaped as 'the machinery of the government'. Hence, we could state the modernization agenda of public administration is based on a rather mechanistic and rational perspective. Moreover, one could also conclude that the different public innovation agendas as we have studied them in the previous chapters, have a rather general and top down character. It is primarily framed at the system's level of public administration.

This also colors the way in which ICT is being used in modernization projects. ICT is defined as a rather neutral set of tools, which in the hand of the right persons and under the right conditions, can be applied to enhance the efficiency of public administration. ICT makes it possible to redesign the cogwheels within the government's machinery, so that not only their functioning but also the interplay between them may operate more smoothly, more efficiently to produce more effective outputs and outcomes. This mechanistic modernization perspective has a number of important consequences, which will be addressed when discussing the next issues.

The Ecology of ICT-driven Public Innovation

First, a mechanistic perspective tends to overestimate the contribution of ICT; while at the same time the unintended and indirect consequences of ICT are very often neglected. The results of ICT are being influenced by the complex and dynamic institutional setting in which it is developed, introduced and used and in which other factors play an important role. Therefore it is important to understand ICT driven innovations in public administration from an ecological perspective. Results are the product of the contingent, and thus unique and local, co-evolution of developments in different environments (technological, political, economic and socio-cultural) and in which at the same time different stakeholders operate, which try to influence the way in which problems are conceived and solutions are developed and implemented [1]. For instance, the cases of two Belgian Crossroads Banks in the social security show quite convincingly, how rather subtle the interaction between technological, political and organizational factors and actors has taken place.

Neglect of Implementation Conditions

The importance of an ecological perspective on ICT-driven innovation is also demonstrated by the fact that implementation conditions are very important. Acknowledgement of these feasibility conditions contributes at forehand to the success of an innovation. Relevant factors are for instance the need to acquire support (e.g. chapter 3, 5, 8), to generate trust (e.g. chapter 3, 5, 10), the availability of resources chapter (like financial funds, people and knowledge, see e.g. chapter 9, 10) a more ore less equal distribution of costs and benefits among relevant stakeholders (e.g. chapter 4 and 5). Moreover, in many cases ICT-driven innovation has not only implied the standardization and formalization of information systems, data formats but also working processes, routines and procedures, which could generate resistance (e.g. chapter 3, 4, 5, 6 and 8). This stresses the essence of having an implementation agenda, which can also consists of a number of paradoxes, which should be handled (e.g. chapter 8). However, the interesting point is that, although the importance of all these and other factors have been known in the literature and practice of public administration modernization, these issues are forgotten rather quickly, if a technology driven innovation is proposed. Ingeniousness prevails, due to a strong belief in the blessings of technology. This attitude of technology optimism is being strengthened by the idea that the implementation of such a technology driven innovation is about choosing and applying the right set of tools. An interesting example is the strong belief in the blessing of IDTV (chapter, 7) ID-cards (chapter 12) or the concept of e-government (chapter 13).

An Evolutionary Perspective on Public Innovation

Another important consequence of an ecological approach of ICT driven public innovation is that it stresses the importance of a more evolutionary approach when assessing the impact of a public innovation instead of a more revolutionary approach [2]. Many case descriptions show that revolutionary changes in the division of power between public organizations and between government and citizens did not have occurred (perhaps with an exception to Estonia – see the chapter of Driessen). In many cases we see that the transformation of public administration (and the accompanying legal regimes) has come down to more or less small steps (e.g. due changes in the allocations of tasks, resources or the improvement of the information and knowledge position of citizens) instead of a more radical change of organizational structures and institutional relations. On the short term this may look like the reinforcement of existing practices, interests and positions, which is also being described in the literature on the effects of ICT [see for an overview 3, 4 and 5]. However, it would also be possible, after some time has passed and also indirect effects have been studied, that profound and more qualitative changes in practices, interests and positions could be described. This also points us at one of the minor points of the content of this book. An evolutionary perspective in the case study description and analysis did not prevail. Most case studies can be viewed as random indications.

The Social Embeddedness of Public Innovation

Furthermore, several case studies show that the social and political embeddedness of the interactions and relationships between relevant actors, – organizations and institutions – are important to foster an innovative ICT climate [2]. In the Belgian and Dutch social security sector cases (chapters 3 and 5) trustworthy relationships – e.g. between different organizations within the public sector and between the private and public sector – have been explicitly defined as an important factor which has contributed to the ability to develop new practices. In a more mechanistic approach to ICT driven public innovations one tends to forget this [6].

    There is also another reason to stress the importance of the social and political embeddedness of ICT driven public innovation. Due to the linkage capacity of modern technology and the penetration of ICT into the primary processes of public administration, we can observe that many ICT innovations have an interorganizational and/or relational character. This observation stresses the necessity of collaboration between relevant stakeholders and the emergence of intermediary organizations, like trusted third parties or shared service centres, which facilitate collaboration (e.g. chapter 3, 4, 9, 10, 11 and 12).

Different partners in a transformation process concerning new ways of working (together), interacting, formulating and implementing public policy (service delivery, law enforcement) hold at least a minimum of mutual trust in each other and in each others data, information and knowledge to be able to improve efficiency or to become a more responsive, citizen-oriented part of public administration. In other words: in many cases ICT driven public innovation implies collaborative government, which seems impossible without robust but flexible agreements (see chapter 5) on what role each party involved can and may play in terms of decision-making, policy implementation and control over the information resources that form the basis for the functioning of specific public policy in question. Along with that, other main issues for success or failure of creating new public practices (steered by or) with the help of modern ICT are standardization of information and data exchange, financial aspects such as adequate cost-benefit analysis, (sufficient) economics of scale and/or substantial financial incentives for all parties (especially private parties) involved – not necessarily meaning return on investment on short notice but there must be at least something shining at the faraway horizon.

Therefore, it is important to look at the nature and the degree of social capital, between the most important stakeholders, available in a policy sector in which modernization and innovation takes place [7]. Trust can be seen as an important condition for actors to get engaged in a learning and communication process in which a process of creative destruction actually can take place and actors do not have to be afraid for sheer power politics and opportunism.

Allocation of Values in the 'Polis'

Due to its emphasis on rationality and the efficient use of resources in public administration, the risk exists to forget that public administration is one of the institutions in the 'polis' in which not only economic considerations play an important role. Typical for the life in the polis is that values have to be weighted against each other. Efficiency is one of these values, but other values are also important such as liberty, equity, equality and security and the separation of power (checks and balances). However, does the modernization agenda of public administration recognize the existence of these other values in public administration? Does it recognize the fact that public administration is a part of the 'polis'? Moreover, many interesting innovations are often those innovations, which are able to reconcile conflicting values at a higher level. For instance, CCTV cameras as an example of a technological innovation, makes it possible to contribute to the safety in public places – like streets – while at the same time it is rather efficient, due to the limited number of policy officers which is available to actually patrol in these streets. One officer behind the screen can monitor many locations.

On the other hand we see that two political values, besides efficiency, have been an important trigger for change. These values are accessibility and transparency of government information. In the chapters by Driessen (chapter 4) and Edwards (chapter 10) we see that access to government information, and thus access to knowledge, has led to the empowerment of the citizens versus public administration.

Distinction Between Bureaucracy and Democracy/Politics

In the mechanistic perspective on modernization there is sharp normative distinction between bureaucracy and politics or even between bureaucracy and democracy. In this perspective bureaucracy is defined as a neutral collection of people and other resources (like knowledge), which serve the goals that have been formulated by politicians in a democratic process, according the playing rules of representative democracy. This has four major implications for the innovation agenda of public administration.

First, it strengthens the internal orientation on modernization and the use of ICT, focusing on improving internal efficiency (e.g. reducing red tape, improving the speediness or length of working processes and routines).

Secondly, external modernization is primarily seen as improving the efficiency of the service delivery process to citizens and companies on the one hand; and improving and monitoring the 'rule of the law' when laws and regulations are applied (in terms of legal security and equality) on the other hand. This also influences the way in which citizens are being approached: primarily as a consumer as well a (legal) subject. The implication is that another possible role of citizens is being neglected, namely citizens as co-producers of public policies (based on their role as active citizens, as 'citoyen', who can bring in specific knowledge, experience, ideas and preferences; see also Edward's chapter). This also entails the neglect of a possible alternative public innovation agenda.

Thirdly, it does not focus on innovations in relation to political renewal. In order to do so it is important to look at the essence of politics. Politics deal with the question how communities are trying to achieve something as a community. Politics and public policy are about communities trying to formulate and achieve collective goals in relation to the specific problems with which a community is confronted [8]. Possible collective goals are how to achieve economic growth when the population of the people in the community is aging, how to create safe neighbourhoods, a sustainable environment or a transport infrastructure. The international comparison, as well as several case studies, shows that the modernization agenda is very weakly related to specific societal problems.

Fourthly, due to this distinction a lot of attention is paid to political responsibility and accountability. How can politicians but also top level administrators, make sure that bureaucratic agencies comply to their political goals, which are laid down in all kinds of policy programs that have to be implemented, and that political risks could be minimized? In many governments this challenge is being translated in an increased intention for installing all kinds of elaborated internal, efficiency based accountability regimes, in risk-avoiding behaviour, which does not stimulate innovation and in a weak external accountability orientation, focussing on public or societal accountability.

Hence, there is a risk that the modernization agenda of public administration is too narrowly and too internally focused. One could even say that a managerial perspective on ICT-driven prevails. Is it possible to break this open?

4. An Alternative Public Innovation Strategy

In our opinion an important challenge for public administration is to connect its own internal, managerial innovation agenda to the broader societal agenda. How to achieve this? How does such an alternative innovation strategy look like? We would like to present the following steps, which are based on a method that we have been using several times, when involved in drafting an ICT driven innovation agenda in different public sectors [9].

First, it is important that ICT driven public innovation should focus more on the real manifestation of specific societal problems, like the social quality of a neighbourhood and the fight against crime or unsafety in this neighbourhood or the provision of all kinds of 'light' medical and house keeping services to elderly and ill people at their home, now the number of elderly people is increasing, due to the aging of the population.

Secondly, it is important to focus on the concrete manifestation of the problems at the micro-level. In relation to the social quality of neighbourhoods this would imply that we focus on the quality of life (or the lack of quality) in a street or on a square. In the case of the elderly people who require care, this would suggest that the living room or bedroom of this man or woman would be at the centre of our attention.

The next step is to get different pictures of how different stakeholders who fulfil different roles in this street or neighbourhood, experience the specific problems or challenges in this street and what kind of solutions they imagine. In the case of the social quality of the neighbourhood this would imply that the perceptions of problems and solutions of different kinds of residents – e.g. house owners, shop owners – and visitors (like shopping people) or street level bureaucrats or other professionals who work at the street level (like the neighbourhood police officer, the social worker of the housing company, the public cleansing service, the youth workers, teachers of the local school, the local family doctor etc.) have to be described and analyzed. However, this is only one circle c.q. group of stakeholders that could be identified.

There is also another relevant group. If one looks at the problems with which many of these stakeholders, especially professional street level workers, are confronted with, one could see that a number of problems refer to the relationships between these local 'front offices' with their own back offices or with the back offices in other organizations with which they have to deal. That's why it is important to draw a second circle of 'hidden' stakeholders, which operate at different level of scale. For instance, for the police officer this is the police station in the neighbourhood or even police headquarters, but also the offices of other organizations, which deliver specific services important to him, like the health care or social care organizations.

Focussing on the perceptions and the framing of problems and solutions by different groups of stakeholders has the advantage that we will be able to take into consideration the 'real life' needs, preferences and experiences of these actors. It is not the policy agenda at the abstract system level that determines our view of relevant problems and possible solutions, and thus the kind of innovations needed. Moreover, we try to get a better understanding of the interdependencies of the network of the relevant actors, which can be discerned around a specific problem.

The next step is to bring these perceptions of problems and possible solutions – of which are some ICT-driven and some not – into a creative setting, in which all relevant stakeholders (also the 'weak' and unorganised ones) are present. The aim is to get a better and more shared understanding about the nature and characteristics of the specific problem. However, it is important that problems and possible solutions are discussed, challenged and tested in a creative way. In order to simulate a process of 'creative destruction' one can organize this setting as a 'garbage can' as it has been described by Cohen, March and Olson [10] and has been worked out in relation to agenda change by Kingdon [11]. Following this line of reasoning, innovations are not only the results of a searching process in which a specific solution is formulated for a specific problem. Problems and solutions can also be seen as separate streams, which can be coupled together under the right circumstances, for instance if the 'policy window' is open. This way of working has several advantages, we have noticed. First, that it is worthwhile to look for innovations designed in complete different sectors as possible solutions, not only as an instrumental solution but also as a lens (a perspective on problem-solving), which can be used to look for dedicated and tailor-made solutions. Secondly, participants are asked to make the conditions explicit under which they think problems and solutions can be matched, under which the policy window can be opened. Implementation conditions are made visible at forehand. Moreover, it is easier to get a better insight in the support or the resistance of relevant stakeholders. Thirdly, the innovations put forward are rather demand driven, because they take the real life manifestation of specific problems in the public sector as a starting point instead of rather abstract policy frameworks.

The advantage of this approach is that ICT-driven public innovations relate to the different (and sometimes conflicting) values, which are embedded in daily problems with which citizens, companies, societal organizations and government organizations are confronted with. It tries to overcome the one-sidedness of the present public innovation agenda, in which ICT is primarily defined as a tool to achieve efficiency. Moreover, this approach tries to recognize the fact that effective public innovations are contextually based innovations. This does not imply that innovations, which are developed elsewhere, cannot be adopted by other organizations. It recognizes the importance of shaping and re-shaping of public innovations (and re-inventions), due to the local and contingent co-evolutions of different environments and different stakeholders.

References

[1]   V. Bekkers and V. Homburg, E-Government as an Information Ecology: Backgrounds and Concepts, in: *The Information Ecology of E-Government*, V. Bekkers and V. Homburg (eds.), IOS Press, Amsterdam/Berlin/Oxford/Tokyo/Washington DC, 2005.
[2]   S. Zouridis and K. Termeer, Never the Twain Shall Meet. Een oxymoron: innovatie in het openbaar bestuur, *Bestuurskunde* **14**(7/8) (2006), 13-23.
[3]   K. Kraemer and R. King, Computing and Public Organizations, *Public Administration Review* (1986), 488-496.
[4]   I.Th.M. Snellen and W.B.J.H. van de Donk (eds.), *Public Administration in an Information Age*, IOS Press, Amsterdam/Berlin/Oxford/Tokyo/Washington, 1998.
[5]   K.V. Andersen and J.N. Danziger, Impacts of IT on Politics and the Public Sector: Methodological, Epistemological, and Substantive Evidence from the "Golden Age" of Transformation, *International Journal of Public Administration*, **25**(5) (2001), 13-32.
[6]   M. Granovetter, Economic Action and Social Structure: the Problem of Embeddedness, *American Journal of Sociology*, **91** (1985), 481-510.
[7]   F. Fukuyama, *Trust*, Hamish Hamilton, London, 1995.
[8]   D. Stone, *The Policy Paradox. The Art of Political Decision-Making*, Norton and Company, New York/London, 2002.
[9]   V.J.J.M. Bekkers (ed.), H.P.M. van Duivenboden, R. Feenstra, V. Frissen, J. de Mul, A. Ponsioen, M. de Rooij, C. Terhoeven, M. Thaens, A. van Venrooy, J. van Wamelen and S. Zouridis, *De buurt in het web, het web in de buurt. Een ICT-kanskaart voor sociale cohesie*, Lemma, Utrecht, 2004.
[10] M.D. Cohen, J.G. March and J. Olson, A Garbage Can Model of Organizational Choice, *Administrative Science Quarterly*, **17**(1) (1972), 1-25.
[11] J.W. Kingdon, *Agendas, Alternatives and Public Policies*, Harper, New York, 1995.

Information and Communication Technology and Public Innovation
V.J.J.M. Bekkers et al. (Eds.)
IOS Press, 2006

Author Index